POOR ARNOLD'S
ALMANAC

by

ARNOLD ROTH

FANTAGRAPHICS BOOKS

FANTAGRAPHICS BOOKS
7563 Lake City Way NE
Seattle, WA 98115

Poor Arnold's Almanac © 1998 Arnold Roth
Introduction © 1998 John Updike

Gary Groth, editor
Ilse Thompson, assistant editor
Carrie Whitney, art director
Gary Groth & Kim Thompson, publishers

First Fantagraphics Books edition: June 1998

ISBN: 1-56097-322-6

Printed in Canada

FANTAGRAPHICS BOOKS

Table Of Contents

WAXING ROTH by John Updike

All cartoonists are geniuses, but Arnold Roth especially so. The first time I saw a Roth drawing, I was zapped. Those shaggy zigzag lines! Those pointy noses! Those infinitely rubbery limbs! Those big, big eyes with every eyelash in place! And amid the linear hyperactivity lurks a curious clarity — every detail "reads"; there is no fudging. A superabundant creative spirit surges through a Roth drawing like electricity; his cup of invention overfloweth.

Consider this sheaf of strips, done for the New York Herald-Tribune Syndicate, Sundays only, between May of 1959 and 1961, and revived a bit in 1989. Originally titled *Poor Richard's Encyclopedia*, it shows an encyclopedic scope: Roth was game to produce a dozen panels, ten or so separate gags, on topics ranging from Dogs to Sleep, Alaska to Lions. Though he has described in interviews how the strip was untimely dropped by the syndicate, it is hard to believe he could have indefinitely maintained the stream of ideas. The strip was drawn in a relatively tight, early Roth style — notice the exquisitely neat lettering — but in specimens like "Gardening" and "Books" we can see traces of the fearless exaggerations of the mature, full-feathered Roth.

Born in 1929, he comes from Philadelphia, a city with a long, proud tradition of art and illustration. He graduated from Central High and was expelled from the Philadelphia College of Art; he kept leaving class to have a smoke, and he was late in the morning from staying up all night playing alto sax in jazz bands. Though his main ambition was always to be a cartoonist, the jazzman in him can be detected in the lyrical visual swoops and his preference for improvisation with the pen, as opposed to careful preliminary drawings in pencil. On his way to commercial success he worked in a picture factory painting tree foliage with a sponge and in a toy factory painting eyes on ducks. He also executed little Pennsylvania Dutch lampshades for Woolworth's. Like most of his ilk, he wanted to be a *New Yorker* cartoonist, but when an interview showed him the extent of control the art department expected to have over its artists, Roth walked away. He has been free-lancing on the wild side ever since. He is allergic to editorial interference; it takes away from the jazz. He has worked for *Playboy*, and for a magazine called *Trump* that Hefner founded and folded, and for one called *Humbug* that lasted a year. For a time he lived in England and was a steady contributor to *Punch*. These days he appears most everywhere, from *Esquire* to *Time* — wherever the paper is glossy. To my lasting delight, he has done three beautiful book jackets for me, at my invitation. He is not only a linear wizard but a fine colorist, in the delicate English style. English artists — Gilray, Rowlandson, Cruikshank — have meant a lot to him; he reminds us, a bit, of Searle and Scarfe. Nevertheless, he is an American original, irreverent, tireless, manicky, and secretly efficient. He can *draw*, is what it comes down to, and his work jumps with joy.

JAZZ
HEY, YOU! PLAY THE MELODY!
THAT WAS THE MELODY!

POOR ARNOLD'S
ALMANAC
BASE BALL
THE INVENTOR OF BASEBALL WAS CAPTAIN ABNER DOUBLEDAY---SO THEY TELL ME!
IT IS PLAYED ON A DIAMOND-SHAPED INFIELD WITH FOUR BASES IN IT; AND AN OUTFIELD WITH EMPTY BOTTLES, OLD NEWSPAPERS, CUPS, ETC., IN IT!
H
THE UMPIRE MUST MAKE SPLIT-SECOND DECISIONS!
EVERY TEAM HAS ITS ARDENT FANS
FEH!
THE MANAGER PLANS STRATEGY IN THE DUGOUT...
HOROSCOPE
MAP OF STADIUM
WIND DIREC
WEATHE REPORT
DREAM BOOK
...THEN HE DIRECTS HIS PLAYERS WITH HIS SAGE DECISIONS.
PSSST! STRIKE HIM OUT!
P
THE CATCHER GIVES SECRET INSTRUCTIONS TO THE PITCHER.
STRIKE HIM OUT!
IS THAT **YOU**, HARRY?
USING HIS LONG STRETCH, THE FIRST-BASEMAN MAKES THE MOST PUT-OUTS!
C
YOUNG TALENTS RECEIVE LARGE BONUSES FOR PLAYING.
5-31
ALL MAJOR LEAGUE PLAYERS MUST EXCEL IN FOUR THINGS:....
STRIKE THREE!
..HITTING....
..THROWING...
..FIELDING....
SKRINCH!
SHAV
..SHAVING!
BASEBALL IS AMERICA'S FAVORITE *OUTDOOR* SPORT!
ZZZZZZZ
SUDS BREW
ARNOLD ROTH

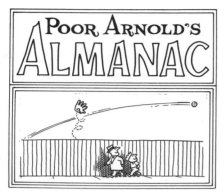

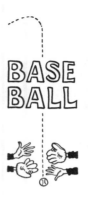

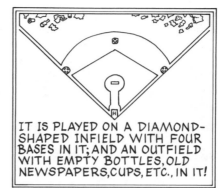

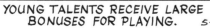

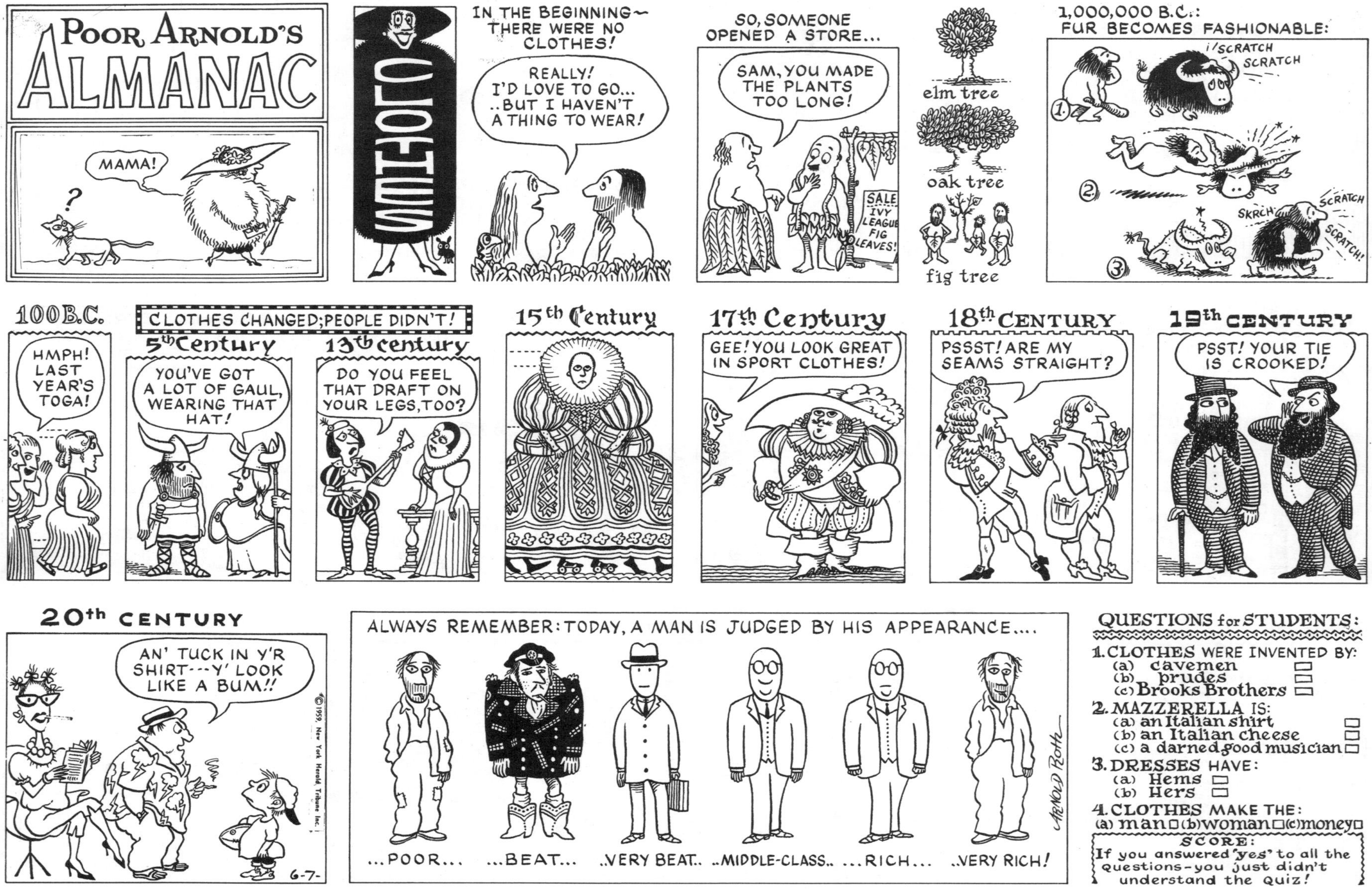
POOR ARNOLD'S
ALMANAC
MAMA!
?
CLOTHES
IN THE BEGINNING~ THERE WERE NO CLOTHES!
REALLY! I'D LOVE TO GO... ..BUT I HAVEN'T A THING TO WEAR!
SO, SOMEONE OPENED A STORE...
SAM, YOU MADE THE PLANTS TOO LONG!
SALE IVY LEAGUE FIG LEAVES!
elm tree
oak tree
fig tree
1,000,000 B.C.: FUR BECOMES FASHIONABLE:
1.
SCRATCH
SCRATCH
2.
3.
SKRCH
SCRATCH
SCRATCH!
100B.C.
HMPH! LAST YEAR'S TOGA!
CLOTHES CHANGED; PEOPLE DIDN'T!
5th Century
YOU'VE GOT A LOT OF GAUL, WEARING THAT HAT!
13th century
DO YOU FEEL THAT DRAFT ON YOUR LEGS, TOO?
15th Century
17th Century
GEE! YOU LOOK GREAT IN SPORT CLOTHES!
18th CENTURY
PSSST! ARE MY SEAMS STRAIGHT?
19th CENTURY
PSST! YOUR TIE IS CROOKED!
20th CENTURY
AN' TUCK IN Y'R SHIRT---Y' LOOK LIKE A BUM!!
© 1959, New York Herald Tribune Inc.
6-7-
ALWAYS REMEMBER: TODAY, A MAN IS JUDGED BY HIS APPEARANCE....
...POOR...
...BEAT...
..VERY BEAT..
..MIDDLE-CLASS..
...RICH...
..VERY RICH!
ARNOLD ROTH
QUESTIONS for STUDENTS:
1. CLOTHES WERE INVENTED BY:
(a) cavemen ☐
(b) prudes ☐
(c) Brooks Brothers ☐
2. MAZZERELLA IS:
(a) an Italian shirt ☐
(b) an Italian cheese ☐
(c) a darned good musician ☐
3. DRESSES HAVE:
(a) Hems ☐
(b) Hers ☐
4. CLOTHES MAKE THE:
(a) man ☐ (b) woman ☐ (c) money ☐
SCORE:
If you answered 'yes' to all the questions - you just didn't understand the Quiz!

POOR ARNOLD'S ALMANAC
SAY AAH!
AWK!
The History of MEDICINE
Rx
WITCH DOCTORS STARTED THE WHOLE THING!
DOC, I FEEL AWFUL!
AW! IT'S ALL IN YOUR HEAD.
BY 1200 A.D. A CRUDE SYSTEM OF ANATOMY EXISTED.
OH, DE TOE BONE'S CONNECTED TO DE FOOT BONE AN' DE FOOT BONE'S CONNECTED...
ONE TECHNIQUE HAS NEVER CHANGED....
SMACK!
WHAT'D I DO?
BARBERS USED TO BE SURGEONS.
OOPS!
BLOOD-LETTING WAS OVERDONE...
FEEL BETTER?
HOW DRY I AM!
..IT STILL IS.. SOMETIMES!
Rx BILL
ROENTGEN INVENTED THE X-RAY MACHINE.
1.
2.
3.
4.
RESEARCH HAS ALWAYS BEEN AN IMPORTANT ELEMENT...
YES! THIS ONE IS MILDER... MUCH MILDER!
A DRAMATIZATION
.....NOW, CLASS, REPEAT AFTER ME.. ..'BOIL WATER-AND PLENTY OF IT.' 'ONLY TIME WILL TELL!' 'SHE'LL NEVER YODEL AGAIN...'
SCHOOL OF MOTION PICTURE MEDICINE
PSYCHIATRY IS A NEW FORM OF TREATMENT.
..AND, SO, DOCTOR, MY PROBLEM IS THAT PEOPLE THINK I'M A BORE!
ZZZZZZZ
ARNOLD Roth
IN THE FUTURE, SURGEONS WILL USE ARTIFICIAL ORGANS.
Be Mine
6-14
FACTS to REMEMBER
1. A Doctor is man's best friend.
2. Dog is man's best friend.
3. When you're poor, you lose all your friends.
4. There is no cure for Exitdortonitis
5. There is no Exitdortonitis.
6. An apple a day costs $36.50 PER YEAR
7. Blood is thicker than water.

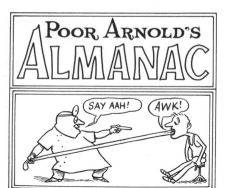

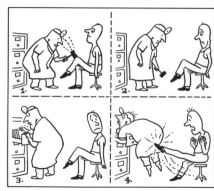

POOR ARNOLD'S ALMANAC

DOGS

THROUGH THE AGES, DOGS HAVE SERVED MANKIND....

...IN PEACE..... AND WAR!

HE WENT THATAWAY!

WHY, IT'S RIM-TIM-TIM, THE WONDER DOG!

SIC 'EM, BOY!

CERTAIN DOGS ARE USED IN MEDICAL EXPERIMENTS!

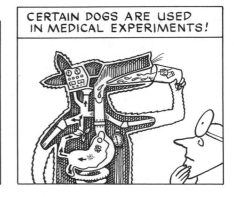

THERE IS A DOG CONSTELLATION!

PURE-BREDS COMPETE IN SHOWS.

MIMI ♪ YOU CRAZY, LEETLE ♪ GOOD FOR NUSSING MIMI

WHAT A ROTTEN VOICE!

JUDGES

TAP   TAP

SOME DOGS ARE ALMOST HUMAN!

IT'S FOR YOU... ...AGAIN!

ALL HOUNDS ARE NATURAL HUNTERS......

YOICKS

YIPES

THANKS

FOR SALE HUNTING DOG

MOST DOGS MAKE WONDERFUL PETS....

PWITTY, WIDDLE SNOOKUMS! YOU MAMA HAVE A PWESENT FAW YOU! SAY SUMFING, SWEETIEPOO!

ARF!

6-21

THERE ARE MANY KINDS OF DOG.
* * *
HERE IS A SCRAPBOOK OF SOME FAMOUS SPECIES.

POINTER

SCOTCH TERRIER

BEYON BONNIE ♪ ♪ BANKSH

AFGHAN HOUND

ST. BERNARD

HIC!

WATER SPANIEL

GREYHOUND

NEXT TIME TAKE THE TRAIN

100% PURE MUTT!

ARNOLD ROTH

4

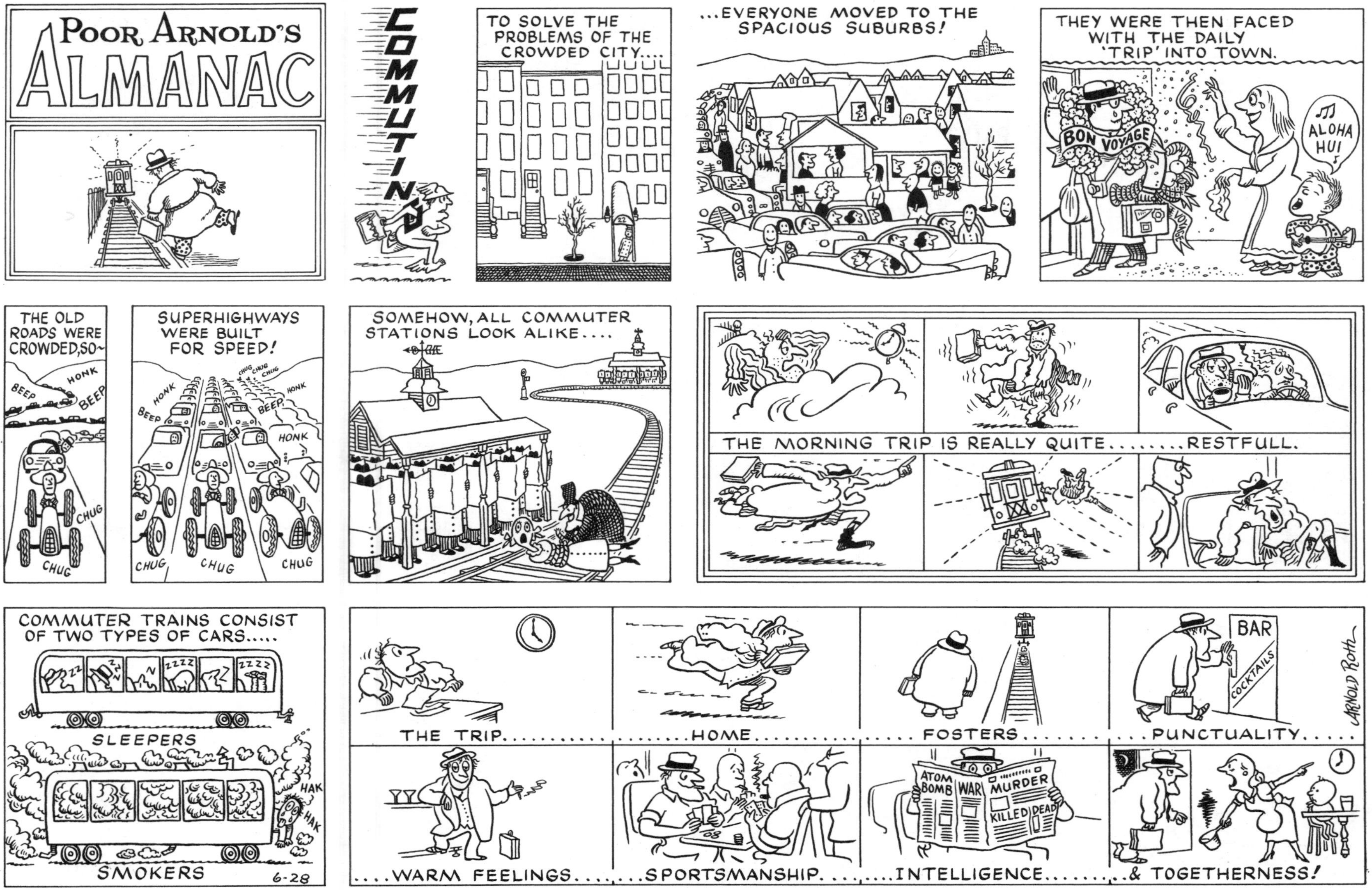
POOR ARNOLD'S
ALMANAC
COMMUTING
TO SOLVE THE PROBLEMS OF THE CROWDED CITY....
...EVERYONE MOVED TO THE SPACIOUS SUBURBS!
THEY WERE THEN FACED WITH THE DAILY 'TRIP' INTO TOWN.
BON VOYAGE
ALOHA HUI
THE OLD ROADS WERE CROWDED,SO~
HONK
BEEP
BEEP
CHUG
CHUG
SUPERHIGHWAYS WERE BUILT FOR SPEED!
HONK
BEEP
CHUG CHUG CHUG
BEEP
HONK
HONK
CHUG
CHUG
CHUG
SOMEHOW, ALL COMMUTER STATIONS LOOK ALIKE....
THE MORNING TRIP IS REALLY QUITE........RESTFULL.
COMMUTER TRAINS CONSIST OF TWO TYPES OF CARS.....
SLEEPERS
HAK
HAK
SMOKERS
6-28
BAR
COCKTAILS
ARNOLD ROTH
THE TRIP.........
........HOME.........
.....FOSTERS.....
...PUNCTUALITY....
ATOM BOMB
WAR
MURDER
KILLED
DEAD
....WARM FEELINGS....
....SPORTSMANSHIP....
....INTELLIGENCE........
..& TOGETHERNESS!

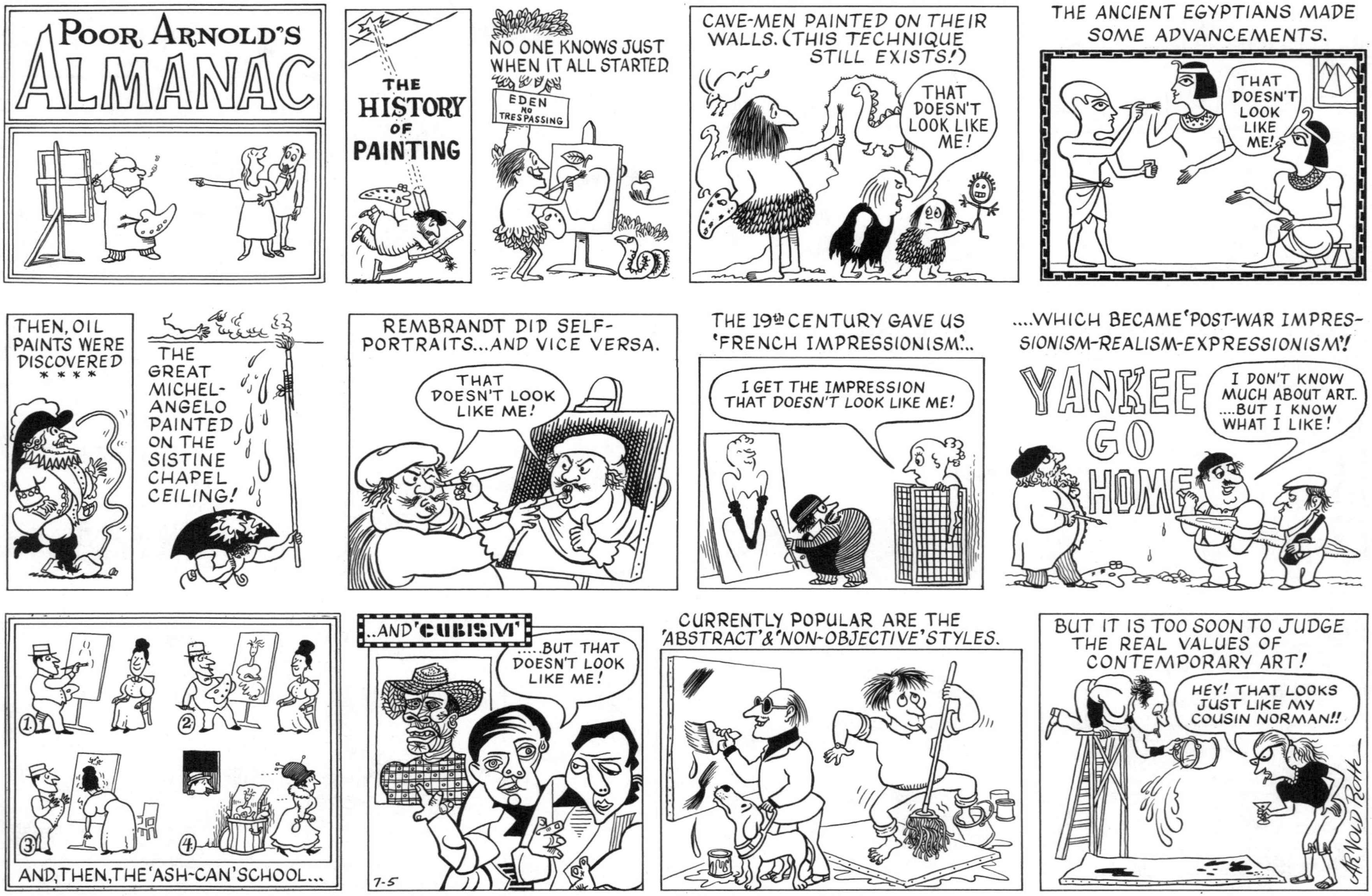
POOR ARNOLD'S
ALMANAC
THE HISTORY OF PAINTING
NO ONE KNOWS JUST WHEN IT ALL STARTED.
EDEN
NO TRESPASSING
CAVE-MEN PAINTED ON THEIR WALLS. (THIS TECHNIQUE STILL EXISTS!)
THAT DOESN'T LOOK LIKE ME!
THE ANCIENT EGYPTIANS MADE SOME ADVANCEMENTS.
THAT DOESN'T LOOK LIKE ME!
THEN, OIL PAINTS WERE DISCOVERED
* * * *
THE GREAT MICHEL-ANGELO PAINTED ON THE SISTINE CHAPEL CEILING!
REMBRANDT DID SELF-PORTRAITS...AND VICE VERSA.
THAT DOESN'T LOOK LIKE ME!
THE 19th CENTURY GAVE US 'FRENCH IMPRESSIONISM'...
I GET THE IMPRESSION THAT DOESN'T LOOK LIKE ME!
....WHICH BECAME 'POST-WAR IMPRES-SIONISM-REALISM-EXPRESSIONISM'!
YANKEE GO HOME
I DON'T KNOW MUCH ABOUT ART.. ....BUT I KNOW WHAT I LIKE!
AND, THEN, THE 'ASH-CAN' SCHOOL...
..AND 'CUBISM'
.....BUT THAT DOESN'T LOOK LIKE ME!
7-5
CURRENTLY POPULAR ARE THE 'ABSTRACT' & 'NON-OBJECTIVE' STYLES.
BUT IT IS TOO SOON TO JUDGE THE REAL VALUES OF CONTEMPORARY ART!
HEY! THAT LOOKS JUST LIKE MY COUSIN NORMAN!!
ARNOLD ROTH

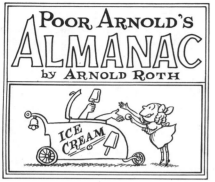

Poor Arnold's Almanac by Arnold Roth

ICE CREAM

NERO ENJOYED THE FIRST ICE CREAM (SNOW MIXED WITH FRUIT JUICE)!

THROW SOME WATER ON THAT CITY—IT'S MELTING MY DESSERT!

FOR YEARS THIS FORMULA REMAINED UNCHANGED.

IMAGINE! 28 Flavors of Snow!

Ye Howard Jontsons

MARCO POLO BROUGHT BACK IMPROVEMENTS FROM CHINA!

'AY, MARCO, GIMME A CHOCOLATS, VANILLAS, WONTON & EGG ROLL.

NO, NO! YOU GET ONLY **ONE** FROM COLUMN 'A' AND **TWO** FROM COLUMN 'B'.....

TINGLE DINGLE

ICA CREME

BUT ONLY ROYALTY COULD AFFORD IT.

GIVE ME A KING-SIZE DIP!

BUT—YOU'RE ONLY A DUKE.

ICE CREAM CAME TO AMERICA WITH THE EARLY COLONISTS...

SAY, BOY! LET'S HAVE ANOTHER OF THOSE WILD TURKEY SUNDAES!

I'LL SAY THEY'RE WILD!

ICE CREAM PARLOURS BECAME EXTREMELY POPULAR.

SET UP ANOTHER, JOE!

MOTHER, DEAR MOTHER, COME HOME WITH ME, NOW!

KIDS LOVE IT—ADULTS DO, TOO!

BOY! COULD I GO FOR A CONE OF VANILLA RIGHT NOW!

7-12

IT COMES IN MANY FORMS....

ICH! — IN CONES

ICH! — ON A STICK

ICH! — IN A 'SANDWICH'

ICH! PLOP — IN A DISH

IN SUMMER, ICE CREAM IS SOLD EVERYWHERE.

ICE CREAM

TINGLE LINGLE

ICE CREAM

ICE CREAM

TINGLE LINGLE

TINGLING

TINGLE!

ICE CREAM

ICE CREAM

BLINGLB TBLING

ICE CREAM

ORDERING ICE CREAM REQUIRES DEEP THOUGHT & CLEAN-CUT DECISION...

I WANT A CONE OF ICE CREAM. UH—WHAT FLAVORS YA GOT?

I'VE GOT VANILLA, CHOCOLATE, STRAWBERRY, JUNIPER, LIME, LEMON, RASPBERRY-MINT, CHOPPED LIVER-MINT, OLIVE-CHIP, BANANA, CHERRY, ORANGE, COFFEE, TEA-FLAKE, EGG-NOG, LICORICE, MAYONAISSE-NUT, VANILLA-FUDGE, OAT, BUTTERSCOTCH-FIG, RUMMY-RAISINS, WATERMELON-DRIP, AVOCADO-NUT, SPAGHETTI-FUDGE, BOURBON-MASH, SPLIT-PEA-CARAMEL AND MACKEREL-MINT!

ARNOLD Roth

UH—UMMN—EH—IH—HMMM—

—I'LL HAVE AN EGG SALAD SANDWICH, INSTEAD!

POOR ARNOLD'S ALMANAC
by ARNOLD ROTH

TENNIS COURTS

Tennis

TENNIS IS PLAYED ON TWO KINDS OF COURT.

ON CLAY COURTS

AND GRASS COURTS.

NECESSARY EQUIPMENT:

A FEW BALLS

ONE RACQUET

A NET

AN EASY OPPONENT

REFRESH-MENTS

REACH

EVEN GIRLS CAN EXCEL

OBJECT OF GAME: MAKE YOUR OPPO-NENT MISS THE BALL!

A GOOD, HARD, FAST SERVE IS IMPORTANT!
✳ ☆ ✳ ☆ ✳

STUDENTS: LEARN THE CORRECT FORM AS SHOWN IN THIS SLOW-MOTION PICTURE OF A FORMER CHAMPION!

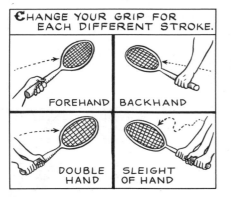

CHANGE YOUR GRIP FOR EACH DIFFERENT STROKE.

FOREHAND

BACKHAND

DOUBLE HAND

SLEIGHT OF HAND

GOOD PLAYERS ARE RELAXED - ALWAYS!

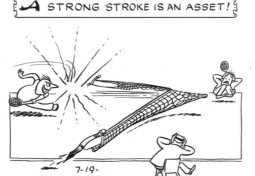

A STRONG STROKE IS AN ASSET!

7-19-

ALWAYS SHOW GOOD SPORTSMANSHIP!

© 1959, New York Herald Tribune Inc.

ARNOLD ROTH

8

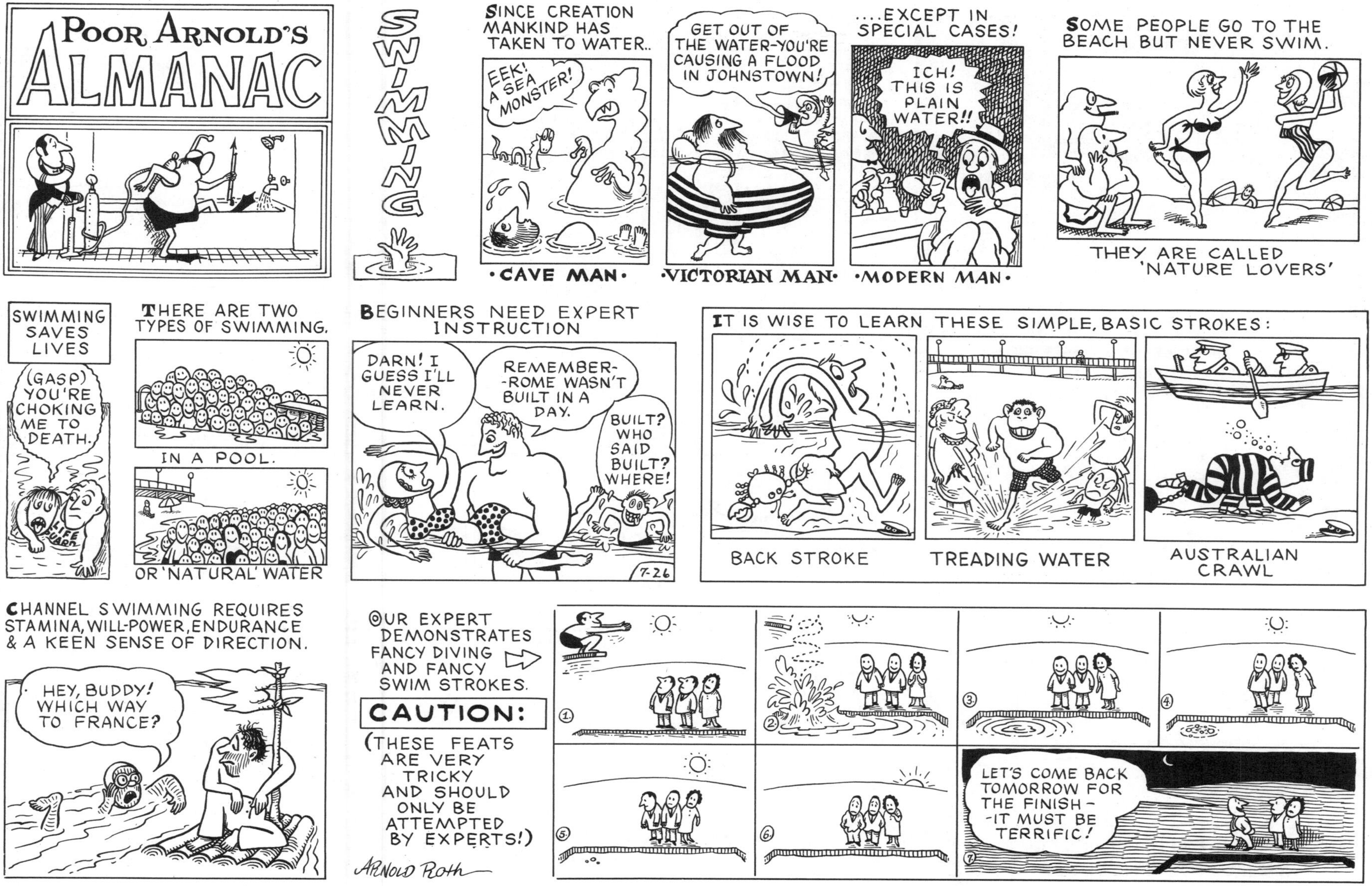
POOR ARNOLD'S
ALMANAC
SWIMMING
SINCE CREATION MANKIND HAS TAKEN TO WATER..
EEK! A SEA MONSTER!
•CAVE MAN•
GET OUT OF THE WATER-YOU'RE CAUSING A FLOOD IN JOHNSTOWN!
•VICTORIAN MAN•
....EXCEPT IN SPECIAL CASES!
ICH! THIS IS PLAIN WATER!!
•MODERN MAN•
SOME PEOPLE GO TO THE BEACH BUT NEVER SWIM.
THEY ARE CALLED 'NATURE LOVERS'
SWIMMING SAVES LIVES
(GASP) YOU'RE CHOKING ME TO DEATH.
LIFE GUARD
THERE ARE TWO TYPES OF SWIMMING.
IN A POOL.
OR 'NATURAL' WATER
BEGINNERS NEED EXPERT INSTRUCTION
DARN! I GUESS I'LL NEVER LEARN.
REMEMBER--ROME WASN'T BUILT IN A DAY.
BUILT? WHO SAID BUILT? WHERE!
7-26
IT IS WISE TO LEARN THESE SIMPLE, BASIC STROKES:
BACK STROKE
TREADING WATER
AUSTRALIAN CRAWL
CHANNEL SWIMMING REQUIRES STAMINA, WILL-POWER, ENDURANCE & A KEEN SENSE OF DIRECTION.
HEY, BUDDY! WHICH WAY TO FRANCE?
OUR EXPERT DEMONSTRATES FANCY DIVING AND FANCY SWIM STROKES.
CAUTION:
(THESE FEATS ARE VERY TRICKY AND SHOULD ONLY BE ATTEMPTED BY EXPERTS!)
ARNOLD ROTH
1
2
3
4
5
6
7
LET'S COME BACK TOMORROW FOR THE FINISH--IT MUST BE TERRIFIC!

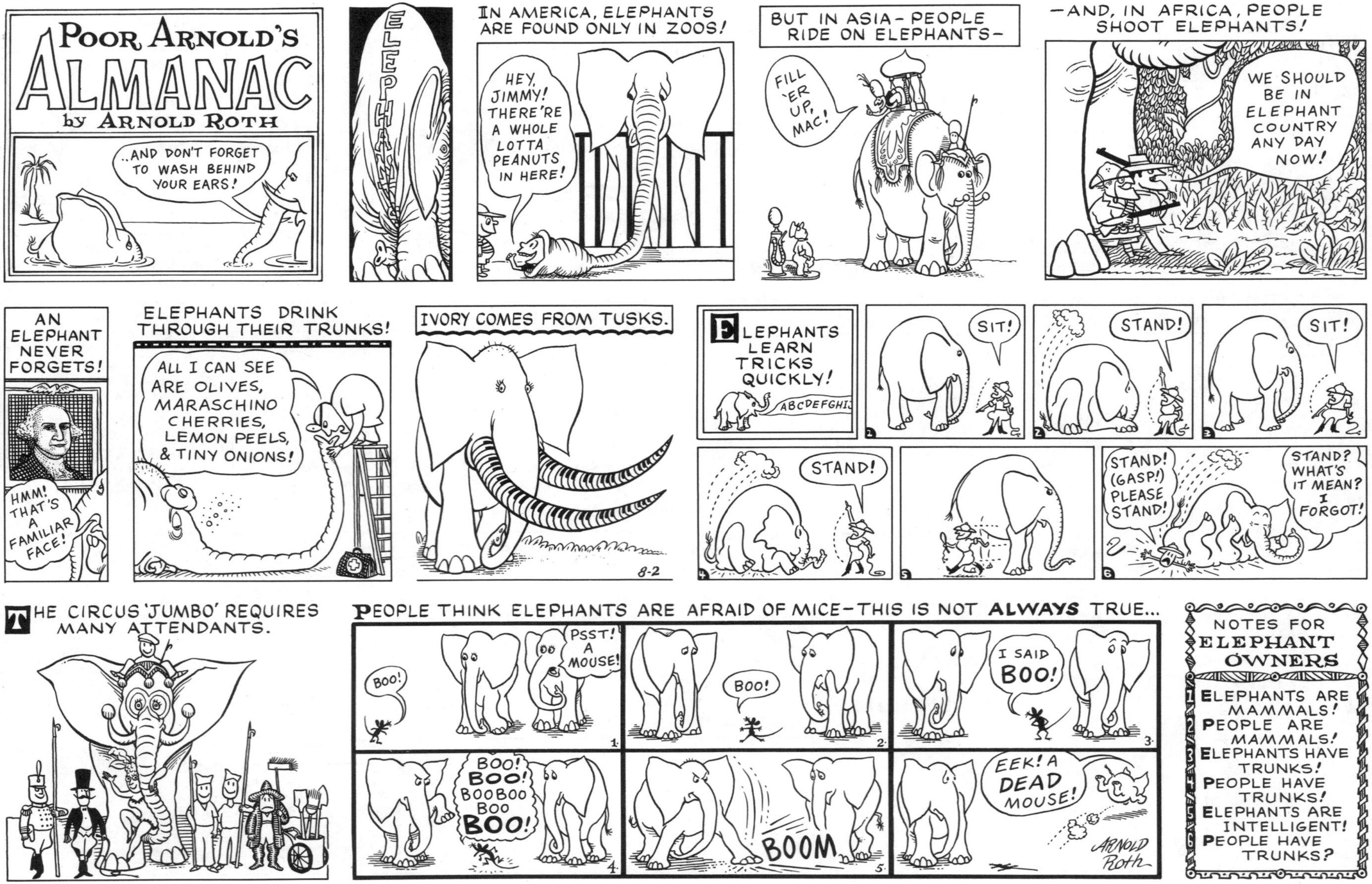
POOR ARNOLD'S ALMANAC
by ARNOLD ROTH
..AND DON'T FORGET TO WASH BEHIND YOUR EARS!
ELEPHANTS
IN AMERICA, ELEPHANTS ARE FOUND ONLY IN ZOOS!
HEY, JIMMY! THERE'RE A WHOLE LOTTA PEANUTS IN HERE!
BUT IN ASIA - PEOPLE RIDE ON ELEPHANTS -
FILL 'ER UP, MAC!
— AND, IN AFRICA, PEOPLE SHOOT ELEPHANTS!
WE SHOULD BE IN ELEPHANT COUNTRY ANY DAY NOW!
AN ELEPHANT NEVER FORGETS!
HMM! THAT'S A FAMILIAR FACE!
ELEPHANTS DRINK THROUGH THEIR TRUNKS!
ALL I CAN SEE ARE OLIVES, MARASCHINO CHERRIES, LEMON PEELS, & TINY ONIONS!
IVORY COMES FROM TUSKS.
8-2
ELEPHANTS LEARN TRICKS QUICKLY!
ABCDEFGHIJ
SIT!
STAND!
SIT!
STAND!
STAND! (GASP!) PLEASE STAND!
STAND? WHAT'S IT MEAN? I FORGOT!
THE CIRCUS 'JUMBO' REQUIRES MANY ATTENDANTS.
PEOPLE THINK ELEPHANTS ARE AFRAID OF MICE—THIS IS NOT ALWAYS TRUE...
BOO!
PSST! A MOUSE!
BOO!
I SAID BOO!
BOO! BOO! BOOBOO BOO BOO!
BOOM
EEK! A DEAD MOUSE!
ARNOLD Roth
NOTES FOR ELEPHANT OWNERS
1 ELEPHANTS ARE MAMMALS!
2 PEOPLE ARE MAMMALS!
3 ELEPHANTS HAVE TRUNKS!
4 PEOPLE HAVE TRUNKS!
5 ELEPHANTS ARE INTELLIGENT!
6 PEOPLE HAVE TRUNKS?

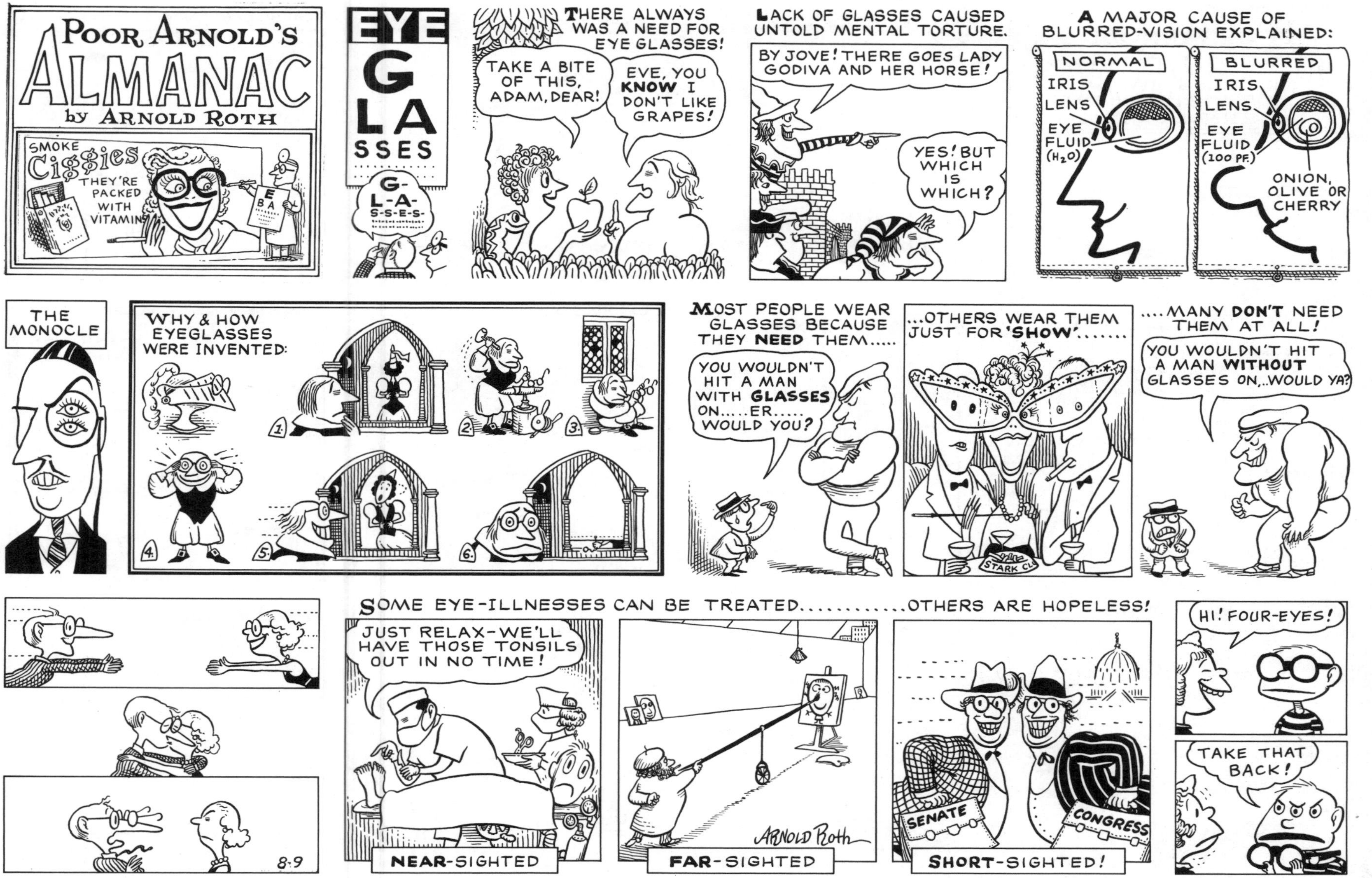

POOR ARNOLD'S
ALMANAC
by ARNOLD ROTH
SMOKE
Ciggies
THEY'RE PACKED WITH VITAMIN
EYE
G
LA
SSES
G-
L-A-
S-S-E-S-
THERE ALWAYS WAS A NEED FOR EYE GLASSES!
TAKE A BITE OF THIS, ADAM, DEAR!
EVE, YOU KNOW I DON'T LIKE GRAPES!
LACK OF GLASSES CAUSED UNTOLD MENTAL TORTURE.
BY JOVE! THERE GOES LADY GODIVA AND HER HORSE!
YES! BUT WHICH IS WHICH?
A MAJOR CAUSE OF BLURRED-VISION EXPLAINED:
NORMAL
IRIS
LENS
EYE FLUID (H_2O)
BLURRED
IRIS
LENS
EYE FLUID (100 PF.)
ONION, OLIVE OR CHERRY
THE MONOCLE
WHY & HOW EYEGLASSES WERE INVENTED:
1.
2.
3.
4.
5.
6.
MOST PEOPLE WEAR GLASSES BECAUSE THEY NEED THEM.....
YOU WOULDN'T HIT A MAN WITH GLASSES ON.....ER..... WOULD YOU?
...OTHERS WEAR THEM JUST FOR 'SHOW'.......
STARK CL
....MANY DON'T NEED THEM AT ALL!
YOU WOULDN'T HIT A MAN WITHOUT GLASSES ON,..WOULD YA?
8-9
SOME EYE-ILLNESSES CAN BE TREATED.............OTHERS ARE HOPELESS!
JUST RELAX-WE'LL HAVE THOSE TONSILS OUT IN NO TIME!
NEAR-SIGHTED
ARNOLD ROTH
FAR-SIGHTED
SENATE
CONGRESS
SHORT-SIGHTED!
HI! FOUR-EYES!
TAKE THAT BACK!

POOR ARNOLD'S ALMANAC
by ARNOLD ROTH
22SP
MOTORING
SUMMER VACATION—AND ALL AMERICA TAKES TO THE ROAD.
1.
OMIGOSH!
SCREEEE
2.
WE FORGOT THE KIDS!
3.
4.
5.
ROADSIDE STANDS ARE IRRESISTABLE.
POTTERY
1.
2.
3.
4.
TRAVEL BROADENS THE VOCABULARY.
DRAT! DRAT! DRAT!
DARN! DARN! DARN!
GIVE
FUNNY HOW A NEW DIMENSION IN A PERSON'S...
..CHARACTER EVOLVES WHEN THEY GET BEHIND A WHEEL!
TURNPIKE DRIVING CAN BECOME MONOTONOUS.
A SPORTCAR DRIVER READING A ROAD MAP!
©1958, New York Herald Tribune Inc.
CAUTION: DEER CROSSING
DEER CROSSI
HIGHWAY COURTESY IS ALWAYS APPRECIATED!
OOPS! I BEG YOUR PARDON!
LIKEWISE, I'M SURE!
YOU'LL NEVER CATCH ME DRIVING ON THESE HOLIDAY WEEKENDS! I STAY HOME WHERE IT'S SAFE!
8-16
ARNOLD Roth
DRIVING QUIZ: TIME LIMIT: 2 HRS.
QUESTION: CAR 'X' LEAVES CHICAGO GOING 80 M.P.H. AND CAR 'Y' LEAVES NEW YORK GOING 90 M.P.H. —— WHERE WILL THEY MEET?
ANSWER: IN A JAIL - IN INDIA SINCE CAR 'X' WENT WEST AND CAR 'Y' WENT EAST - BESIDES, THE LIMIT IN INDIA IS 35 M.P.H.
QUESTION: IF SODIUM-NITRATE IS ADDED TO NITROGEN-OXIDE, WHAT IS THE RESULT?
ANSWER: THIS IS NOT A QUESTION ABOUT DRIVING! CLASS DISMISSED!

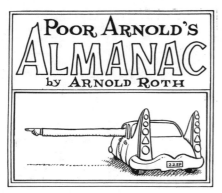

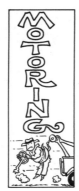

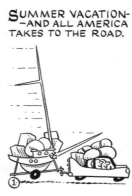

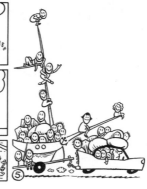

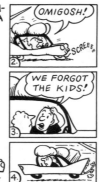

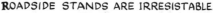

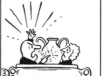

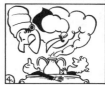

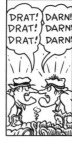

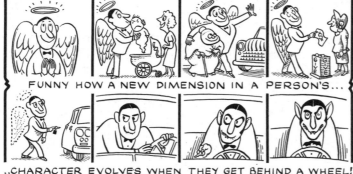

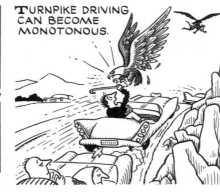

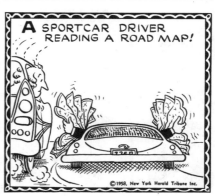

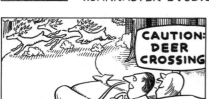

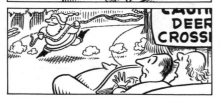

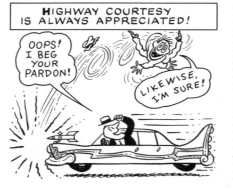

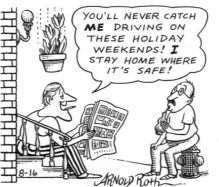

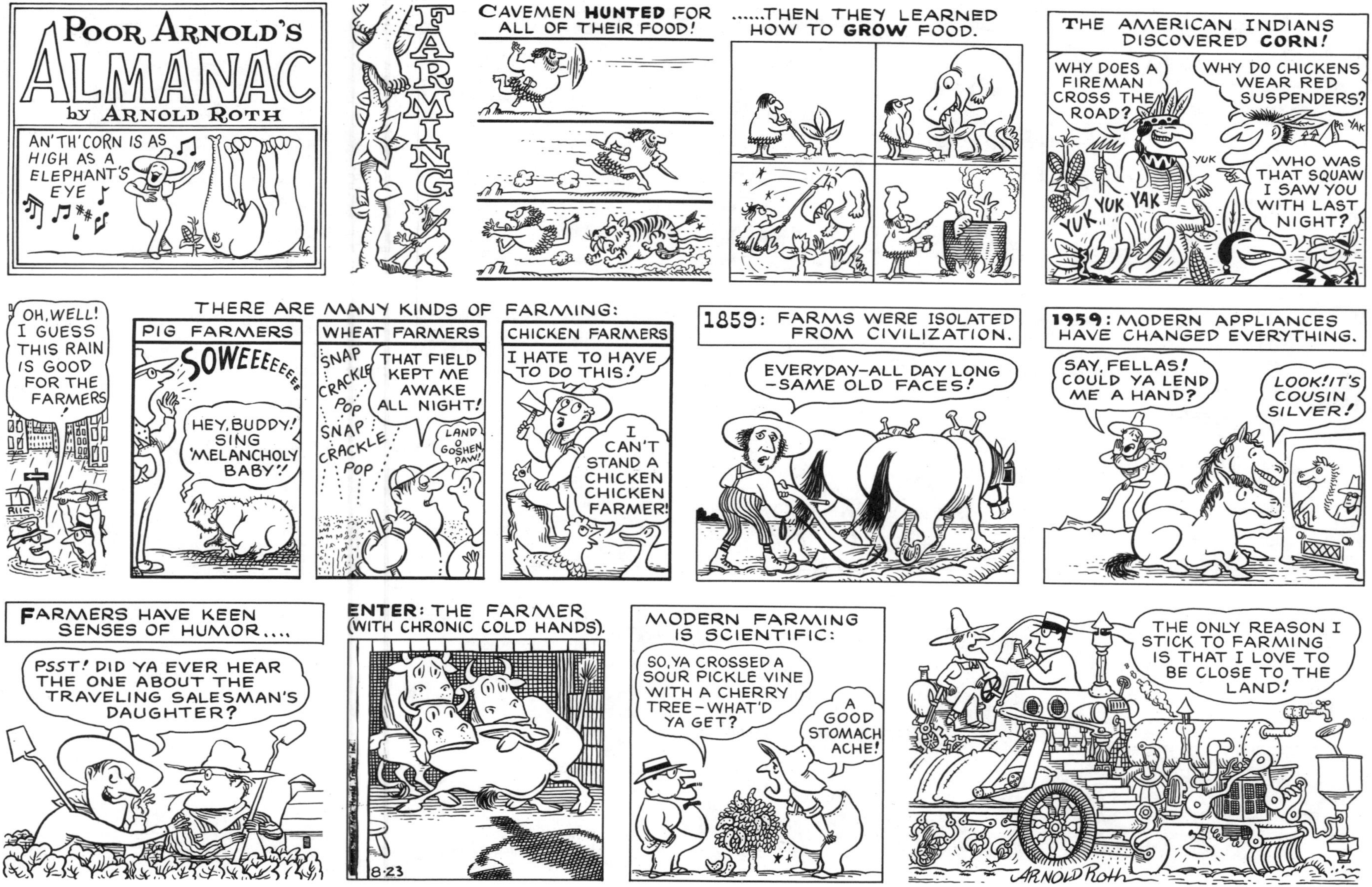
POOR ARNOLD'S ALMANAC
by ARNOLD ROTH
AN' TH' CORN IS AS HIGH AS A ELEPHANT'S EYE
FARMING
CAVEMEN **HUNTED** FOR ALL OF THEIR FOOD!
......THEN THEY LEARNED HOW TO **GROW** FOOD.
THE AMERICAN INDIANS DISCOVERED **CORN**!
WHY DOES A FIREMAN CROSS THE ROAD?
WHY DO CHICKENS WEAR RED SUSPENDERS?
YAK
YUK
WHO WAS THAT SQUAW I SAW YOU WITH LAST NIGHT?
YUK YUK YAK
OH, WELL! I GUESS THIS RAIN IS GOOD FOR THE FARMERS!
THERE ARE MANY KINDS OF FARMING:
PIG FARMERS
SOWEEEEeeeee
HEY, BUDDY! SING 'MELANCHOLY BABY'!
WHEAT FARMERS
SNAP CRACKLE POP SNAP CRACKLE POP
THAT FIELD KEPT ME AWAKE ALL NIGHT!
LAND O GOSHEN, PAW!
CHICKEN FARMERS
I HATE TO HAVE TO DO THIS!
I CAN'T STAND A CHICKEN CHICKEN FARMER!
1859: FARMS WERE ISOLATED FROM CIVILIZATION.
EVERYDAY—ALL DAY LONG —SAME OLD FACES!
1959: MODERN APPLIANCES HAVE CHANGED EVERYTHING.
SAY, FELLAS! COULD YA LEND ME A HAND?
LOOK! IT'S COUSIN SILVER!
FARMERS HAVE KEEN SENSES OF HUMOR....
PSST! DID YA EVER HEAR THE ONE ABOUT THE TRAVELING SALESMAN'S DAUGHTER?
ENTER: THE FARMER (WITH CHRONIC COLD HANDS).
8·23
MODERN FARMING IS SCIENTIFIC:
SO, YA CROSSED A SOUR PICKLE VINE WITH A CHERRY TREE—WHAT'D YA GET?
A GOOD STOMACH ACHE!
THE ONLY REASON I STICK TO FARMING IS THAT I LOVE TO BE CLOSE TO THE LAND!
ARNOLD ROTH

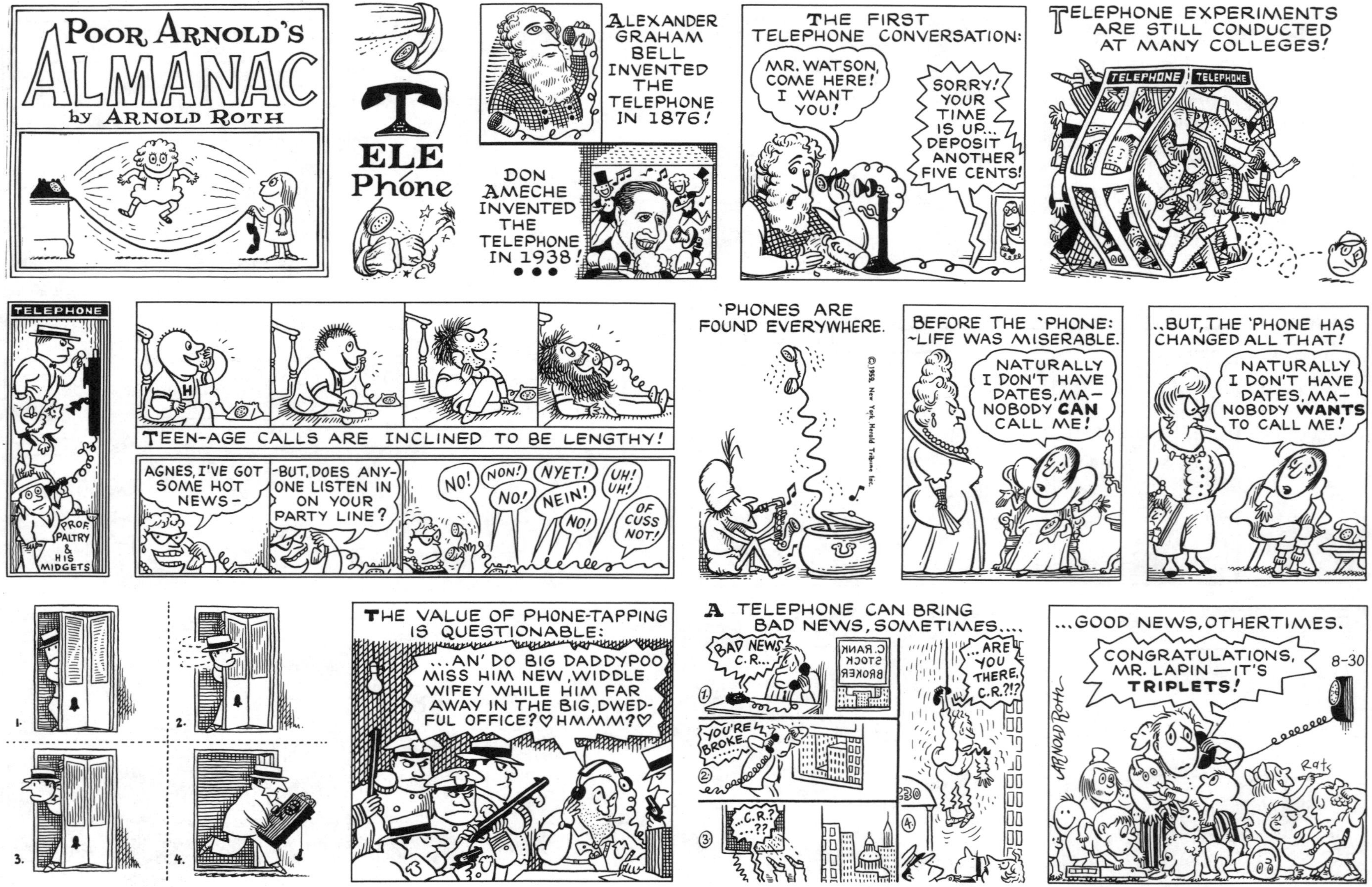

POOR ARNOLD'S ALMANAC
by ARNOLD ROTH
TELEPhone
ALEXANDER GRAHAM BELL INVENTED THE TELEPHONE IN 1876!
DON AMECHE INVENTED THE TELEPHONE IN 1938! • • •
THE FIRST TELEPHONE CONVERSATION:
MR. WATSON, COME HERE! I WANT YOU!
SORRY! YOUR TIME IS UP... DEPOSIT ANOTHER FIVE CENTS!
TELEPHONE EXPERIMENTS ARE STILL CONDUCTED AT MANY COLLEGES!
TELEPHONE
TELEPHONE
TELEPHONE
PROF. PALTRY & HIS MIDGETS
TEEN-AGE CALLS ARE INCLINED TO BE LENGTHY!
AGNES, I'VE GOT SOME HOT NEWS–
–BUT, DOES ANYONE LISTEN IN ON YOUR PARTY LINE?
NO!
NON!
NO!
NYET!
NEIN!
NO!
UH! UH!
OF CUSS NOT!
'PHONES ARE FOUND EVERYWHERE.
© 1952, New York Herald Tribune Inc.
BEFORE THE 'PHONE: ~LIFE WAS MISERABLE.
NATURALLY I DON'T HAVE DATES, MA– NOBODY **CAN** CALL ME!
..BUT, THE 'PHONE HAS CHANGED ALL THAT!
NATURALLY I DON'T HAVE DATES, MA– NOBODY **WANTS** TO CALL ME!
1.
2.
3.
4.
THE VALUE OF PHONE-TAPPING IS QUESTIONABLE:
...AN' DO BIG DADDYPOO MISS HIM NEW, WIDDLE WIFEY WHILE HIM FAR AWAY IN THE BIG, DWEDFUL OFFICE?♡HMMM?♡
A TELEPHONE CAN BRING BAD NEWS, SOMETIMES....
BAD NEWS, C.R...
C. RANK STOCK BROKER
1.
YOU'RE BROKE......
2.
...ARE YOU THERE, C.R.?!?
...C.R.? ...??
3.
4.
...GOOD NEWS, OTHERTIMES.
CONGRATULATIONS, MR. LAPIN—IT'S **TRIPLETS!**
8-30
ARNOLD ROTH
Rats

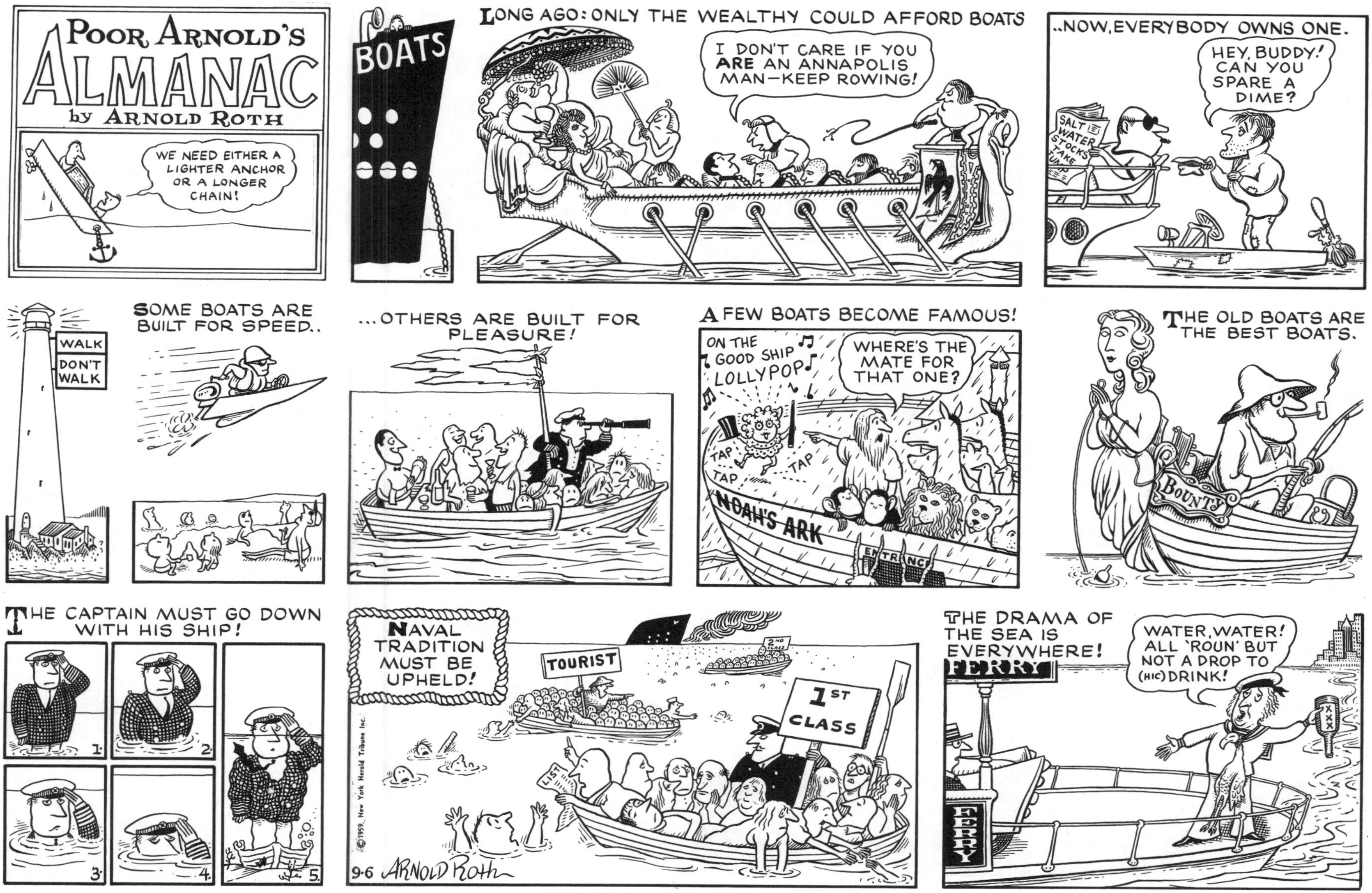
POOR ARNOLD'S ALMANAC
by ARNOLD ROTH
WE NEED EITHER A LIGHTER ANCHOR OR A LONGER CHAIN!
BOATS
LONG AGO: ONLY THE WEALTHY COULD AFFORD BOATS
I DON'T CARE IF YOU ARE AN ANNAPOLIS MAN—KEEP ROWING!
..NOW, EVERYBODY OWNS ONE.
SALT WATER STOCKS TAKE
HEY, BUDDY! CAN YOU SPARE A DIME?
WALK
DON'T WALK
SOME BOATS ARE BUILT FOR SPEED..
...OTHERS ARE BUILT FOR PLEASURE!
A FEW BOATS BECOME FAMOUS!
ON THE GOOD SHIP LOLLYPOP
TAP TAP TAP
WHERE'S THE MATE FOR THAT ONE?
NOAH'S ARK
ENTRANCE
THE OLD BOATS ARE THE BEST BOATS.
BOUNTY
THE CAPTAIN MUST GO DOWN WITH HIS SHIP!
1. 2. 3. 4. 5.
NAVAL TRADITION MUST BE UPHELD!
TOURIST
2ND CLASS
1ST CLASS
LIST
©1959, New York Herald Tribune Inc.
9·6 ARNOLD ROTH
THE DRAMA OF THE SEA IS EVERYWHERE!
FERRY
WATER, WATER! ALL 'ROUN' BUT NOT A DROP TO (HIC) DRINK!
XXX
FERRY

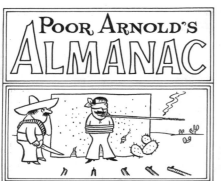

POOR ARNOLD'S ALMANAC

WHAT WAS IT LIKE BEFORE PEOPLE SMOKED?

YE READER'S DIGESTE MAGAZINE

EGAD! NOT A THING TO WRITE ABOUT!

YE EDITOR

THE AMERICAN INDIANS INVENTED SMOKING.

WHAT'VE YA GOT WITH CORK-TIP, NITROTITE-FILTER, KING-SIZE IN A FLIPPED-TOP BOX, CHIEF?

ARE YOU OLD ENUFF TO SMOKE?

SIR WALTER RALEIGH INTRODUCED IT TO EUROPEANS.......

SMOKE! SMOKE! SMOKE! ALL THE TIME – HE SMOKES!

YEAH! A REGULAR CHIMNEY.

GAD! I WISH I HAD SAID THAT!

HAMLET

THEN, EVERYBODY LEARNED!

INHALE! EXHALE! INHALE! EXHALE! INHALE!

TO SOME, IT IS A GRAND ADVENTURE..

ARE YOU OLD ENOUGH TO SMOKE?

....TO OTHERS – A PROBLEM.....

HEY, BUDDY! GOT A MATCH?

..& TO MANY–JUST PLAIN RELAXING!

ARE YOU OLD ENOUGH TO SMOKE?

AT FIRST–ONLY MEN SMOKED.

BLOW SOME MY WAY!

SURE!

OMIGOSH! GERT! SPEAK TO ME!

MOST WOMEN STARTED IN THE 1920'S.

CHARLESTON

RAZZ A MA TAZZ

WHAT A DISGRACE! SMOKING!

ARNOLD ROTH

NOW, JUST ABOUT EVERYBODY DOES IT.

HEY! YOU'RE NOT OLD ENOUGH TO SMOKE!

©1959, New York Herald Tribune Inc.

MANY AUTHORITIES DISAPPROVE OF THE WHOLE IDEA!

ED, YOU'LL HAVE TO STOP SMOKING. YOU KNOW IT'S NO GOOD FOR YOU!

MOST POPULAR FORMS OF SMOKING ARE:

PIPE

CIGAR

CIGARETTE

CORN SILK

CONTRARY TO PUBLIC OPINION, SMOKING IS **NOT** A HABIT ~

DON'T BOTHER DADDY! HE'S GIVING UP SMOKING.

9-13

~AND IS NOT **ALWAYS** INJURIOUS TO THE HEALTH.

DON'T BLAME ME! I TOLD YOU THAT SMOKING WOULD STUNT YOUR GROWTH.

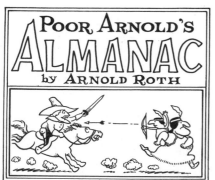

POOR ARNOLD'S
ALMANAC
by ARNOLD ROTH
AMERICAN
INDIANS
INDIANS WERE THE ONLY INHABITANTS OF AMERICA..
I'M SORRY! BUT YOU'LL HAVE TO LEAVE.... YOU'RE NO INDIAN!
SAYS WHO!?
HIS.
....UNTIL THE WHITE-MAN ARRIVED!
OBVIOUSLY A CASE OF VITAMIN DEFICIENCY!
BUT THEY SOON LEARNED WHITE-MAN'S WAYS!
I'LL RAISE IT!
O.K.! POKER FACE!
WE GIVE TRADING STAMPS
THERE ARE MANY DIFFERENT KINDS OF INDIANS....
EASTERN INDIANS
WESTERN INDIANS
PSST! GOT A LIGHT?
CIGAR-STORE INDIANS
YANKS GO HOME
Cleveland Indians
HIAWATHA
LAKE GITCHY GOOMIE
WHAT'S YOUR NAME?
MINNIE!
LAKE GITCHY GOOMIE
MINNIE? HA! HA!
NO WONDER THEY'RE CALLED LAUGHING WATERS!
9-20
INDIANS SOLD MANHATTAN FOR $24.
NEW WORLD REAL ESTATE CO. SPECIALS ·TODAY·
I KNOW THOSE INDIAN-GIVERS! YOU'LL SEE– THEY'LL WANT IT BACK SOMEDAY!
THE RAIN DANCE
INDIANS SOMETIMES SCALPED PEOPLE (FEH!)
HEY, LOOK! A PRE-FAB!
© 1959, New York Herald Tribune Inc.
These Summit Meetings are nothin' but a waste o' time!
CUSTER'S LAST STAND!
THE INDIAN WARS ENDED WITH THE SMOKING OF THE PEACE-PIPE.
(COUGH! COUGH!) O.K.! O.K.! (HACK!) WE GIVE UP! (COUGH!) YOU WIN!
ARNOLD ROTH

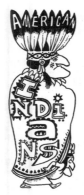

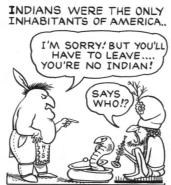

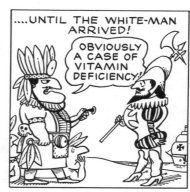

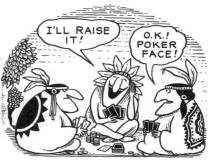

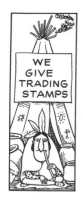

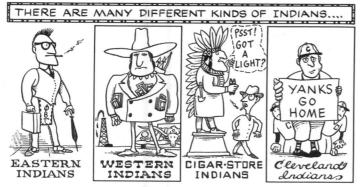

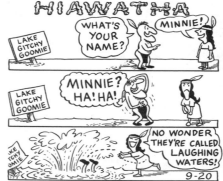

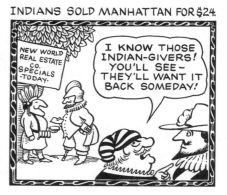

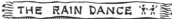

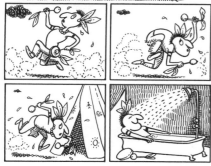

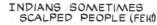

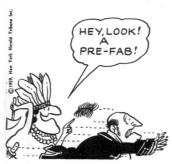

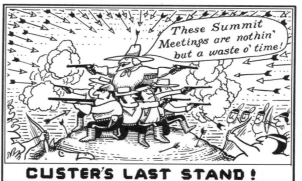

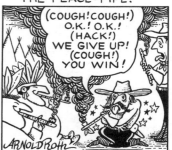

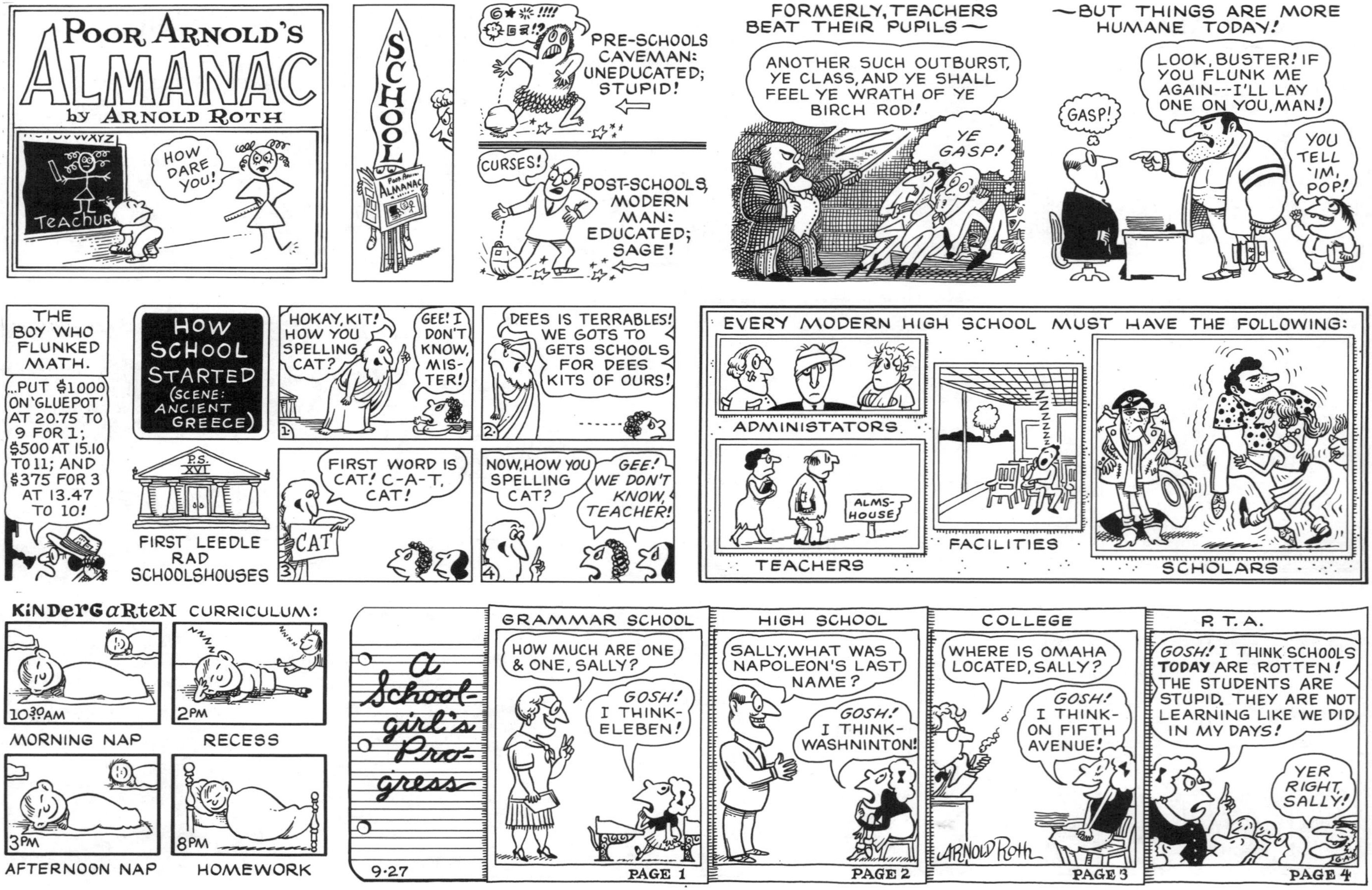
POOR ARNOLD'S ALMANAC
by ARNOLD ROTH
TEACHUR
HOW DARE YOU!
SCHOOL
POOR ARNOLD'S ALMANAC
PRE-SCHOOLS CAVEMAN: UNEDUCATED; STUPID!
CURSES!
POST-SCHOOLS, MODERN MAN: EDUCATED; SAGE!
FORMERLY, TEACHERS BEAT THEIR PUPILS—
ANOTHER SUCH OUTBURST, YE CLASS, AND YE SHALL FEEL YE WRATH OF YE BIRCH ROD!
YE GASP!
—BUT THINGS ARE MORE HUMANE TODAY!
LOOK, BUSTER! IF YOU FLUNK ME AGAIN---I'LL LAY ONE ON YOU, MAN!
GASP!
YOU TELL 'IM, POP!
THE BOY WHO FLUNKED MATH.
...PUT $1000 ON 'GLUEPOT' AT 20.75 TO 9 FOR 1; $500 AT 15.10 TO 11; AND $375 FOR 3 AT 13.47 TO 10!
HOW SCHOOL STARTED (SCENE: ANCIENT GREECE)
P.S. XVI
FIRST LEEDLE RAD SCHOOLSHOUSES
HOKAY, KIT! HOW YOU SPELLING CAT?
GEE! I DON'T KNOW, MISTER!
DEES IS TERRABLES! WE GOTS TO GETS SCHOOLS FOR DEES KITS OF OURS!
FIRST WORD IS CAT! C-A-T, CAT!
CAT
NOW, HOW YOU SPELLING CAT?
GEE! WE DON'T KNOW, TEACHER!
EVERY MODERN HIGH SCHOOL MUST HAVE THE FOLLOWING:
ADMINISTATORS
TEACHERS
ALMS-HOUSE
FACILITIES
SCHOLARS
KINDERGARTEN CURRICULUM:
10:30 AM
MORNING NAP
2 PM
RECESS
3 PM
AFTERNOON NAP
8 PM
HOMEWORK
a School-girl's Pro-gress
9·27
GRAMMAR SCHOOL
HOW MUCH ARE ONE & ONE, SALLY?
GOSH! I THINK-ELEBEN!
PAGE 1
HIGH SCHOOL
SALLY, WHAT WAS NAPOLEON'S LAST NAME?
GOSH! I THINK-WASHNINTON!
PAGE 2
COLLEGE
WHERE IS OMAHA LOCATED, SALLY?
GOSH! I THINK-ON FIFTH AVENUE!
ARNOLD ROTH
PAGE 3
P.T.A.
GOSH! I THINK SCHOOLS TODAY ARE ROTTEN! THE STUDENTS ARE STUPID. THEY ARE NOT LEARNING LIKE WE DID IN MY DAYS!
YER RIGHT, SALLY!
PAGE 4

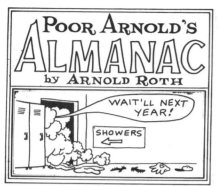

Poor Arnold's ALMANAC
by ARNOLD ROTH

WAIT'LL NEXT YEAR!
SHOWERS →

The WORLD SERIES

BALL! FIVE

EVERY YEAR, AROUND THIS TIME, NORMAL ACTIVITIES CEASE......

HELP! HELP! HELP! HELP!

WHEW! WHAT A NAG!

......PEOPLE ARE PRE-OCCUPIED... AND, **WHY**, YOU ASK?.........

WAIT, MARSHAL! I'LL BE BACK-NEXT WEEK!

INSTITUTE FOR ADVANCED STUDIES

QUIET, YOU FOOL, SIR! IT'S THE WORLD SERIES!

STRIKE FOUR

THE STRATEGIST

BUNT!

SERIES TICKETS ARE HARD TO GET:

...AND TO MY NEPHEW, ROY, I BEQUEATH MY WORLD SERIES TICKETS!

LAST WILL & TESTY MENT

ONLY THE **REAL** FANS GET TICKETS:

YESSIR! THIS IS THE FIRST GAME I'VE BEEN TO ALL YEAR!

THE SERIES 'GOAT'

GULP!

BOO FEH! FOOEY! BOO S-S-S-S FEH!

THE SERIES 'HERO'

HOORAY! YIPPEE! RAH!

YIPPEE! HUZZAHS! UNFEH! HOORAY!

THE PLAYER'S ONLY THOUGHT IS OF THE **PRESTIGE** OF WINNING!

$ $ $ $

IF YOU ARE CONFUSED **NOW**... THINK OF WHAT THE WORLD SERIES WILL BE LIKE WHEN THERE ARE **THREE** MAJOR LEAGUES!

10-4

ArNoLd RoTh

5   22   30

19

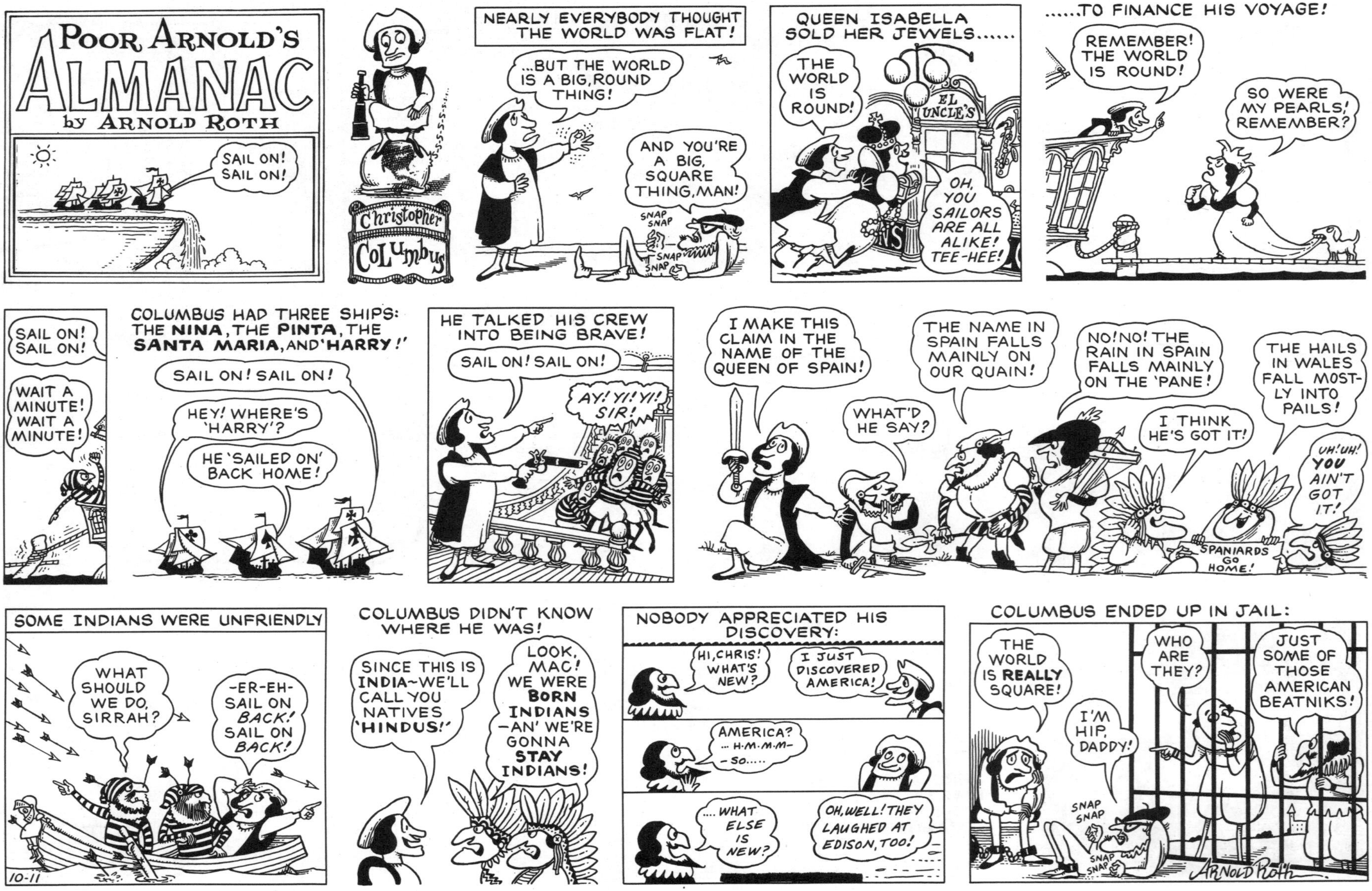
POOR ARNOLD'S
ALMANAC
by ARNOLD ROTH
SAIL ON! SAIL ON!
Christopher Columbus
NEARLY EVERYBODY THOUGHT THE WORLD WAS FLAT!
...BUT THE WORLD IS A BIG, ROUND THING!
AND YOU'RE A BIG, SQUARE THING, MAN!
SNAP SNAP
SNAP SNAP
QUEEN ISABELLA SOLD HER JEWELS......
THE WORLD IS ROUND!
EL UNCLE'S
OH, YOU SAILORS ARE ALL ALIKE! TEE-HEE!
......TO FINANCE HIS VOYAGE!
REMEMBER! THE WORLD IS ROUND!
SO WERE MY PEARLS! REMEMBER?
SAIL ON! SAIL ON!
WAIT A MINUTE! WAIT A MINUTE!
COLUMBUS HAD THREE SHIPS: THE NINA, THE PINTA, THE SANTA MARIA, AND 'HARRY!'
SAIL ON! SAIL ON!
HEY! WHERE'S 'HARRY'?
HE 'SAILED ON' BACK HOME!
HE TALKED HIS CREW INTO BEING BRAVE!
SAIL ON! SAIL ON!
AY! YI! YI! SIR!
I MAKE THIS CLAIM IN THE NAME OF THE QUEEN OF SPAIN!
WHAT'D HE SAY?
THE NAME IN SPAIN FALLS MAINLY ON OUR QUAIN!
NO! NO! THE RAIN IN SPAIN FALLS MAINLY ON THE 'PANE!
I THINK HE'S GOT IT!
THE HAILS IN WALES FALL MOSTLY INTO PAILS!
UH! UH! YOU AIN'T GOT IT!
SPANIARDS GO HOME!
SOME INDIANS WERE UNFRIENDLY
WHAT SHOULD WE DO, SIRRAH?
-ER-EH- SAIL ON BACK! SAIL ON BACK!
10-11
COLUMBUS DIDN'T KNOW WHERE HE WAS!
SINCE THIS IS INDIA~WE'LL CALL YOU NATIVES 'HINDUS!'
LOOK, MAC! WE WERE BORN INDIANS —AN' WE'RE GONNA STAY INDIANS!
NOBODY APPRECIATED HIS DISCOVERY:
HI, CHRIS! WHAT'S NEW?
I JUST DISCOVERED AMERICA!
AMERICA? ...H-M-M-M- -SO.....
....WHAT ELSE IS NEW?
OH, WELL! THEY LAUGHED AT EDISON, TOO!
COLUMBUS ENDED UP IN JAIL:
THE WORLD IS REALLY SQUARE!
WHO ARE THEY?
JUST SOME OF THOSE AMERICAN BEATNIKS!
I'M HIP, DADDY!
SNAP SNAP
SNAP SNAP
ARNOLD ROTH

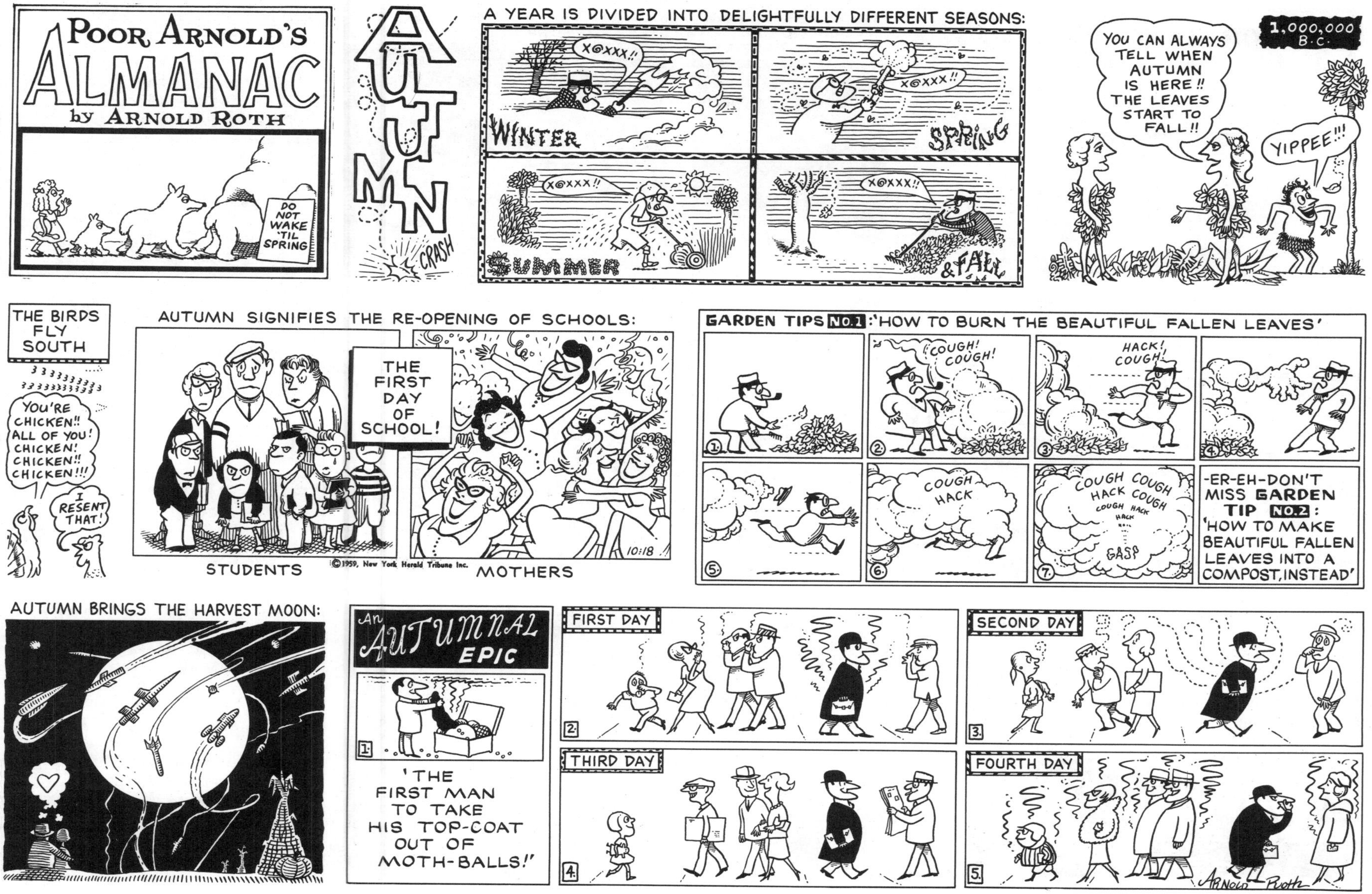
POOR ARNOLD'S ALMANAC
by ARNOLD ROTH
DO NOT WAKE 'TIL SPRING
AUTUMN
CRASH
A YEAR IS DIVIDED INTO DELIGHTFULLY DIFFERENT SEASONS:
X@XXX!!
WINTER
X@XXX!!
SPRING
X@XXX!!
SUMMER
X@XXX!!
&FALL
1,000,000 B.C.
YOU CAN ALWAYS TELL WHEN AUTUMN IS HERE!! THE LEAVES START TO FALL!!
YIPPEE!!!
THE BIRDS FLY SOUTH
YOU'RE CHICKEN!! ALL OF YOU! CHICKEN! CHICKEN!! CHICKEN!!!
I RESENT THAT!
AUTUMN SIGNIFIES THE RE-OPENING OF SCHOOLS:
THE FIRST DAY OF SCHOOL!
10:18
STUDENTS
©1959, New York Herald Tribune Inc.
MOTHERS
GARDEN TIPS NO.1: 'HOW TO BURN THE BEAUTIFUL FALLEN LEAVES'
1.
2. COUGH! COUGH!
3. HACK! COUGH!
4.
5.
6. COUGH HACK
7. COUGH COUGH HACK COUGH COUGH HACK HACK GASP
-ER-EH-DON'T MISS GARDEN TIP NO.2: 'HOW TO MAKE BEAUTIFUL FALLEN LEAVES INTO A COMPOST, INSTEAD'
AUTUMN BRINGS THE HARVEST MOON:
An AUTUMNAL EPIC
1.
'THE FIRST MAN TO TAKE HIS TOP-COAT OUT OF MOTH-BALLS!'
FIRST DAY
2.
SECOND DAY
3.
THIRD DAY
4.
FOURTH DAY
5.
ARNOLD ROTH

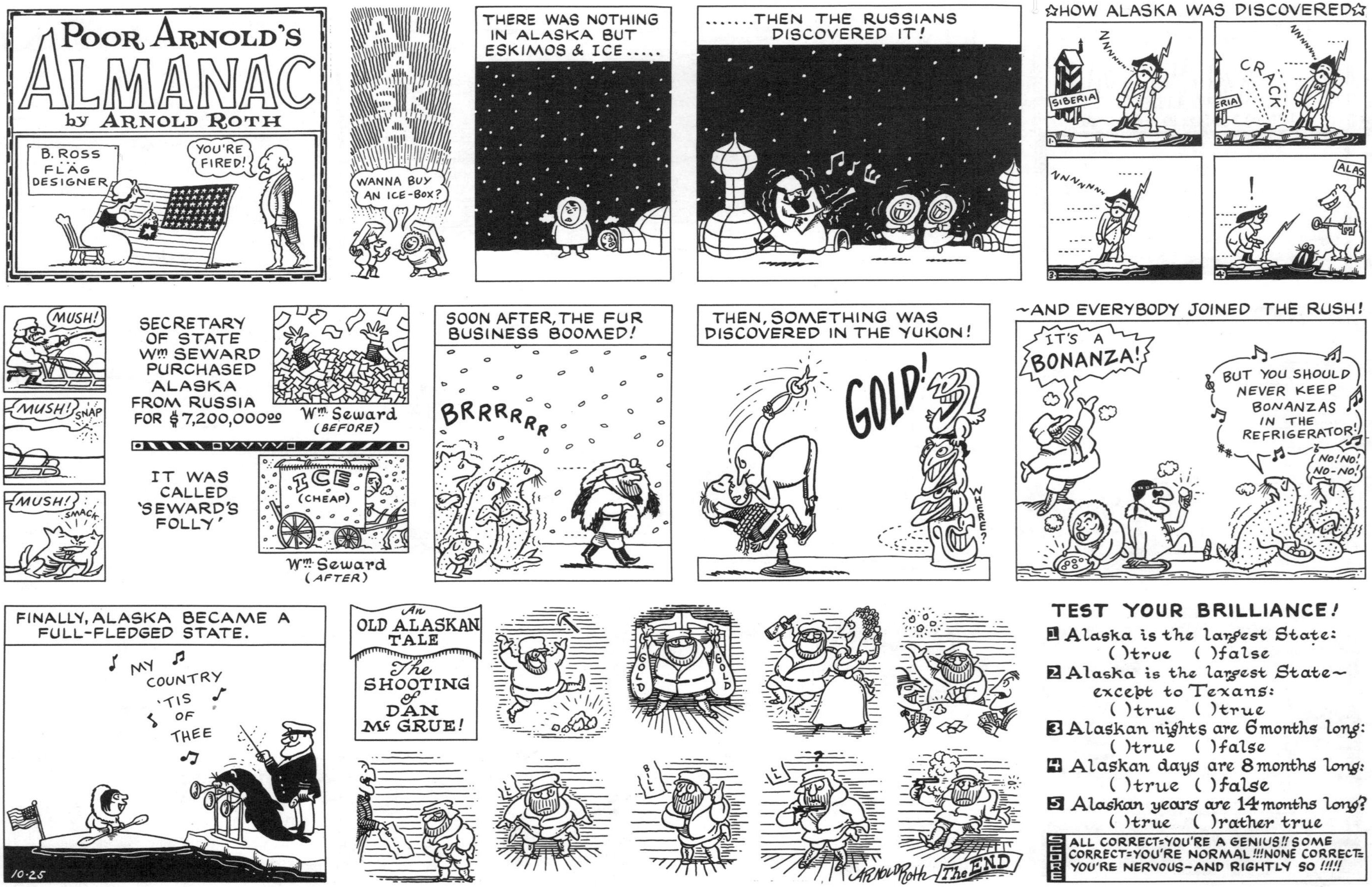

POOR ARNOLD'S ALMANAC
by ARNOLD ROTH
B. ROSS FLAG DESIGNER
YOU'RE FIRED!
ALASKA
WANNA BUY AN ICE-BOX?
THERE WAS NOTHING IN ALASKA BUT ESKIMOS & ICE.....
.......THEN THE RUSSIANS DISCOVERED IT!
☆HOW ALASKA WAS DISCOVERED☆
SIBERIA
ZZZZ
CRACK
ERIA
!
ALAS
MUSH!
MUSH! SNAP
MUSH! SMACK
SECRETARY OF STATE Wm SEWARD PURCHASED ALASKA FROM RUSSIA FOR $7,200,000.00
Wm Seward (BEFORE)
IT WAS CALLED 'SEWARD'S FOLLY'
ICE (CHEAP)
Wm Seward (AFTER)
SOON AFTER, THE FUR BUSINESS BOOMED!
BRRRRRRR
THEN, SOMETHING WAS DISCOVERED IN THE YUKON!
GOLD!
WHERE?
~AND EVERYBODY JOINED THE RUSH!
IT'S A BONANZA!
BUT YOU SHOULD NEVER KEEP BONANZAS IN THE REFRIGERATOR!
NO! NO! NO-NO!
FINALLY, ALASKA BECAME A FULL-FLEDGED STATE.
MY COUNTRY 'TIS OF THEE
10-25
An OLD ALASKAN TALE
The SHOOTING of DAN McGRUE!
GOLD
GOLD
BILL
BILL
BILL
BILL
?
ARNOLD ROTH
The END
TEST YOUR BRILLIANCE!
1 Alaska is the largest State: ( )true ( )false
2 Alaska is the largest State~ except to Texans: ( )true ( )true
3 Alaskan nights are 6 months long: ( )true ( )false
4 Alaskan days are 8 months long: ( )true ( )false
5 Alaskan years are 14 months long? ( )true ( )rather true
SCORE
ALL CORRECT=YOU'RE A GENIUS!! SOME CORRECT=YOU'RE NORMAL!!! NONE CORRECT=YOU'RE NERVOUS-AND RIGHTLY SO!!!!!

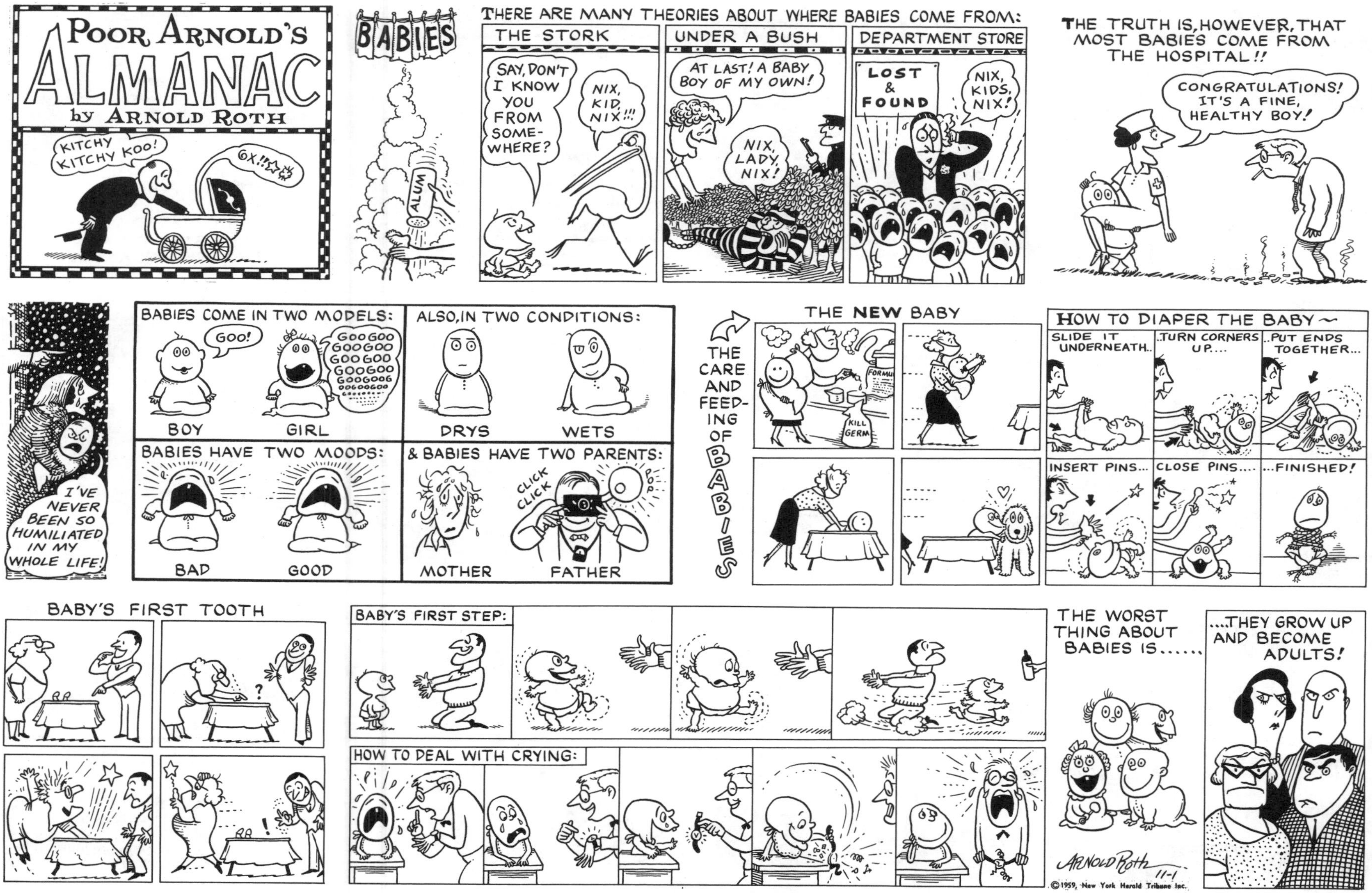
POOR ARNOLD'S
ALMANAC
by ARNOLD ROTH
KITCHY KITCHY KOO!
GX!!
BABIES
ALUM
THERE ARE MANY THEORIES ABOUT WHERE BABIES COME FROM:
THE STORK
SAY, DON'T I KNOW YOU FROM SOME-WHERE?
NIX, KID, NIX!!!
UNDER A BUSH
AT LAST! A BABY BOY OF MY OWN!
NIX, LADY, NIX!
DEPARTMENT STORE
LOST & FOUND
NIX, KIDS, NIX!
THE TRUTH IS, HOWEVER, THAT MOST BABIES COME FROM THE HOSPITAL!!
CONGRATULATIONS! IT'S A FINE, HEALTHY BOY!
I'VE NEVER BEEN SO HUMILIATED IN MY WHOLE LIFE!
BABIES COME IN TWO MODELS:
GOO!
GOOGOO GOOGOO GOOGOO GOOGOO GOOGOO
BOY
GIRL
ALSO, IN TWO CONDITIONS:
DRYS
WETS
BABIES HAVE TWO MOODS:
BAD
GOOD
& BABIES HAVE TWO PARENTS:
CLICK CLICK
POP
MOTHER
FATHER
THE CARE AND FEED-ING OF BABIES
THE NEW BABY
FORMULA
KILL GERM
HOW TO DIAPER THE BABY ~
SLIDE IT UNDERNEATH..
..TURN CORNERS UP....
..PUT ENDS TOGETHER...
INSERT PINS...
CLOSE PINS....
...FINISHED!
BABY'S FIRST TOOTH
?
!
BABY'S FIRST STEP:
HOW TO DEAL WITH CRYING:
THE WORST THING ABOUT BABIES IS......
....THEY GROW UP AND BECOME ADULTS!
ARNOLD ROTH 11-1
©1959, New York Herald Tribune Inc.

ALMANAC

COLLEGE FOOTBALL

Is there a Doctor in the house?

er~would I do? I'm a medical student!

THE MODERN FOOTBALL FIELD IS 100 YDS. LONG, 53⅓ YDS. WIDE, AND IS COVERED WITH WHITE STRIPES AND INJURED PLAYERS.

• A TYPICAL 'GRIDIRON ELEVEN' •

GO TEAM GO

THE ENGLISH DEPARTMENT SHALL HEAR ABOUT THAT!

LEFT HALF-BACK

QUARTER-BACK

RIGHT HALF-BACK

FULL-BACK

BURP

RIGHT END | RIGHT TACKLE | RIGHT GUARD | CENTER | WRONG GUARD | WRONG TACKLE | WRONG END

MODERN MAN | MODERN PLAYER

THE MODERN PLAYER IS WELL CLOTHED AND PROTECTED

OUCH!

HE IS ALSO WELL FED, TRAINED...

...AND WELL INSTRUCTED!

COACH

ARNOLD ROTH

COLLEGE ALUMNI ARE EVERYWHERE SEARCHING FOR TALENT~

WE'RE TOO LATE-OHIO GOT HIM!

ANOTHER 'SLINGIN' SAMMY'!

ACTION PICTURES

THE KICK-OFF | THE TACKLE | THE FUMBLE | THE RECOVERY | THE PASS | THE CATCH

THE OPPOSITION | THE TACKLE | THE RECOVERY | THE COACH | THE CROWD

FOURSCORE AND SEVEN TOUCHDOWNS AGO, YOU MEN....

WOW! WHAT A PEP-TALK!

MY MELANCHOLY BABY

THE END!

POOR ARNOLD'S ALMANAC
by ARNOLD ROTH
TV
T ELE V ISION
1000 B.C.
300 B.C.
700 A.D.
1700 A.D.
VO-DE-O VO-DE-O AN' IT COMES OUT HERE
1935 A.D.
AN' YOU'RE SWELL, TOO, JACK!!!
15 T.V.
A THREE-DIMENSIONAL PORTRAIT 'THE TV REPAIRMAN' AS SEEN BY.....
...HIMSELF....
SOB BLESS YOU, SIR, BLESS YOU!
...HIS MOTHER...
..HIS CUSTOMERS!
THERE ARE DIFFERENT SHOWS FOR ALL AGE GROUPS:
GOSH
GEE
GOOLLY
THE KIDDIES...
BLANDSTAND?
ROCK
LIKE-I DIG IT!
LIKE-WISE!
..THE TEEN-AGERS..
GOSH
GEE!
...THE ADULTS!
..AND, NOW, AN ON-THE-SPOT-DIRECT-TO-YOU-LIVE-TELECAST-SPEECH BY THE PRESIDENT OF THE UNITED STATES!
AW! I'VE SEEN THIS PICTURE BEFORE!
HMM!!...
....BUT...
I FORGET....
..WHO'S IN IT?
'SHOCK THEATER'
GASP
THIS IS TOO SCAIRY...
I'M GOING TO BED!!
GOODNIGHT, DAHLINK!
11-15
HELLO, ED....
ARNOLD ROTH
A MAN WATCHING A TV COMEDY SHOW...
..WATCHING A SERIOUS TV COMMERCIAL...
YAWN
A WOMAN WATCHING TV HORROR SHOW...
ECH!
..WATCHING TV PATENT-MEDICINE AD!!
© 1958, New York Herald Tribune Inc.
IT'S 4 A.M., ALREADY!! GO TO SLEEP!!!
I CAN'T! I NEVER SAW THIS PICTURE BEFORE!!
STATION KROK-TV TEST PATTERN

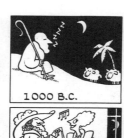

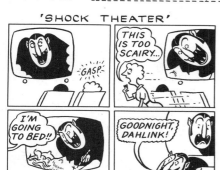

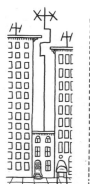

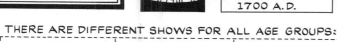

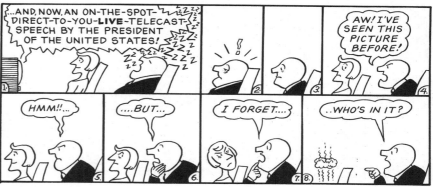

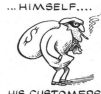

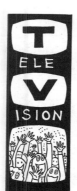

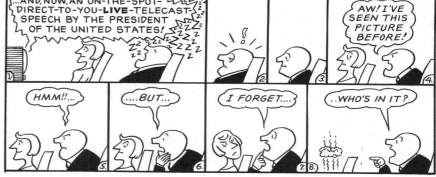

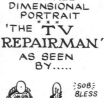

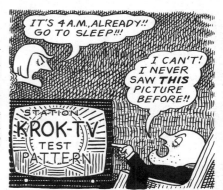

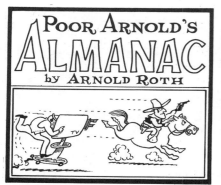

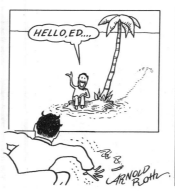

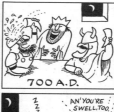

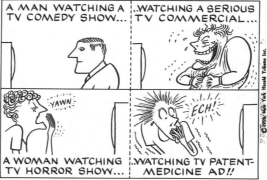

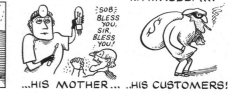

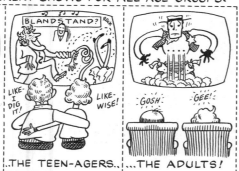

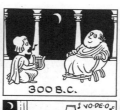

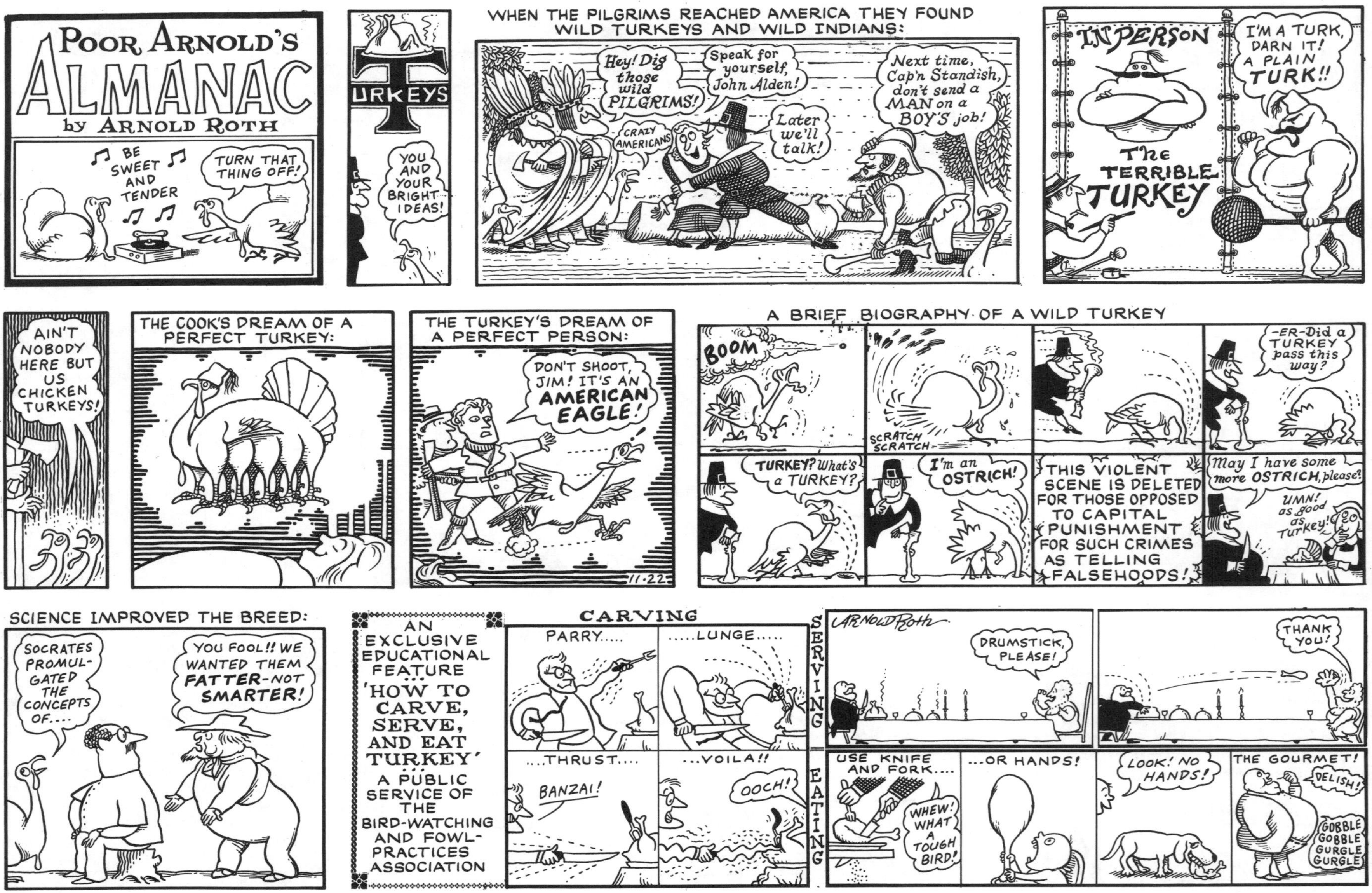
POOR ARNOLD'S ALMANAC
by ARNOLD ROTH
BE SWEET AND TENDER
TURN THAT THING OFF!
TURKEYS
YOU AND YOUR BRIGHT IDEAS!
WHEN THE PILGRIMS REACHED AMERICA THEY FOUND WILD TURKEYS AND WILD INDIANS:
Hey! Dig those wild PILGRIMS!
Speak for yourself, John Alden!
CRAZY AMERICANS
Later we'll talk!
Next time, Cap'n Standish, don't send a MAN on a BOY'S job!
IN PERSON
The TERRIBLE TURKEY
I'M A TURK, DARN IT! A PLAIN TURK!!
AIN'T NOBODY HERE BUT US CHICKEN TURKEYS!
THE COOK'S DREAM OF A PERFECT TURKEY:
THE TURKEY'S DREAM OF A PERFECT PERSON:
DON'T SHOOT, JIM! IT'S AN AMERICAN EAGLE!
11·22·
A BRIEF BIOGRAPHY OF A WILD TURKEY
BOOM
SCRATCH SCRATCH
-ER-Did a TURKEY pass this way?
TURKEY? What's a TURKEY?
I'm an OSTRICH!
THIS VIOLENT SCENE IS DELETED FOR THOSE OPPOSED TO CAPITAL PUNISHMENT FOR SUCH CRIMES AS TELLING FALSEHOODS!
May I have some more OSTRICH, please?
UMN! as good as Turkey!
SCIENCE IMPROVED THE BREED:
SOCRATES PROMULGATED THE CONCEPTS OF....
YOU FOOL!! WE WANTED THEM FATTER-NOT SMARTER!
AN EXCLUSIVE EDUCATIONAL FEATURE ... 'HOW TO CARVE, SERVE, AND EAT TURKEY' ... A PUBLIC SERVICE OF THE BIRD-WATCHING AND FOWL-PRACTICES ASSOCIATION
CARVING
PARRY.....
.....LUNGE.....
....THRUST....
...VOILA!!
BANZAI!
OOCH!
SERVING
ARNOLD ROTH
DRUMSTICK, PLEASE!
THANK YOU!
EATING
USE KNIFE AND FORK....
WHEW! WHAT A TOUGH BIRD!
...OR HANDS!
LOOK! NO HANDS!
THE GOURMET!
DELISH!
GOBBLE GOBBLE GURGLE GURGLE

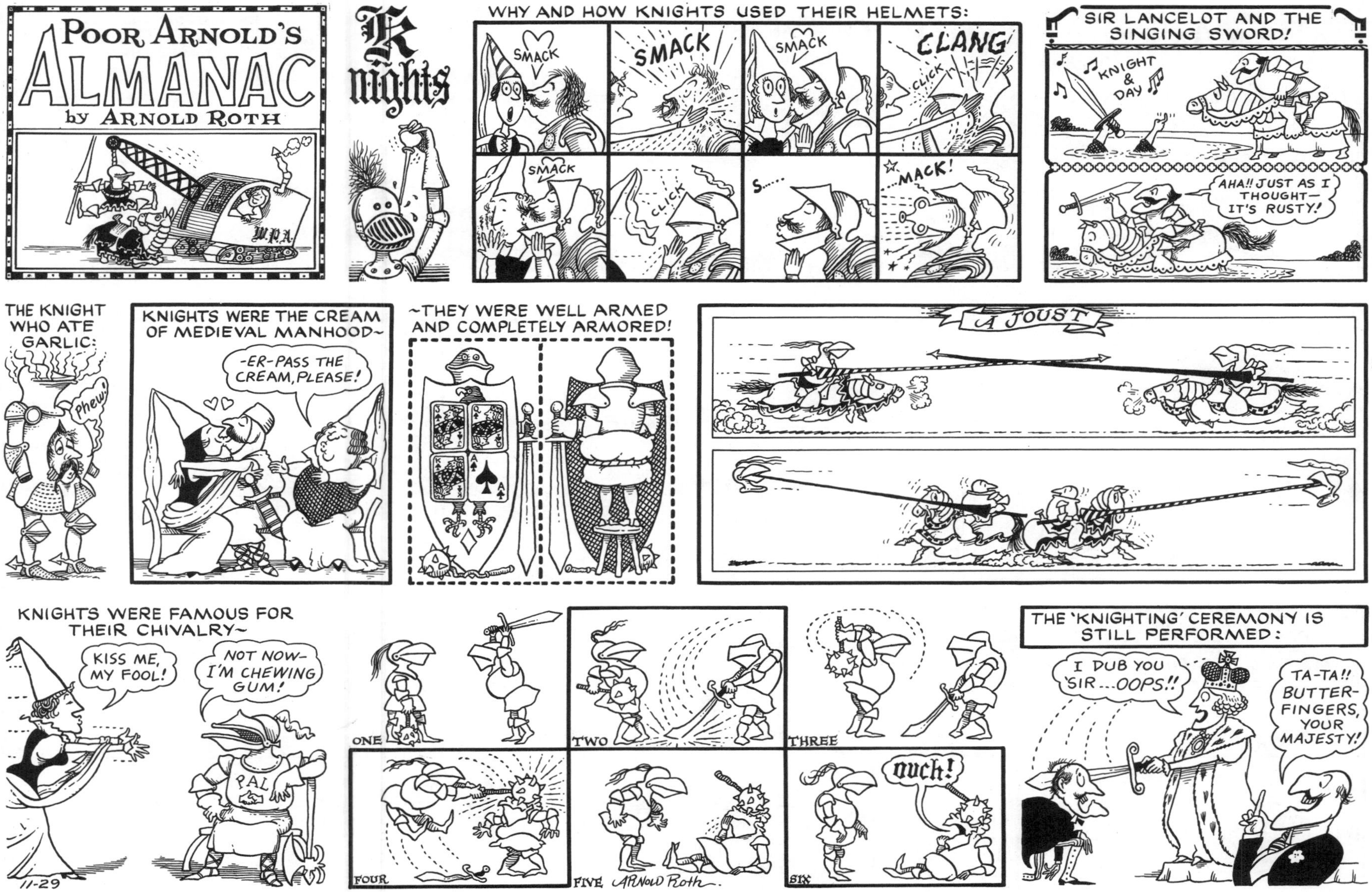
POOR ARNOLD'S
ALMANAC
by ARNOLD ROTH
W.P.A.
Knights
WHY AND HOW KNIGHTS USED THEIR HELMETS:
SMACK
SMACK
SMACK
CLICK
CLANG
SMACK
CLICK
S.....
...MACK!
SIR LANCELOT AND THE SINGING SWORD!
KNIGHT & DAY
AHA!! JUST AS I THOUGHT— IT'S RUSTY!
THE KNIGHT WHO ATE GARLIC:
Phew!
KNIGHTS WERE THE CREAM OF MEDIEVAL MANHOOD~
-ER-PASS THE CREAM, PLEASE!
~THEY WERE WELL ARMED AND COMPLETELY ARMORED!
A JOUST
KNIGHTS WERE FAMOUS FOR THEIR CHIVALRY~
KISS ME, MY FOOL!
NOT NOW- I'M CHEWING GUM!
PAL
11-29
ONE
TWO
THREE
FOUR
FIVE
ARNOLD ROTH
SIX
ouch!
THE 'KNIGHTING' CEREMONY IS STILL PERFORMED:
I DUB YOU SIR...OOPS!!
TA-TA!! BUTTER-FINGERS, YOUR MAJESTY!

POOR ARNOLD'S ALMANAC
by ARNOLD ROTH
AH CHOO
COLDS
SNIFF SNIFF SNFF
COLDS HAVE BEEN WITH US SINCE ANTIQUITY–
AH CHOO!
GESUNDHEIT!
SCIENCE HAS NOT FOUND THE CURE –YET!!
PROFESSOR, I THINK I'VE FOUND A CURE FOR COLDS!
HMM!! YOU ARE OBVIOUSLY A MENTAL CASE– BUT THAT I CAN CURE!
MODERN SCIENCE SCOOPED:
AN ACCURATE PICTURE OF A COMMON COLD GERM:
DOWN WITH PEOPLE ETC.
AN ACCURATE PICTURE OF AN UNCOMMON COLD GERM
DRAT! NOW I'M GETTING A CHILL!
CHARLIE, YOU'RE BLACKBALLED!
POLAR BEAR CLUB
POLAR BEAR CLUB
THE HEAD COLD
THE CHEST COLD
A DRAMATIZATION
SOME VICTIMS RUSH TO THE DOCTOR FOR AID~
HELB ME! I HAB AD AWFUL COLD!
THAD'S A SHABE!
~SOME LEARN FROM TV~
SHAKE COLD MISERIES
ALRIGHT– I'M SHAKING!
~MANY TRY LIQUID DIETS~
Y'SURE THIS'LL HELP ME TO LOSE MY COLD?
ROCK & RYE
LISS'N, WIFF MEDICINE LIKE THAT Y'WON'T WANT TO LOSE IT!!
12·6
~WHILE OTHERS TAKE PREVENTIVE MEASURES!
EEK! A COLD GERM!
DON'T PANIC! I'VE GOT A BEAD ON HIM!
THE COMMON COLD EVEN FIGURES IN OUR FOLKMUSIC
MASSA'S IN DE COLD, COLD GROUND
AH CHOO!
RIP
©1959, New York Herald
© BEATMEN ARCHIVES
SUMMARY: A COLD CAN MAKE ANYONE IRRITABLE, BITTER, MISERABLE AND MEAN!!!
"OLD MOTHER HUBBARD...
MOTHER GOOSE
HONK
...WENT TO THE CUPBOARD...
...TO GET HER POOR DOG A BONE......
COUGH COUGH COUGH COUGH COUGH
...BUD WHED SHE GOT DERE....
SNIFF SNIFF
PLNK
GLP
....THE CUPBOARD WAS BARE.....
..., AND, SO,...
...THE POOR DOG....
...ATE UP MOTHER HUBBARD, INSTEAD!"
YIPPEE!
SLAM
ARNOLD Roth

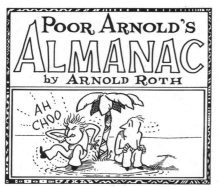

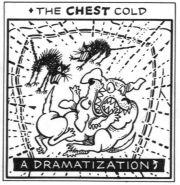

POOR ARNOLD'S
ALMANAC
by ARNOLD ROTH
SNOW
BAR
HOPE VERSUS REALITY
OPULENT GRASS SEED CO.
AT LAST-VACATION TIME!
SNOW PROVIDES MANKIND WITH VITAL ELEMENTS~
~AND THEN THIS CANADIAN FELLOW ORDERS A 'SNOW-BALL!'
McTIPPLE TAVER
ARNOLD ROTH
~IT FOSTERS CULTURE~
SHOW-OFF!
~IT INDUCES SPORT~
LAST ONE TO THE HOSPITAL IS A MONKEY!!
~& TENDERS KNOWLEDGE!!
G☆!!!☼! THIS IS THE LAST TIME I BUY A HOUSE I ONLY SAW IN THE SUMMER!!
IN SOME PLACES IT NEVER SNOWS-
NEXT TIME I'LL PACK THE TRINKETS!
ROCK SALT
~IN OTHERS IT SNOWS ALL THE TIME~
I WONDER WHAT IT'S LIKE OUTSIDE?
ARNOLD ROTH
~BUT IN CERTAIN LOCALES IT ONLY SNOWS OCCASIONALLY!
Welcome to MIAMI
...ALL I HAVE IS A CLOSET FOR $100.00 A DAY!
Hotel FLAGRANT
..BUT $100??
......UNLESS OF COURSE YOU'D PREFER THE ROYAL SUITE FOR $5.00 A WEEK-PLEASE!?!
CRAZY AMERICANS!
Hotel FLAGRANT

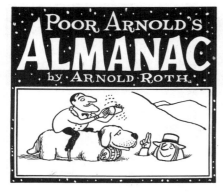

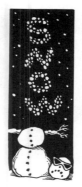

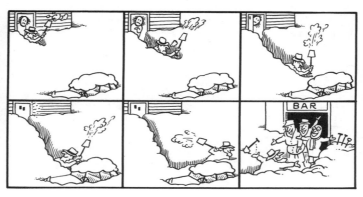

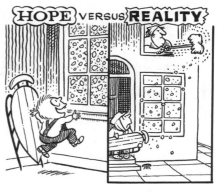

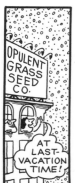

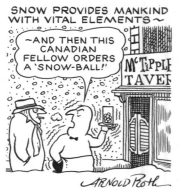

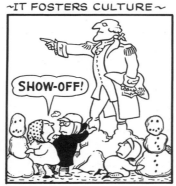

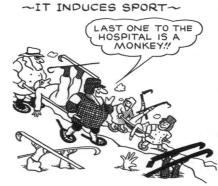

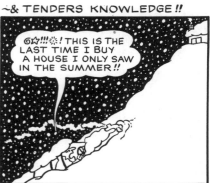

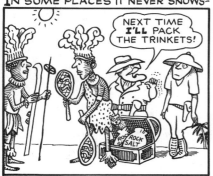

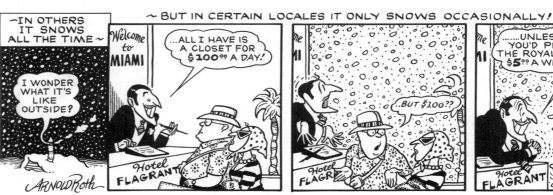

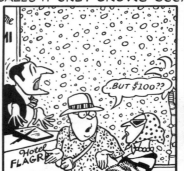

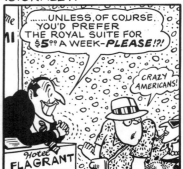

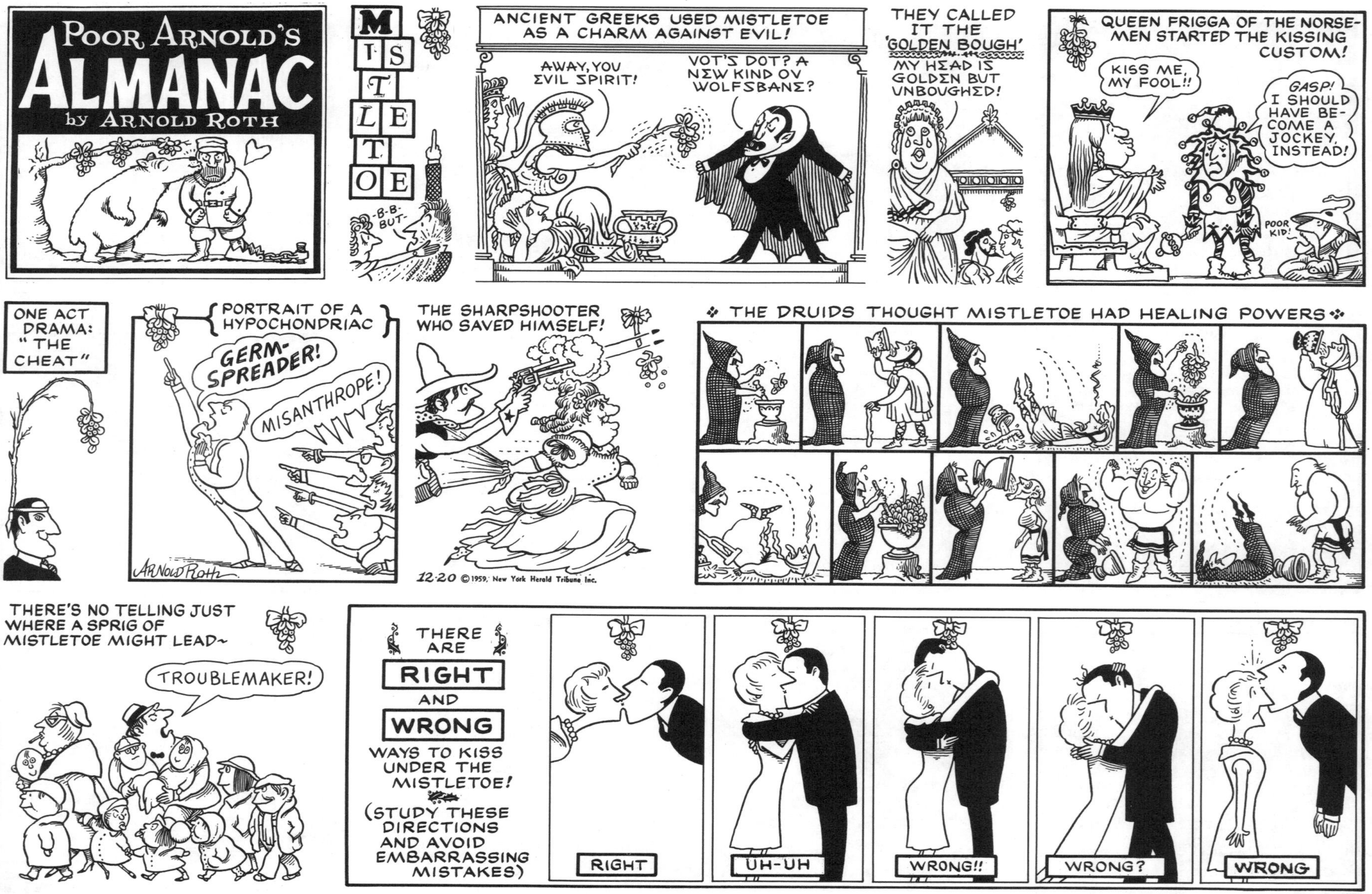
POOR ARNOLD'S ALMANAC
by ARNOLD ROTH
MISTLETOE
-B-B-BUT-
ANCIENT GREEKS USED MISTLETOE AS A CHARM AGAINST EVIL!
AWAY, YOU EVIL SPIRIT!
VOT'S DOT? A NEW KIND OV WOLFSBANE?
THEY CALLED IT THE 'GOLDEN BOUGH'
MY HEAD IS GOLDEN BUT UNBOUGHED!
QUEEN FRIGGA OF THE NORSEMEN STARTED THE KISSING CUSTOM!
KISS ME, MY FOOL!!
GASP! I SHOULD HAVE BECOME A JOCKEY, INSTEAD!
POOR KID!
ONE ACT DRAMA: "THE CHEAT"
PORTRAIT OF A HYPOCHONDRIAC
GERM-SPREADER!
MISANTHROPE!
ARNOLD ROTH
THE SHARPSHOOTER WHO SAVED HIMSELF!
12·20 ©1959, New York Herald Tribune Inc.
THE DRUIDS THOUGHT MISTLETOE HAD HEALING POWERS
THERE'S NO TELLING JUST WHERE A SPRIG OF MISTLETOE MIGHT LEAD~
TROUBLEMAKER!
THERE ARE RIGHT AND WRONG WAYS TO KISS UNDER THE MISTLETOE!
(STUDY THESE DIRECTIONS AND AVOID EMBARRASSING MISTAKES)
RIGHT
UH-UH
WRONG!!
WRONG?
WRONG

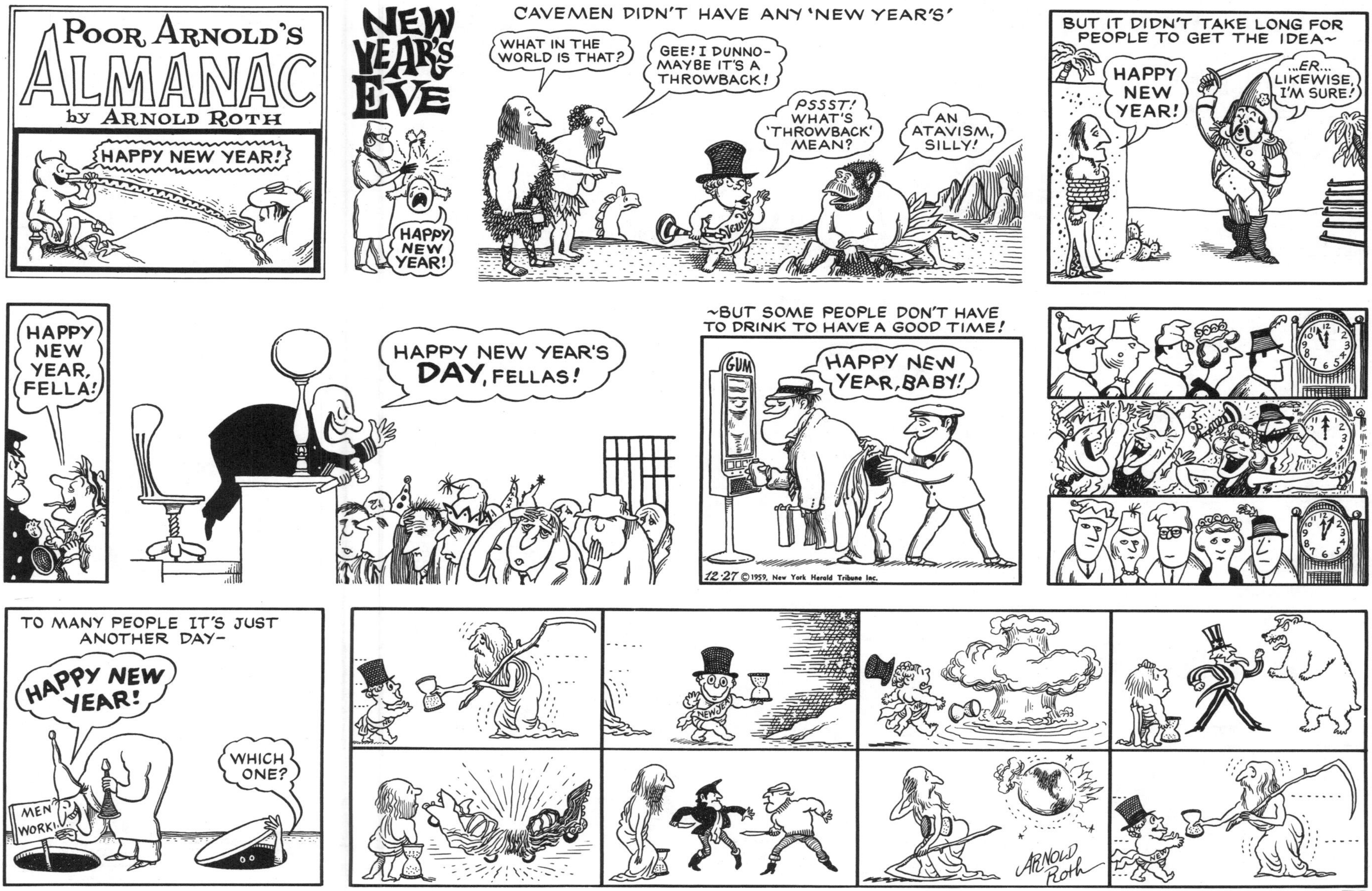

POOR ARNOLD'S ALMANAC
by ARNOLD ROTH
HAPPY NEW YEAR!
NEW YEAR'S EVE
HAPPY NEW YEAR!
CAVEMEN DIDN'T HAVE ANY 'NEW YEAR'S'
WHAT IN THE WORLD IS THAT?
GEE! I DUNNO- MAYBE IT'S A THROWBACK!
PSSST! WHAT'S 'THROWBACK' MEAN?
AN ATAVISM, SILLY!
BUT IT DIDN'T TAKE LONG FOR PEOPLE TO GET THE IDEA~
HAPPY NEW YEAR!
...ER... LIKEWISE, I'M SURE!
HAPPY NEW YEAR, FELLA!
HAPPY NEW YEAR'S DAY, FELLAS!
~BUT SOME PEOPLE DON'T HAVE TO DRINK TO HAVE A GOOD TIME!
GUM
HAPPY NEW YEAR, BABY!
12·27 ©1959, New York Herald Tribune Inc.
TO MANY PEOPLE IT'S JUST ANOTHER DAY-
HAPPY NEW YEAR!
MEN WORKI
WHICH ONE?
ARNOLD ROTH

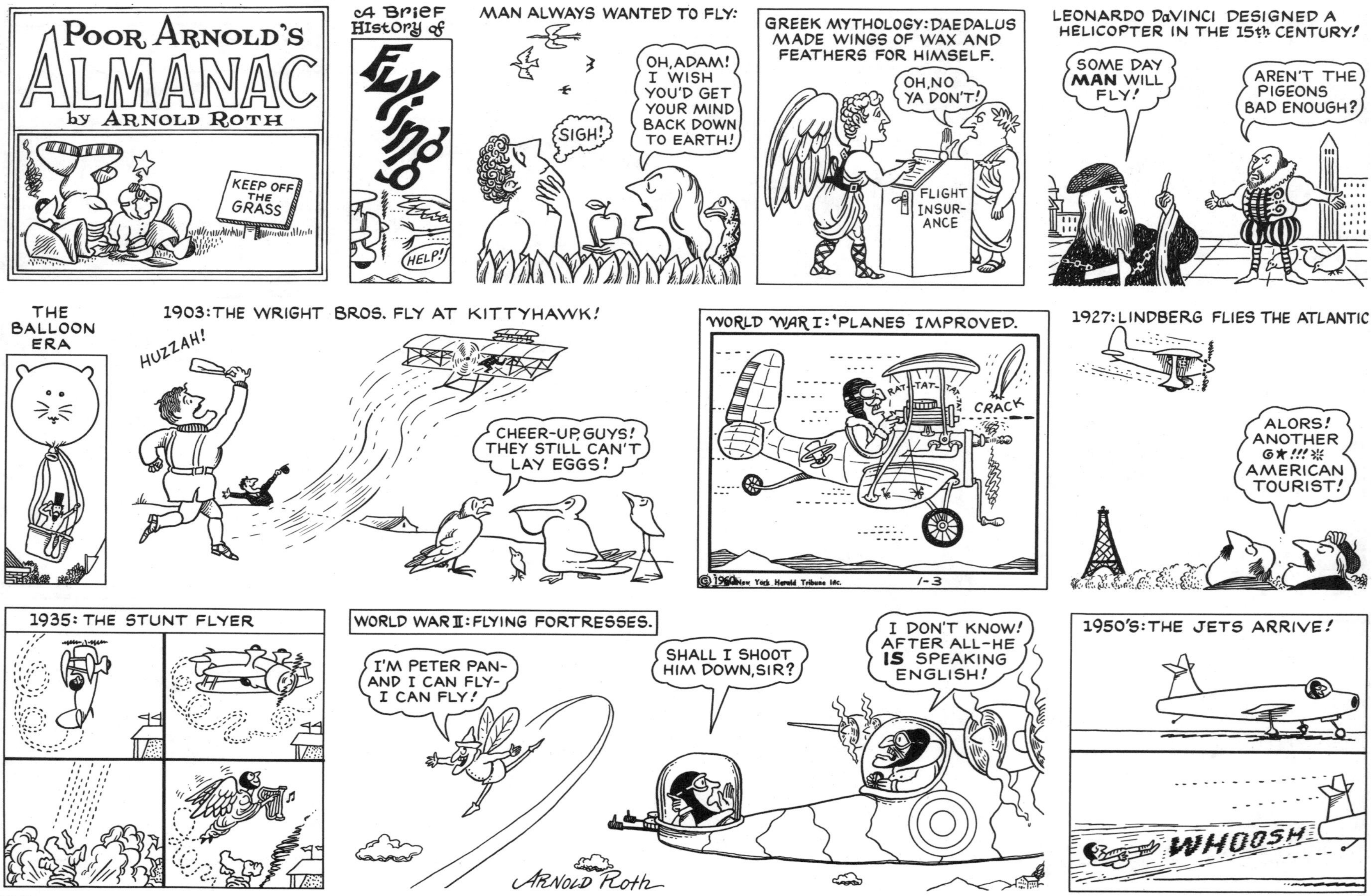

POOR ARNOLD'S
ALMANAC
by ARNOLD ROTH
KEEP OFF THE GRASS
A Brief History of
FLYING
HELP!
MAN ALWAYS WANTED TO FLY:
SIGH!
OH, ADAM! I WISH YOU'D GET YOUR MIND BACK DOWN TO EARTH!
GREEK MYTHOLOGY: DAEDALUS MADE WINGS OF WAX AND FEATHERS FOR HIMSELF.
OH, NO YA DON'T!
FLIGHT INSURANCE
LEONARDO DaVINCI DESIGNED A HELICOPTER IN THE 15th CENTURY!
SOME DAY MAN WILL FLY!
AREN'T THE PIGEONS BAD ENOUGH?
THE BALLOON ERA
1903: THE WRIGHT BROS. FLY AT KITTYHAWK!
HUZZAH!
CHEER-UP, GUYS! THEY STILL CAN'T LAY EGGS!
WORLD WAR I: 'PLANES IMPROVED.
RAT-TAT-TAT-TAT
CRACK
© 1960 New York Herald Tribune Inc.
1-3
1927: LINDBERG FLIES THE ATLANTIC
ALORS! ANOTHER G★!!!※ AMERICAN TOURIST!
1935: THE STUNT FLYER
WORLD WAR II: FLYING FORTRESSES.
I'M PETER PAN- AND I CAN FLY- I CAN FLY!
SHALL I SHOOT HIM DOWN, SIR?
I DON'T KNOW! AFTER ALL-HE IS SPEAKING ENGLISH!
ARNOLD ROTH
1950'S: THE JETS ARRIVE!
WHOOSH

Poor Arnold's Almanac
by Arnold Roth

Bowling

AN EARLY VERSION WAS BOWLING-ON-THE-GREEN

BEGINNER'S LUCK!

BOOM

LITTLE DID THEY REALIZE HOW POPULAR BOWLING WOULD BECOME~

OH, MY BELOVED... ...WILL.....WILL YOU... ...WILL YOU GO BOWLING WITH ME?

I'M AFRAID IT'S A SEVERE CASE OF BOWLER'S CRAMP!

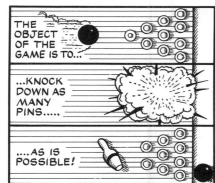

THE OBJECT OF THE GAME IS TO...

...KNOCK DOWN AS MANY PINS.....

....AS IS POSSIBLE!

POOR ARNOLD (HIMSELF) DEMONSTRATES:

INSTRUCTOR

A SMOOTH... ...DELIVERY.... .....PRODUCES.... ...RESULTS?

LADIES LACK STRENGTH- SO, THEY RELY ON SKILL!

BEGINNER'S LUCK!

1-10 ©1960, New York Herald Tribune Inc.

KEEPING SCORE IS A SPORT IN ITSELF!

SUPER BRAIN

A FAST LESSON IN SPORTSMAN- SHIP: NO MATTER WHAT HAPPENS, ALWAYS........

REMEMBER...THE SCORE IS...........NOT EVERYTHING..

..THE IMPORTANT.......THING IS.............MAINTAINING........INTEGRITY!

MOST OF ALL, BOWLING IS GOOD, CLEAN **FAMILY** FUN!

ARNOLD ROTH

33

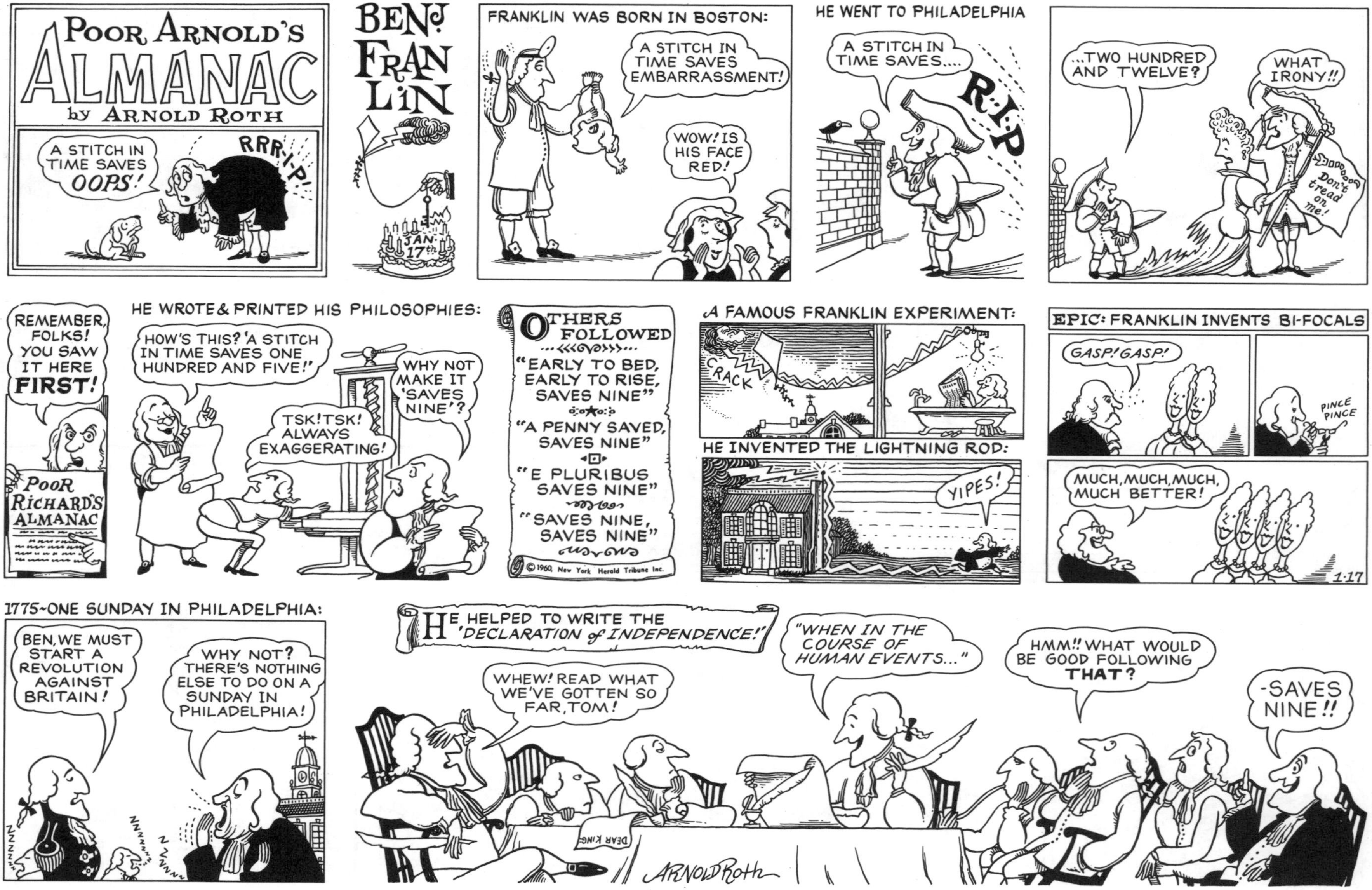
POOR ARNOLD'S ALMANAC
by ARNOLD ROTH
A STITCH IN TIME SAVES OOPS!
RRR-I-P!
BENJ. FRANLIN
JAN. 17th
FRANKLIN WAS BORN IN BOSTON:
A STITCH IN TIME SAVES EMBARRASSMENT!
WOW! IS HIS FACE RED!
HE WENT TO PHILADELPHIA
A STITCH IN TIME SAVES....
R-I-P
...TWO HUNDRED AND TWELVE?
WHAT IRONY!!
Don't tread on me!
REMEMBER, FOLKS! YOU SAW IT HERE FIRST!
POOR RICHARD'S ALMANAC
HE WROTE & PRINTED HIS PHILOSOPHIES:
HOW'S THIS? 'A STITCH IN TIME SAVES ONE HUNDRED AND FIVE!'
TSK! TSK! ALWAYS EXAGGERATING!
WHY NOT MAKE IT 'SAVES NINE'?
OTHERS FOLLOWED
"EARLY TO BED, EARLY TO RISE, SAVES NINE"
"A PENNY SAVED, SAVES NINE"
"E PLURIBUS SAVES NINE"
"SAVES NINE, SAVES NINE"
© 1960, New York Herald Tribune Inc.
A FAMOUS FRANKLIN EXPERIMENT:
CRACK
HE INVENTED THE LIGHTNING ROD:
YIPES!
EPIC: FRANKLIN INVENTS BI-FOCALS
GASP! GASP!
PINCE PINCE
MUCH, MUCH, MUCH, MUCH BETTER!
1·17
1775~ONE SUNDAY IN PHILADELPHIA:
BEN, WE MUST START A REVOLUTION AGAINST BRITAIN!
WHY NOT? THERE'S NOTHING ELSE TO DO ON A SUNDAY IN PHILADELPHIA!
HE HELPED TO WRITE THE 'DECLARATION of INDEPENDENCE!'
WHEW! READ WHAT WE'VE GOTTEN SO FAR, TOM!
"WHEN IN THE COURSE OF HUMAN EVENTS..."
HMM!! WHAT WOULD BE GOOD FOLLOWING THAT?
-SAVES NINE!!
DEAR KING
ARNOLD ROTH

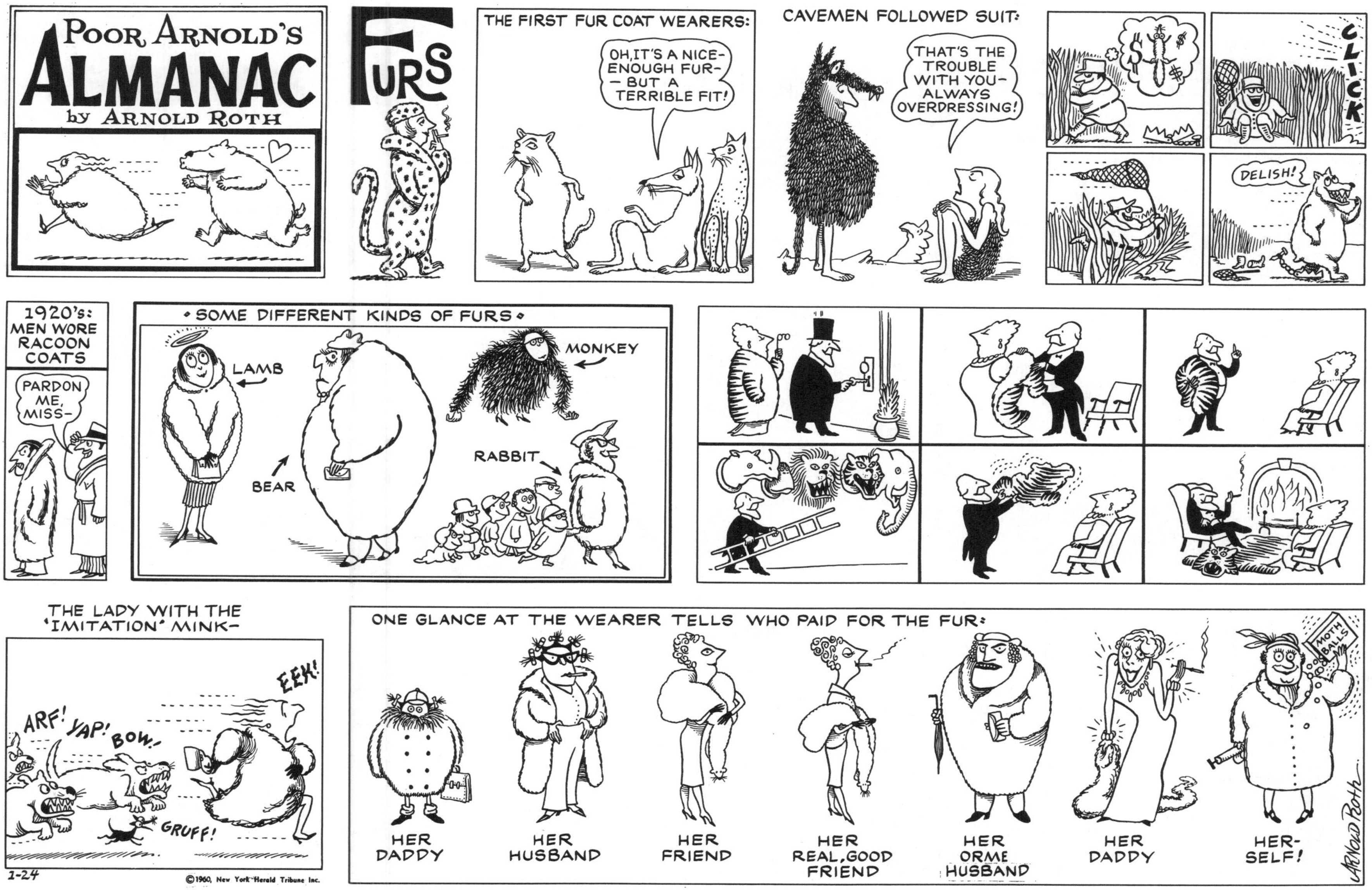
POOR ARNOLD'S
ALMANAC
by ARNOLD ROTH
FURS
THE FIRST FUR COAT WEARERS:
OH, IT'S A NICE-ENOUGH FUR—BUT A TERRIBLE FIT!
CAVEMEN FOLLOWED SUIT:
THAT'S THE TROUBLE WITH YOU—ALWAYS OVERDRESSING!
$
$
$
CLICK
DELISH!
1920's: MEN WORE RACOON COATS
PARDON ME, MISS—
• SOME DIFFERENT KINDS OF FURS •
LAMB
BEAR
MONKEY
RABBIT
THE LADY WITH THE 'IMITATION' MINK—
ARF!
YAP!
BOW!
EEK!
GRUFF!
1-24
©1960, New York Herald Tribune Inc.
ONE GLANCE AT THE WEARER TELLS WHO PAID FOR THE FUR:
HER DADDY
HER HUSBAND
HER FRIEND
HER REAL, GOOD FRIEND
HER ORME HUSBAND
HER DADDY
MOTH BALLS
HER-SELF!
ARNOLD ROTH

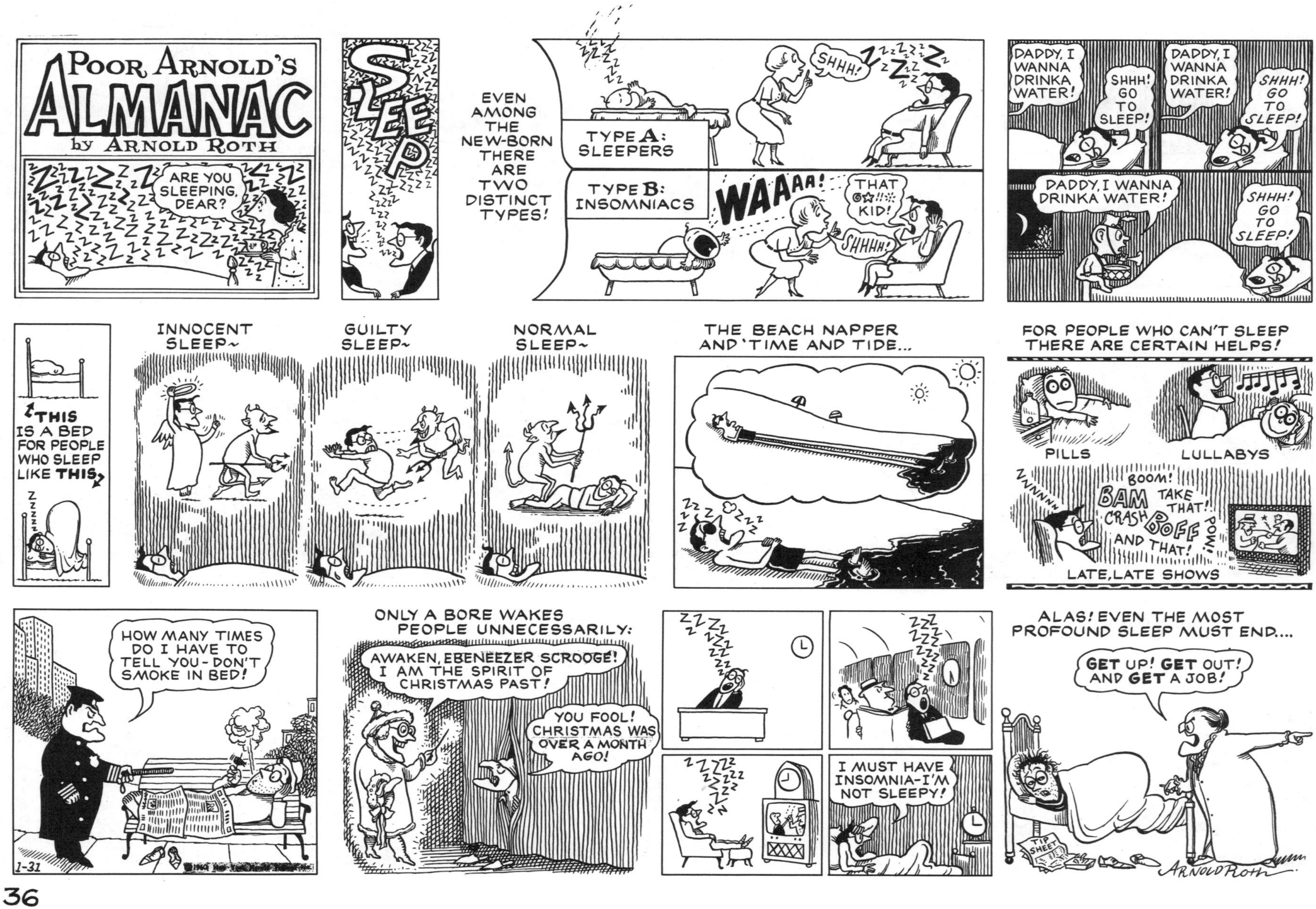
POOR ARNOLD'S ALMANAC
by ARNOLD ROTH
ARE YOU SLEEPING, DEAR?
SLEEP
EVEN AMONG THE NEW-BORN THERE ARE TWO DISTINCT TYPES!
TYPE A: SLEEPERS
SHHH!
TYPE B: INSOMNIACS
WAAAA!
THAT @☆!!※ KID!
SHHHH!
DADDY, I WANNA DRINKA WATER!
SHHH! GO TO SLEEP!
DADDY, I WANNA DRINKA WATER!
SHHH! GO TO SLEEP!
DADDY, I WANNA DRINKA WATER!
SHHH! GO TO SLEEP!
THIS IS A BED FOR PEOPLE WHO SLEEP LIKE THIS
INNOCENT SLEEP~
GUILTY SLEEP~
NORMAL SLEEP~
THE BEACH NAPPER AND 'TIME AND TIDE...
FOR PEOPLE WHO CAN'T SLEEP THERE ARE CERTAIN HELPS!
PILLS
LULLABYS
BOOM!
BAM
TAKE THAT!
CRASH
BOFF
POW!
AND THAT!
LATE, LATE SHOWS
HOW MANY TIMES DO I HAVE TO TELL YOU - DON'T SMOKE IN BED!
1-31
ONLY A BORE WAKES PEOPLE UNNECESSARILY:
AWAKEN, EBENEEZER SCROOGE! I AM THE SPIRIT OF CHRISTMAS PAST!
YOU FOOL! CHRISTMAS WAS OVER A MONTH AGO!
I MUST HAVE INSOMNIA-I'M NOT SLEEPY!
ALAS! EVEN THE MOST PROFOUND SLEEP MUST END....
GET UP! GET OUT! AND GET A JOB!
TIP SHEET
ARNOLD ROTH

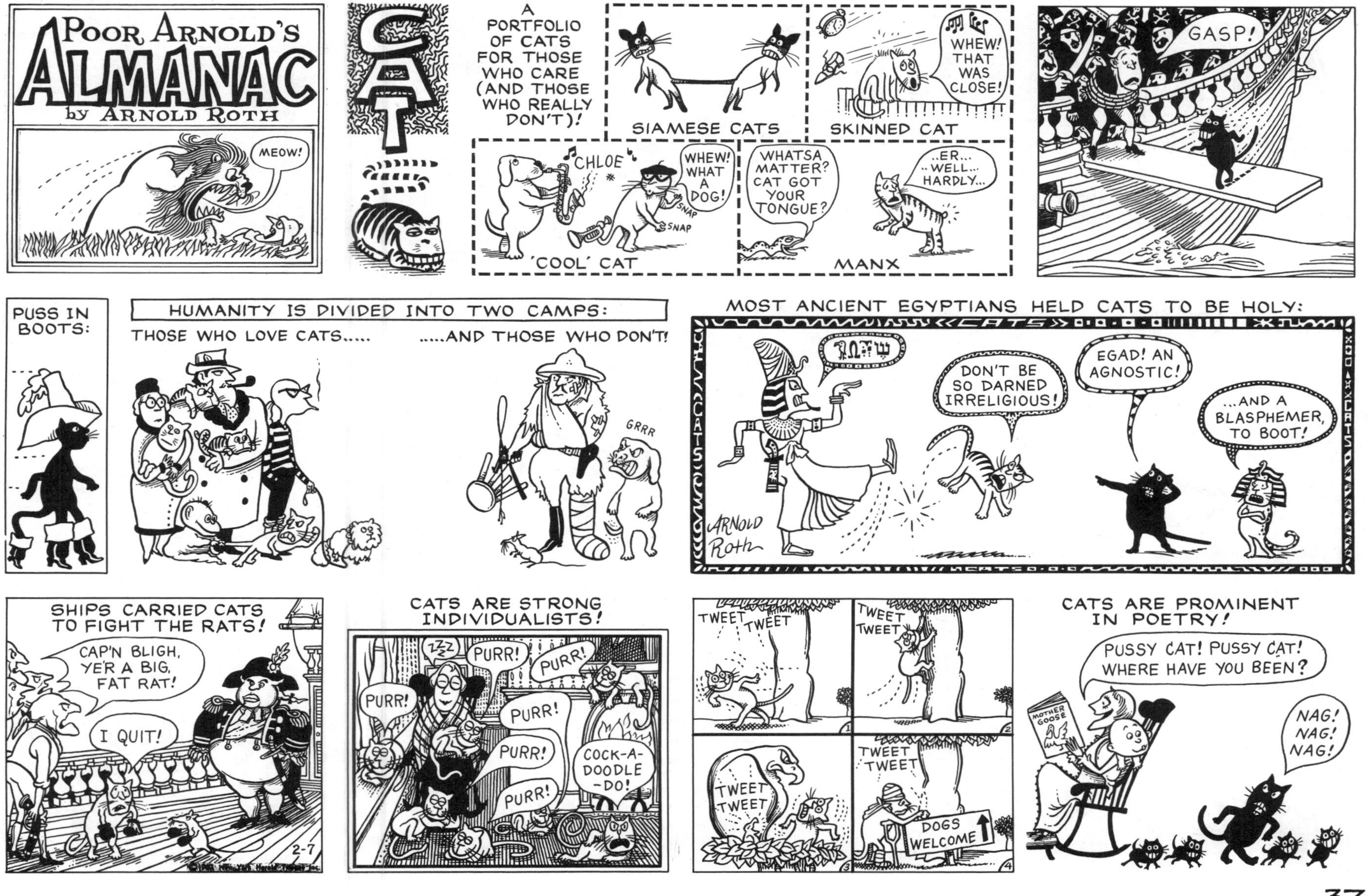
POOR ARNOLD'S
ALMANAC
by ARNOLD ROTH
MEOW!
CAT
A PORTFOLIO OF CATS FOR THOSE WHO CARE (AND THOSE WHO REALLY DON'T)!
SIAMESE CATS
WHEW! THAT WAS CLOSE!
SKINNED CAT
CHLOE
WHEW! WHAT A DOG!
SNAP
SNAP
'COOL' CAT
WHATSA MATTER? CAT GOT YOUR TONGUE?
..ER... ..WELL... HARDLY...
MANX
GASP!
PUSS IN BOOTS:
HUMANITY IS DIVIDED INTO TWO CAMPS:
THOSE WHO LOVE CATS.....
.....AND THOSE WHO DON'T!
GRRR
MOST ANCIENT EGYPTIANS HELD CATS TO BE HOLY:
CATS
DON'T BE SO DARNED IRRELIGIOUS!
EGAD! AN AGNOSTIC!
...AND A BLASPHEMER, TO BOOT!
ARNOLD Roth
SHIPS CARRIED CATS TO FIGHT THE RATS!
CAP'N BLIGH, YE'R A BIG, FAT RAT!
I QUIT!
2-7
CATS ARE STRONG INDIVIDUALISTS!
ZZZ
PURR!
PURR!
PURR!
PURR!
PURR!
PURR!
COCK-A-DOODLE-DO!
TWEET TWEET
TWEET TWEET
TWEET TWEET
TWEET TWEET
DOGS WELCOME
CATS ARE PROMINENT IN POETRY!
PUSSY CAT! PUSSY CAT! WHERE HAVE YOU BEEN?
MOTHER GOOSE
NAG! NAG! NAG!

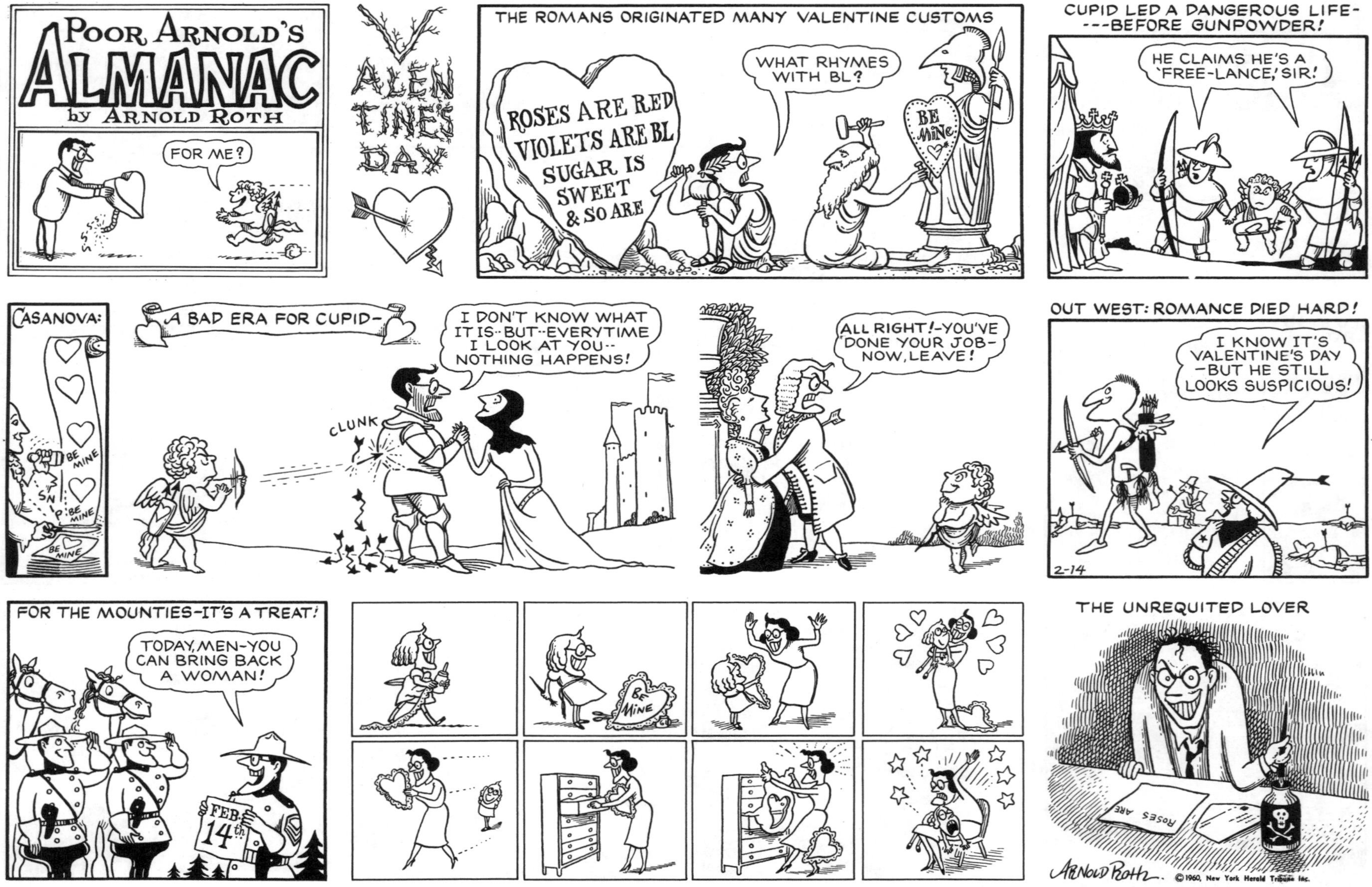

POOR ARNOLD'S
ALMANAC
by ARNOLD ROTH
FOR ME?
VALENTINE'S DAY
THE ROMANS ORIGINATED MANY VALENTINE CUSTOMS
ROSES ARE RED VIOLETS ARE BL SUGAR IS SWEET & SO ARE
WHAT RHYMES WITH BL?
BE MINE
CUPID LED A DANGEROUS LIFE---BEFORE GUNPOWDER!
HE CLAIMS HE'S A 'FREE-LANCE,' SIR!
CASANOVA:
BE MINE
BE MINE
BE MINE
A BAD ERA FOR CUPID-
I DON'T KNOW WHAT IT IS--BUT--EVERYTIME I LOOK AT YOU--NOTHING HAPPENS!
CLUNK
ALL RIGHT!-YOU'VE DONE YOUR JOB-NOW, LEAVE!
OUT WEST: ROMANCE DIED HARD!
I KNOW IT'S VALENTINE'S DAY-BUT HE STILL LOOKS SUSPICIOUS!
2-14
FOR THE MOUNTIES-IT'S A TREAT!
TODAY, MEN-YOU CAN BRING BACK A WOMAN!
FEB. 14th
BE MINE
THE UNREQUITED LOVER
ROSES ARE
ARNOLD ROTH
© 1960, New York Herald Tribune Inc.

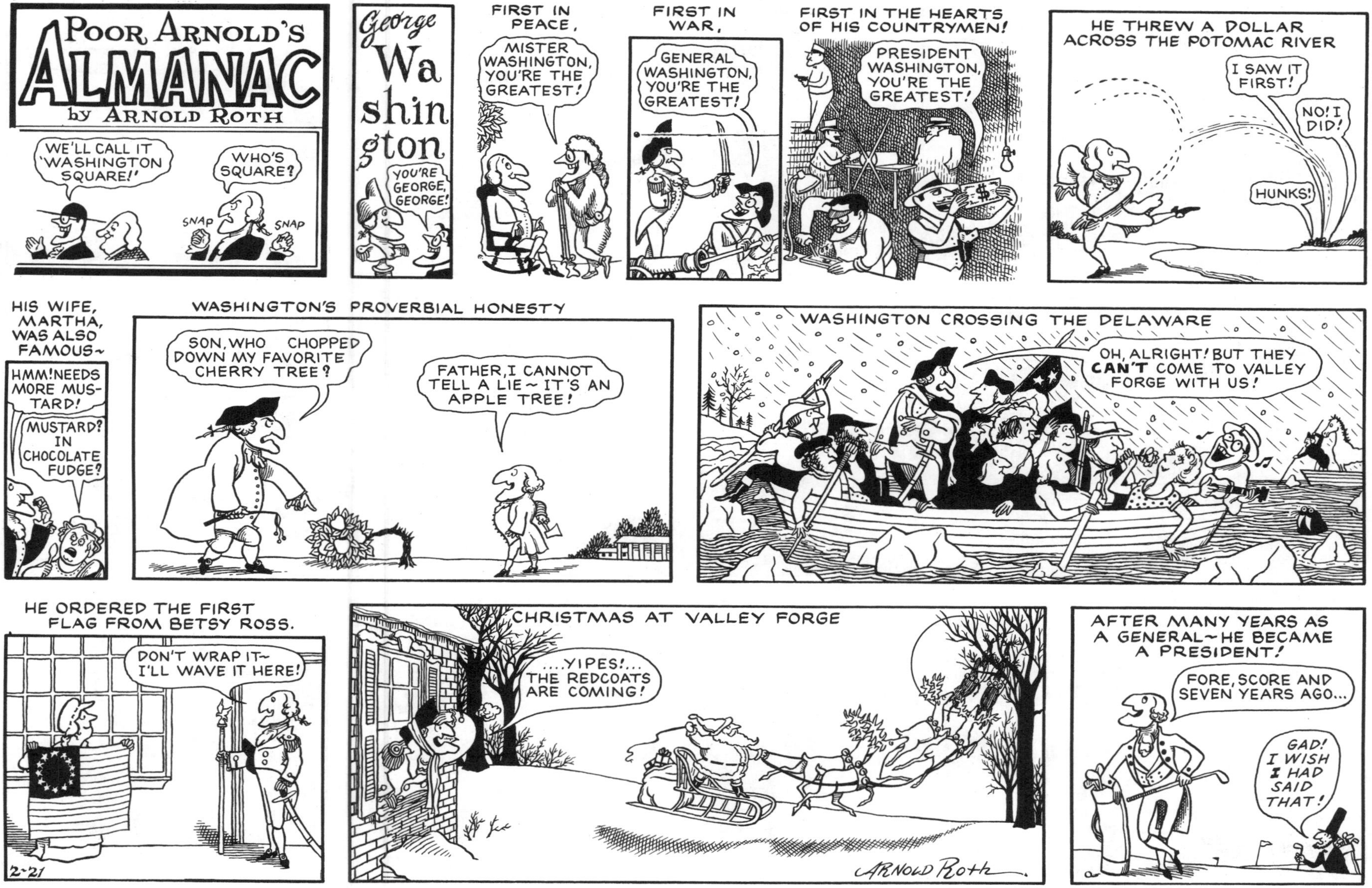
POOR ARNOLD'S
ALMANAC
by ARNOLD ROTH
WE'LL CALL IT 'WASHINGTON SQUARE!'
WHO'S SQUARE?
SNAP
SNAP
George
Washington
YOU'RE GEORGE, GEORGE!
FIRST IN PEACE,
MISTER WASHINGTON, YOU'RE THE GREATEST!
FIRST IN WAR,
GENERAL WASHINGTON, YOU'RE THE GREATEST!
FIRST IN THE HEARTS OF HIS COUNTRYMEN!
PRESIDENT WASHINGTON, YOU'RE THE GREATEST!
HE THREW A DOLLAR ACROSS THE POTOMAC RIVER
I SAW IT FIRST!
NO! I DID!
HUNKS!
HIS WIFE, MARTHA, WAS ALSO FAMOUS~
HMM! NEEDS MORE MUSTARD!
MUSTARD? IN CHOCOLATE FUDGE?
WASHINGTON'S PROVERBIAL HONESTY
SON, WHO CHOPPED DOWN MY FAVORITE CHERRY TREE?
FATHER, I CANNOT TELL A LIE~ IT'S AN APPLE TREE!
WASHINGTON CROSSING THE DELAWARE
OH, ALRIGHT! BUT THEY CAN'T COME TO VALLEY FORGE WITH US!
HE ORDERED THE FIRST FLAG FROM BETSY ROSS.
DON'T WRAP IT~ I'LL WAVE IT HERE!
2-21
CHRISTMAS AT VALLEY FORGE
....YIPES!... THE REDCOATS ARE COMING!
ARNOLD ROTH
AFTER MANY YEARS AS A GENERAL~ HE BECAME A PRESIDENT!
FORE, SCORE AND SEVEN YEARS AGO...
GAD! I WISH I HAD SAID THAT!

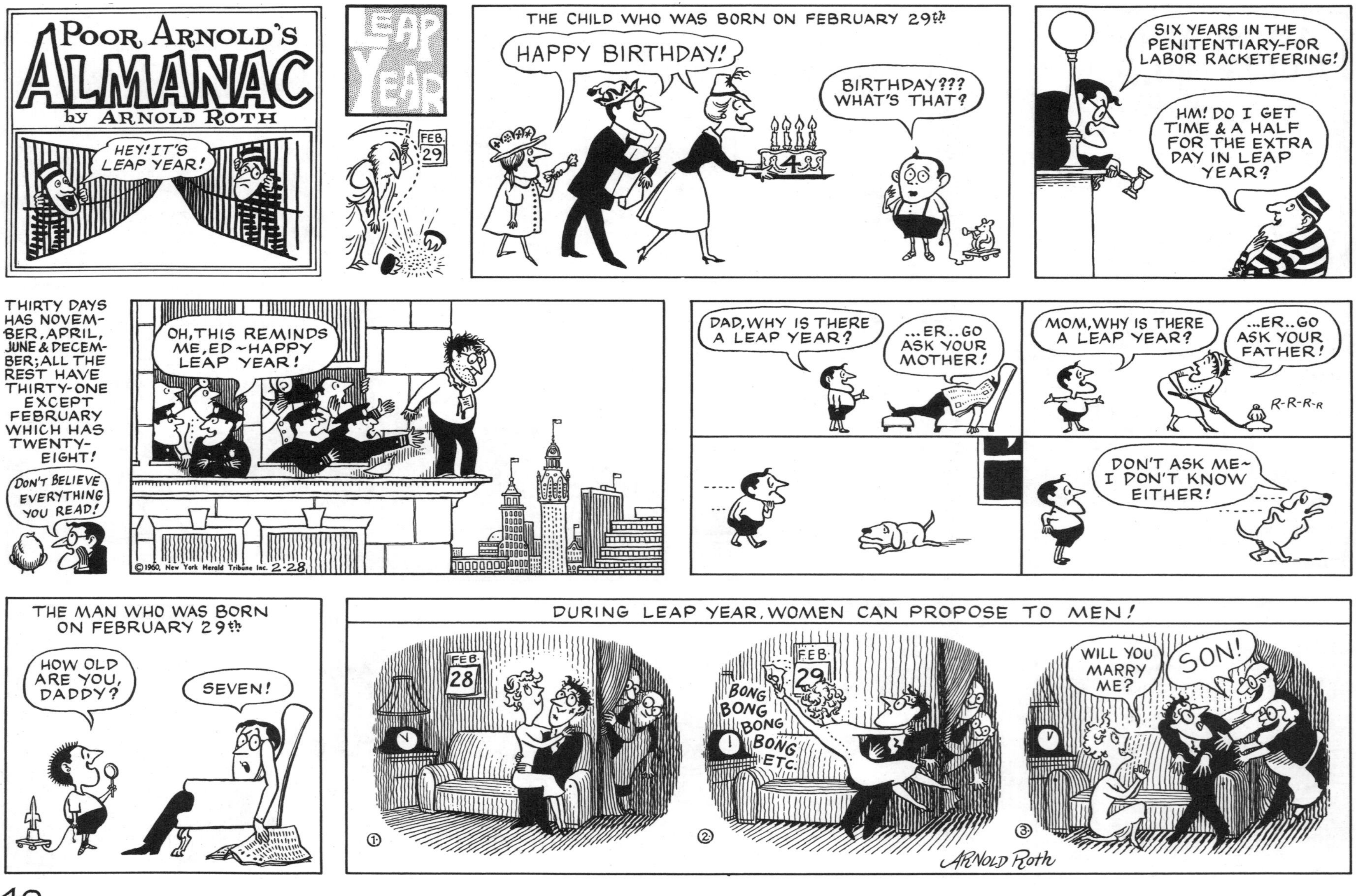
POOR ARNOLD'S
ALMANAC
by ARNOLD ROTH
HEY! IT'S LEAP YEAR!
LEAP YEAR
FEB. 29
THE CHILD WHO WAS BORN ON FEBRUARY 29th
HAPPY BIRTHDAY!
4
BIRTHDAY??? WHAT'S THAT?
SIX YEARS IN THE PENITENTIARY-FOR LABOR RACKETEERING!
HM! DO I GET TIME & A HALF FOR THE EXTRA DAY IN LEAP YEAR?
THIRTY DAYS HAS NOVEMBER, APRIL, JUNE & DECEMBER; ALL THE REST HAVE THIRTY-ONE EXCEPT FEBRUARY WHICH HAS TWENTY-EIGHT!
DON'T BELIEVE EVERYTHING YOU READ!
OH, THIS REMINDS ME, ED~HAPPY LEAP YEAR!
©1960, New York Herald Tribune Inc. 2-28
DAD, WHY IS THERE A LEAP YEAR?
...ER..GO ASK YOUR MOTHER!
MOM, WHY IS THERE A LEAP YEAR?
...ER..GO ASK YOUR FATHER!
R-R-R-R
DON'T ASK ME~ I DON'T KNOW EITHER!
THE MAN WHO WAS BORN ON FEBRUARY 29th
HOW OLD ARE YOU, DADDY?
SEVEN!
DURING LEAP YEAR, WOMEN CAN PROPOSE TO MEN!
FEB. 28
1.
FEB. 29
BONG BONG BONG BONG ETC.
2.
WILL YOU MARRY ME?
SON!
3.
ARNOLD ROTH

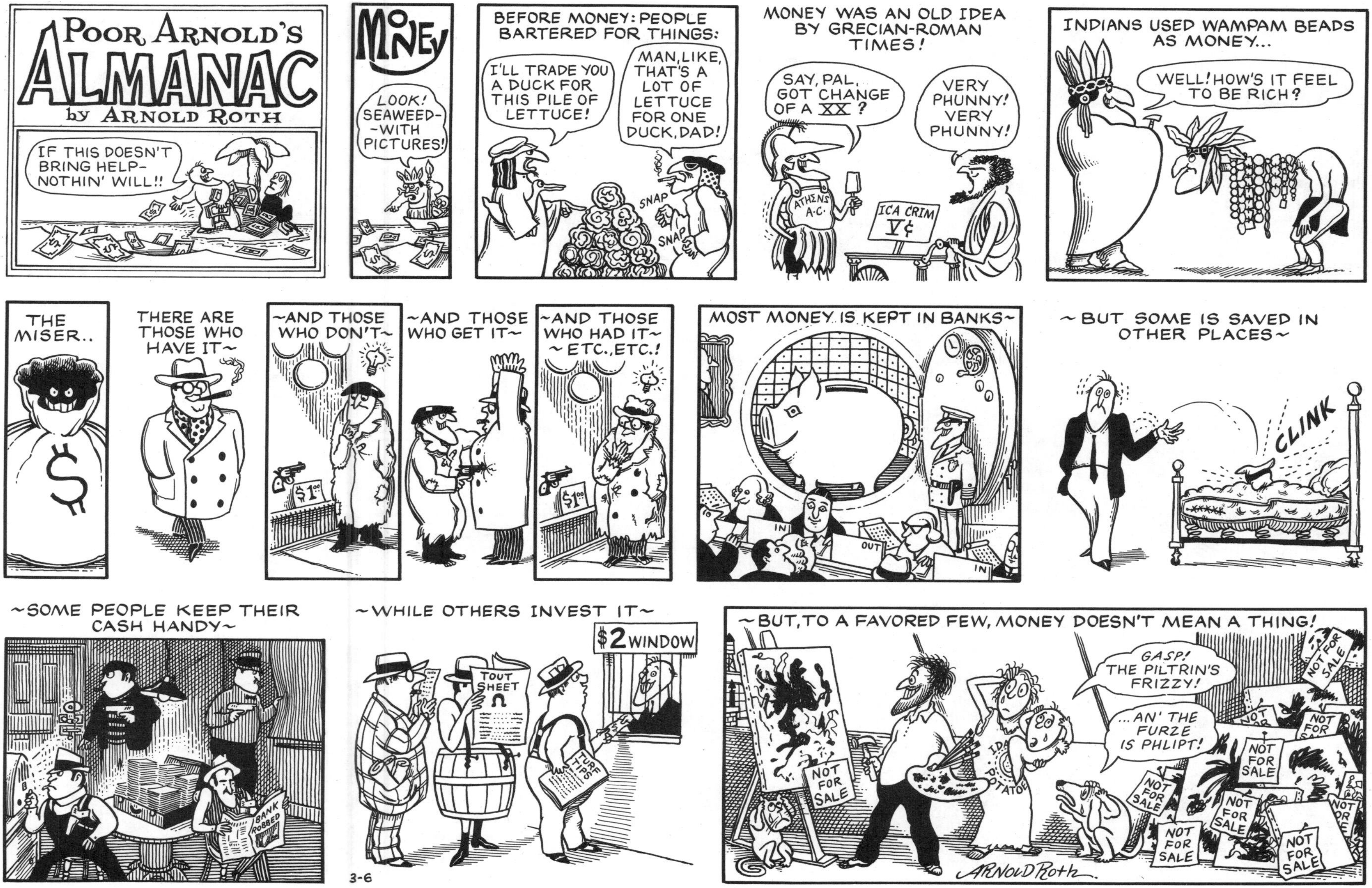
POOR ARNOLD'S
ALMANAC
by ARNOLD ROTH
IF THIS DOESN'T BRING HELP- NOTHIN' WILL!!
MONEY
LOOK! SEAWEED- -WITH PICTURES!
BEFORE MONEY: PEOPLE BARTERED FOR THINGS:
I'LL TRADE YOU A DUCK FOR THIS PILE OF LETTUCE!
MAN, LIKE, THAT'S A LOT OF LETTUCE FOR ONE DUCK, DAD!
SNAP
SNAP
MONEY WAS AN OLD IDEA BY GRECIAN-ROMAN TIMES!
SAY, PAL, GOT CHANGE OF A XX ?
VERY PHUNNY! VERY PHUNNY!
ATHENS A.C.
ICA CRIM
V¢
INDIANS USED WAMPAM BEADS AS MONEY...
WELL! HOW'S IT FEEL TO BE RICH?
THE MISER..
THERE ARE THOSE WHO HAVE IT~
~AND THOSE WHO DON'T~
$1.00
~AND THOSE WHO GET IT~
~AND THOSE WHO HAD IT~ ~ETC., ETC.!
$1.00
MOST MONEY IS KEPT IN BANKS~
IN
OUT
IN
~BUT SOME IS SAVED IN OTHER PLACES~
CLINK
~SOME PEOPLE KEEP THEIR CASH HANDY~
BANK ROBBED
~WHILE OTHERS INVEST IT~
$2 WINDOW
TOUT SHEET
TURF TIPS
3-6
~BUT, TO A FAVORED FEW, MONEY DOESN'T MEAN A THING!
GASP! THE PILTRIN'S FRIZZY!
...AN' THE FURZE IS PHLIPT!
IDA POTATOE
NOT FOR SALE
NOT FOR SALE
NOT FOR SALE
NOT FOR SALE
NOT FOR SALE
NOT FOR SALE
NOT FOR SALE
NOT FOR SALE
ARNOLD ROTH

POOR ARNOLD'S ALMANAC
by ARNOLD ROTH
SCRCH SCRCH SCRCH SCRCH SCRCH SCRCH SCRCH SCRCH
HI FI
BEFORE EDISON: MUSIC COULD ONLY BE HEARD LIVE!
BOOM TLOP
PLIP BOOM BOOM
THE NATIVE IS RESTLESS TONIGHT!
THIS ALL CHANGED WHEN EDISON INVENTED THE PHONOGRAPH—
BOOM TLOP PLIP BOOM BOOM
LISTEN! LOWEST-FI!
FEH!
LOW-FI DISPLEASED MUSIC LOVERS—
I'VE GOT THOSE RUMPOT BLUES
—ONLY HI-FI COULD SOOTHE THEIR SAVAGE EARS!
CAN'T CLICK GET MY CLICK FEET CLICK CLICK INTO MY CLICK SHOES CLICK CLICK
WOW! LISTEN TO THAT— SHE'S GOT FALSE TEETH!
ZZZZ
LOW-FI
© 1960, New York Herald Tribune Inc.
HI-FI
QUESTION: CAN HI-FI REALLY COMPETE WITH LIVE MUSIC?
CLANG CLANG
BONG BONG
HOW AND WHY STEREOPHONIC SOUND WAS INVENTED—
THE PILTRIN'S FRIZZY
AN' THE FURZE IS PHLIPT
3-13
THE ULTIMATE IN HI-FI!
SIGH!
ARNOLD ROTH
BUT TRUE HI-FI IS JUST LIKE BEING AT THE CONCERT IN PERSON—
COUGH! COUGH!
USHER! I DIN'T GETTA PROGRAM!
COUGH
BAM!
BUT THAT'S MY SEAT!
SNEEZE!
COUGH!
BURP!
COUGH

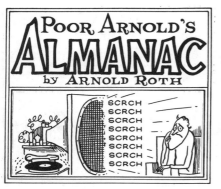

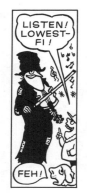

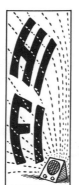

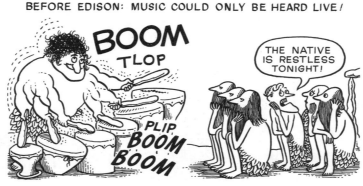

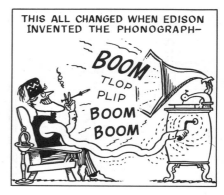

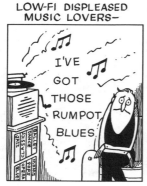

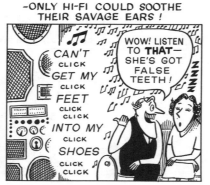

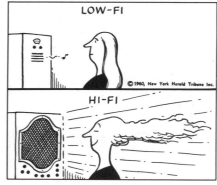

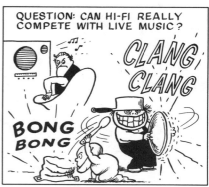

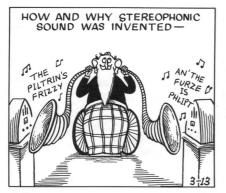

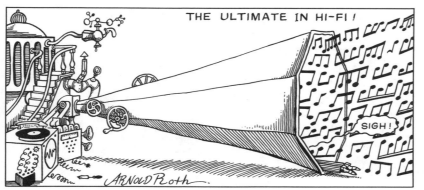

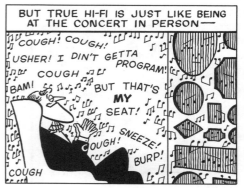

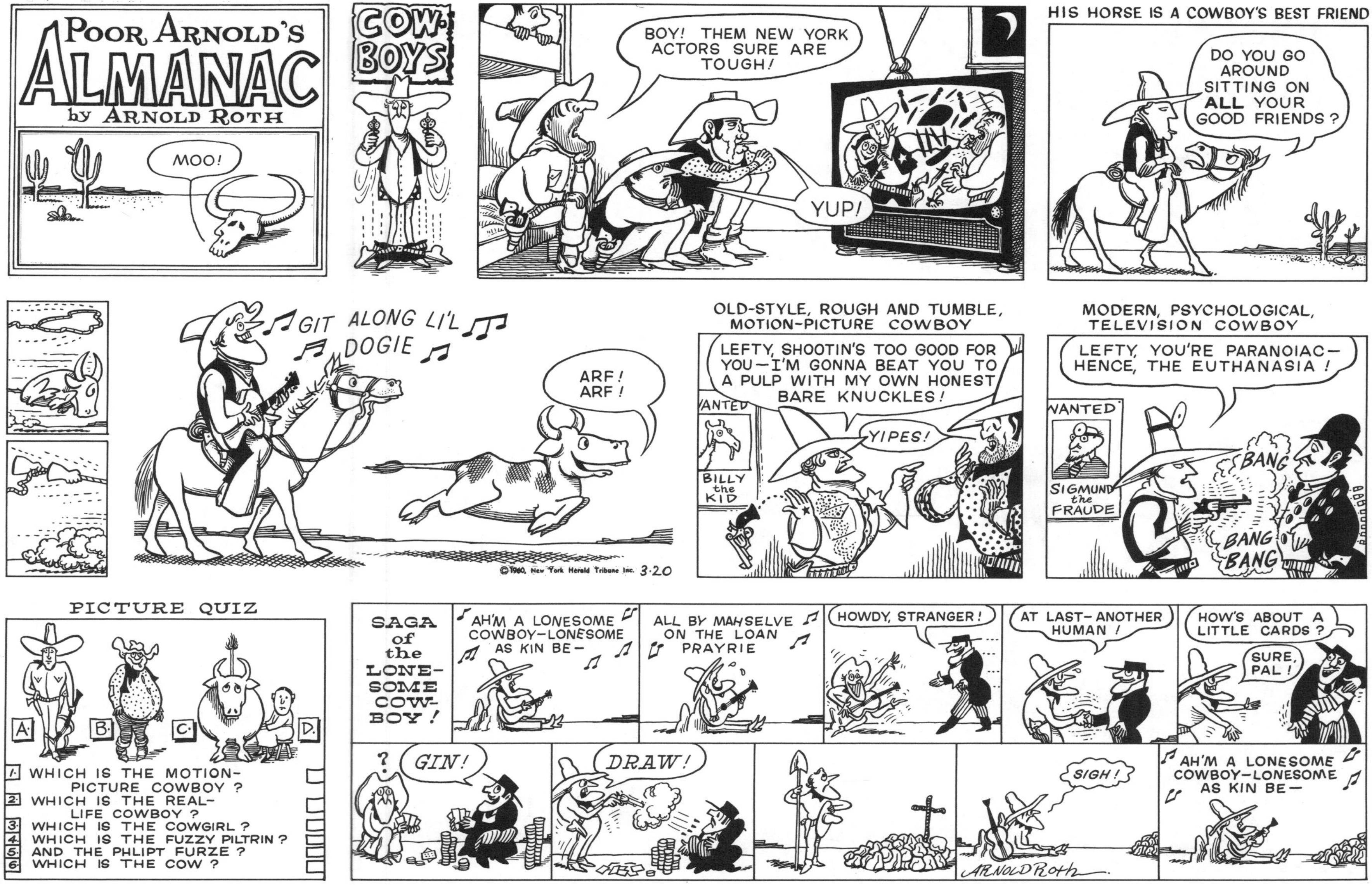
POOR ARNOLD'S
ALMANAC
by ARNOLD ROTH
MOO!
COW-BOYS
BOY! THEM NEW YORK ACTORS SURE ARE TOUGH!
YUP!
HIS HORSE IS A COWBOY'S BEST FRIEND
DO YOU GO AROUND SITTING ON ALL YOUR GOOD FRIENDS?
GIT ALONG LI'L DOGIE
ARF! ARF!
©1960, New York Herald Tribune Inc. 3·20
OLD-STYLE, ROUGH AND TUMBLE, MOTION-PICTURE COWBOY
LEFTY, SHOOTIN'S TOO GOOD FOR YOU—I'M GONNA BEAT YOU TO A PULP WITH MY OWN HONEST BARE KNUCKLES!
WANTED
BILLY the KID
YIPES!
MODERN, PSYCHOLOGICAL, TELEVISION COWBOY
LEFTY, YOU'RE PARANOIAC—HENCE, THE EUTHANASIA!
WANTED
SIGMUND the FRAUDE
BANG
BANG BANG
PICTURE QUIZ
A. B. C. D.
1. WHICH IS THE MOTION-PICTURE COWBOY?
2. WHICH IS THE REAL-LIFE COWBOY?
3. WHICH IS THE COWGIRL?
4. WHICH IS THE FUZZY PILTRIN?
5. AND THE PHLIPT FURZE?
6. WHICH IS THE COW?
SAGA of the LONESOME COWBOY!
AH'M A LONESOME COWBOY—LONESOME AS KIN BE—
ALL BY MAHSELVE ON THE LOAN PRAYRIE
HOWDY, STRANGER!
AT LAST—ANOTHER HUMAN!
HOW'S ABOUT A LITTLE CARDS?
SURE, PAL!
GIN!
DRAW!
SIGH!
AH'M A LONESOME COWBOY—LONESOME AS KIN BE—
ARNOLD ROTH

POOR ARNOLD'S ALMANAC
by ARNOLD ROTH
8
POOL
POOL REQUIRES THE FOLLOWING SIMPLE EQUIPMENT:
A TABLE,
15
8
1
6
3
POOL BALLS,
CUES,—
BUT WHY CAN'T I GO PLAY POOL?
STOP ASKING!
— AND FREEDOM!
A SAGE SAID: "A GOOD POOL PLAYER IS THE RESULT OF A MISSPENT YOUTH."
GOO! ME WINSIES, AGAIN!!
WHY DON'T YOU GO READ A BOOK— OR SOMETHIN'!?
THE BAD LOSER
G★!!
G★!!
POOL WAS ONCE PLAYED BY NOBILITY ONLY—
KING LOUIS XIV, IT'S YOUR SHOT!
VIII BALL IN THE SIDE POCKET!
—AND, SOMETIMES, IT STILL IS!!
O.K., LOUIE! SHOOT!
DOST SPEAK THUSLY TO YOUR SUPERIOR, VASSAL?
©1960, New York Herald Tribune Inc.
PSST! WANNA PLAY?
1.
I JUST MADE UP THIS LI'L GAME!
CLICK
2.
SAY! THIS IS FUN!
CLICK
3.
SAY! THAT LOOKS LIKE FUN!
4.
NO ONE KNOWS WHEN OR WHERE THE GAME STARTED!
WHAT'S IT CALLED?
CALLED?
5.
..ER..EH....POOL!
6.
YOU'RE PLAYING POOL!?
7.
YOU OUGHT TO BE ASHAMED OF YOURSELVES!
SHE'S STARTIN' IN, ALREADY!
8.
A THOROUGH KNOWLEDGE OF GEOMETRY AND PHYSICS IS ESSENTIAL—
I WONDER HOW PYTHAGORAS WOULD PLAY THIS SHOT?
..ER...YOUSE HAS GOT ME THERE, PERFESSOR!
3·27
ONE ACT MELODRAMA: "THE FALLEN IDLE"
EEK! MY SON!
POOL
TSK! TSK! A MOTHER'S HEART!!
Piltrin Frizzy, Furze & Phlipt, Inc.
PO
10 TABLES NO·WAITING
Come In—& Be Healthy!
ARNOLD ROTH
THE TRUTH IS THAT POOL IS A DIFFICULT BUT HEALTHFUL & INTELLECTUAL SPORT!
TO THE OLYMPICS
ATHLETES ENTRANCE

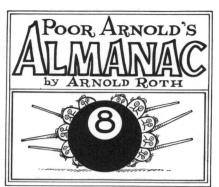

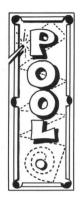

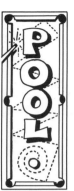

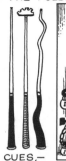

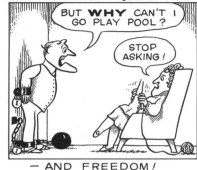

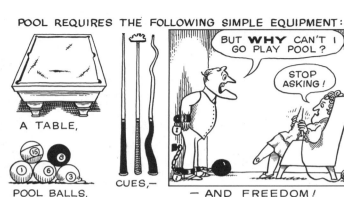

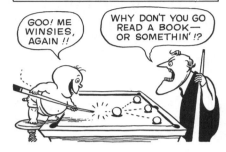

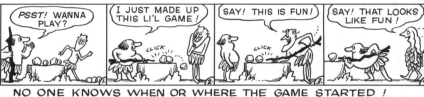

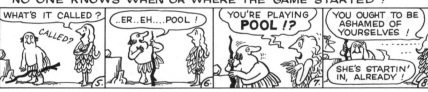

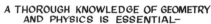

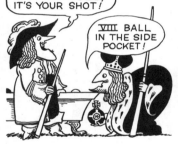

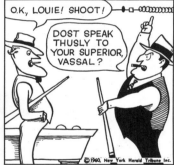

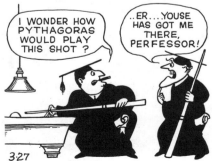

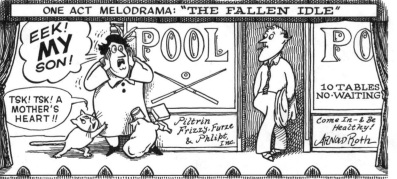

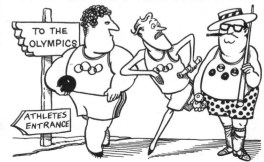

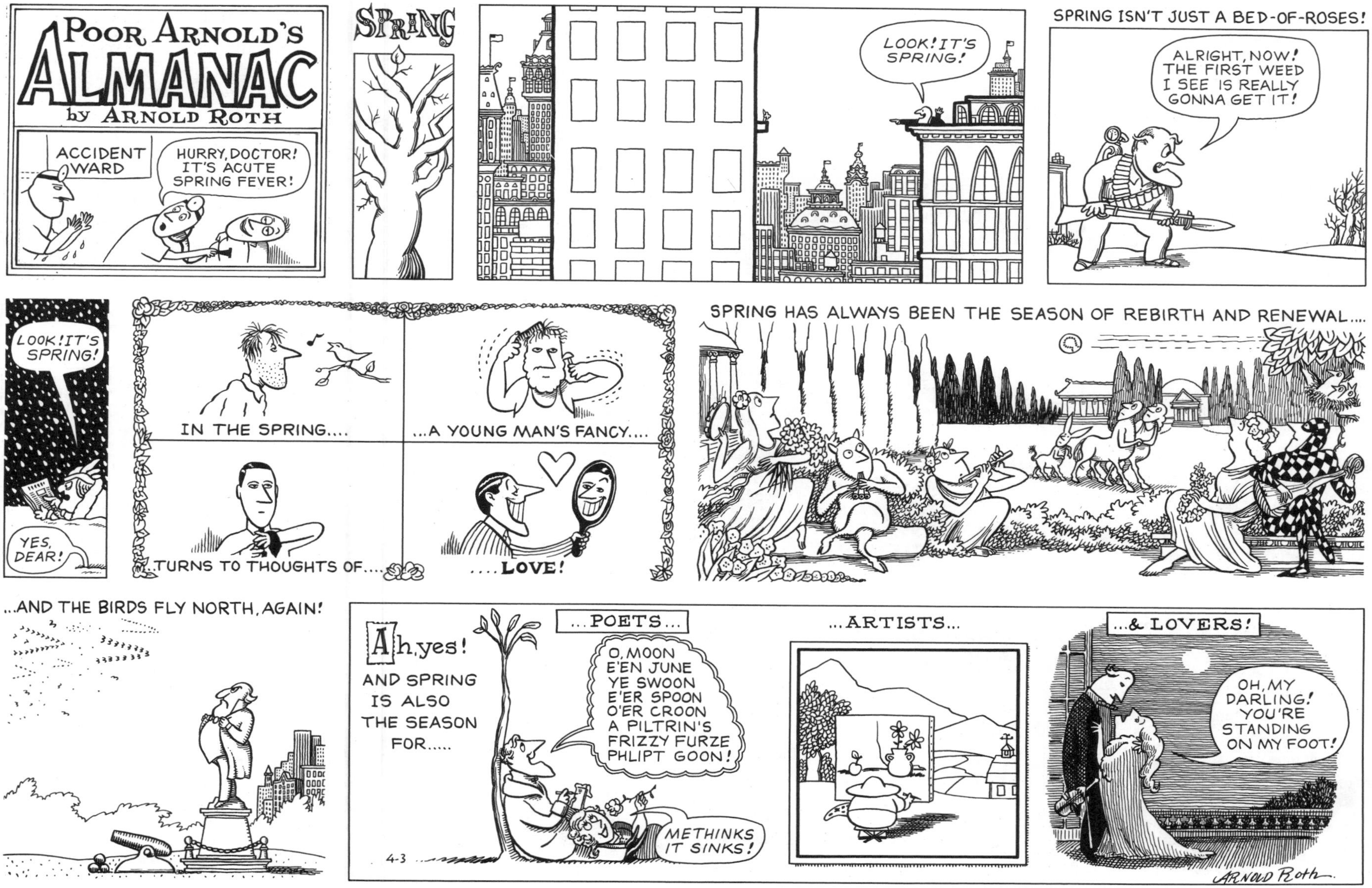
POOR ARNOLD'S
ALMANAC
by ARNOLD ROTH
ACCIDENT WARD
HURRY, DOCTOR! IT'S ACUTE SPRING FEVER!
SPRING
LOOK! IT'S SPRING!
SPRING ISN'T JUST A BED-OF-ROSES!
ALRIGHT, NOW! THE FIRST WEED I SEE IS REALLY GONNA GET IT!
LOOK! IT'S SPRING!
YES, DEAR!
IN THE SPRING....
...A YOUNG MAN'S FANCY....
...TURNS TO THOUGHTS OF....
....LOVE!
SPRING HAS ALWAYS BEEN THE SEASON OF REBIRTH AND RENEWAL....
...AND THE BIRDS FLY NORTH, AGAIN!
Ah, yes! AND SPRING IS ALSO THE SEASON FOR.....
...POETS...
O, MOON E'EN JUNE YE SWOON E'ER SPOON O'ER CROON A PILTRIN'S FRIZZY FURZE PHLIPT GOON!
METHINKS IT SINKS!
4-3
...ARTISTS...
...& LOVERS!
OH, MY DARLING! YOU'RE STANDING ON MY FOOT!
ARNOLD ROTH

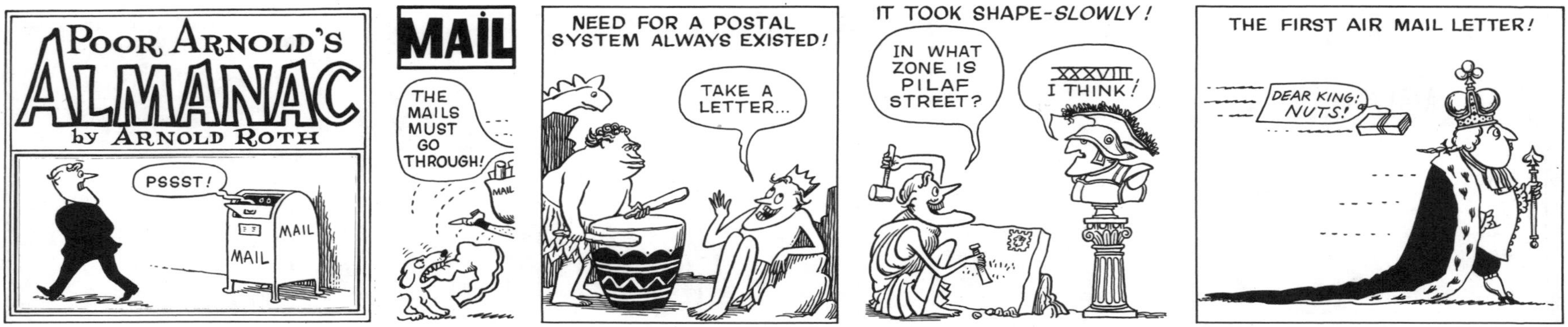

POOR ARNOLD'S
ALMANAC
by ARNOLD ROTH
PSSST!
MAIL
MAIL
MAIL
THE MAILS MUST GO THROUGH!
MAIL
NEED FOR A POSTAL SYSTEM ALWAYS EXISTED!
TAKE A LETTER...
IT TOOK SHAPE-SLOWLY!
IN WHAT ZONE IS PILAF STREET?
XXXVIII I THINK!
THE FIRST AIR MAIL LETTER!
DEAR KING: NUTS!

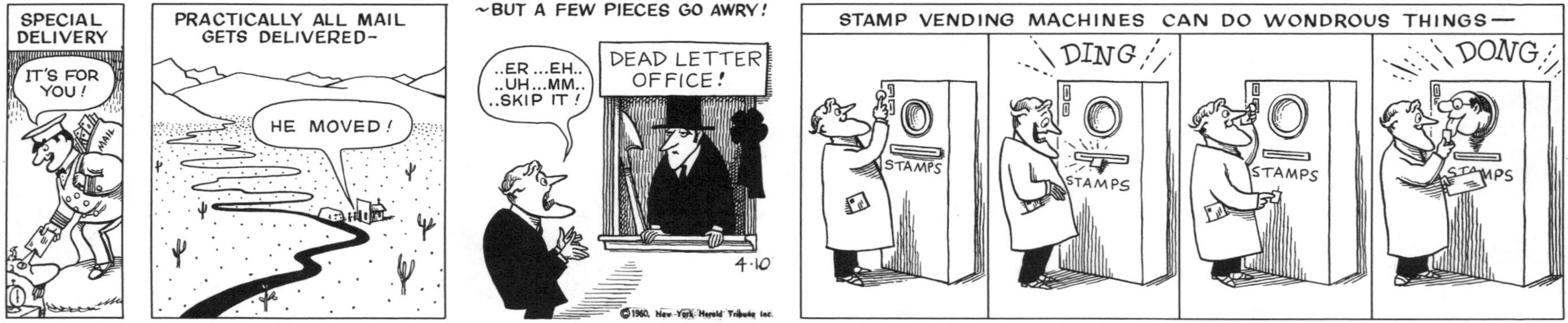

SPECIAL DELIVERY
IT'S FOR YOU!
MAIL
PRACTICALLY ALL MAIL GETS DELIVERED-
HE MOVED!
~BUT A FEW PIECES GO AWRY!
..ER ...EH.. ..UH...MM.. ..SKIP IT!
DEAD LETTER OFFICE!
4·10
© 1960, New York Herald Tribune Inc.
STAMP VENDING MACHINES CAN DO WONDROUS THINGS—
STAMPS
DING
STAMPS
STAMPS
DONG
STAMPS

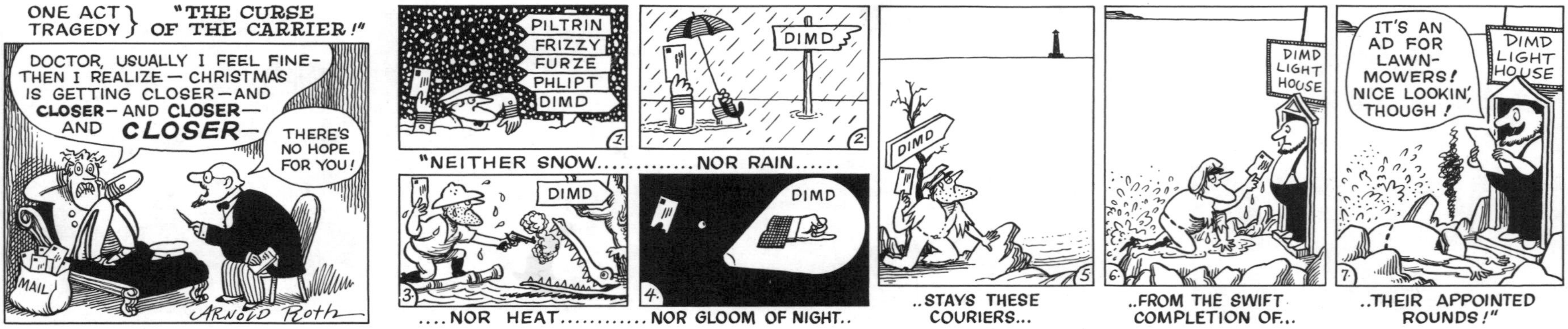

ONE ACT TRAGEDY } "THE CURSE OF THE CARRIER!"
DOCTOR, USUALLY I FEEL FINE-THEN I REALIZE — CHRISTMAS IS GETTING CLOSER—AND CLOSER— AND CLOSER— AND CLOSER-
THERE'S NO HOPE FOR YOU!
MAIL
ARNOLD ROTH
PILTRIN
FRIZZY
FURZE
PHLIPT
DIMD
1.
DIMD
2.
"NEITHER SNOW............NOR RAIN......
DIMD
3.
DIMD
4.
....NOR HEAT...........NOR GLOOM OF NIGHT..
DIMD
5
..STAYS THESE COURIERS...
DIMD LIGHT HOUSE
6.
..FROM THE SWIFT COMPLETION OF...
IT'S AN AD FOR LAWN-MOWERS! NICE LOOKIN', THOUGH!
DIMD LIGHT HOUSE
7.
..THEIR APPOINTED ROUNDS!"

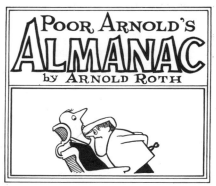

POOR ARNOLD'S
ALMANAC
by ARNOLD ROTH

Den-
Tis-
TRY

BZZZ...

SINCE ALWAYS: TOOTHACHES ACHED ~ & NOTHING HELPED!

HEY, MARTY! — I GOT US DATES!

NOT TONIGHT — I'VE GOT A TOOTHACHE!

FOR AGES, CURES REMAINED ON A DO-IT-YOURSELF BASIS:

BEFORE

AFTER

DENTISTRY PROGRESSED FROM HIT-AND-MISS...

I THINK I GOT IT THAT TIME!

...TO AN EXACT SCIENCE!

X-RAYS SHOW YOU ONLY NEED ONE EXTRACTION!

4-17
©1960, New York Herald Tribune Inc.

...ER...NO! HE'S NOT IN...ER... THAT IS—HE'S NOT OUT...ER.. ..BURP!

① ② ③

R-RING   R-RING RRRING

④ ⑤ ⑥

ARNOLD ROTH

JOY-DAY AT DENTAL SCHOOL:

—AND, THINK, CLASS! EACH AND EVERY ONE CAN BE DRILLED— DOZENS OF TIMES!

The HUMAN HEAD (AS WE KNOW IT!)
YIPPEE!

YUK! YUK! YAK!

SOME PEOPLE JUST HATE TO GO TO THE DENTIST....

...AND THE DENTIST ISN'T ANXIOUS TO HAVE THEM!

'POOR ARNOLD'S' GALLERY OF FAMOUS BUSTS!

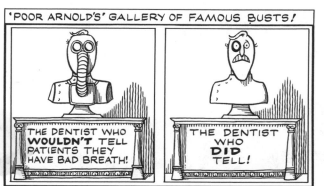

THE DENTIST WHO WOULDN'T TELL PATIENTS THEY HAVE BAD BREATH!

THE DENTIST WHO DID TELL!

47

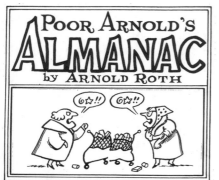

POOR ARNOLD'S ALMANAC
by ARNOLD ROTH
SUPER-MARKETS
DING DING DING DING DING DING
KEY TO SUPER-MARKET SUCCESS: 'SELF-SERVICE'.....
SEA FOOD
FRESH SEA FOOD
...BUT THERE ARE LIMITS!
STOP! THIEF!
MODERN SUPER-MARKETS HAVE EVERYTHING!
DESSERTS
PILTRINS
FRIZZYS
BUTCHER
BAKER
GROCER
LA DE DA
OLD, TIRING MULTI-STORE WAY COMPARED TO NEW, EASY SUPER-WAY!
SUPER DUPER
GASP!
QUESTION: WHAT IS THIS?
ANSWER: IT'S A MAN WHO LOOKED LIKE THIS-
-WHEN HE GOT INTO THE CHECK-OUT LINE!
DING DING DONG DING
ARNOLD ROTH
4·24
©1960, New York Herald Tribune Inc.
GASP!

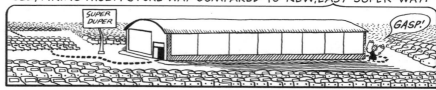

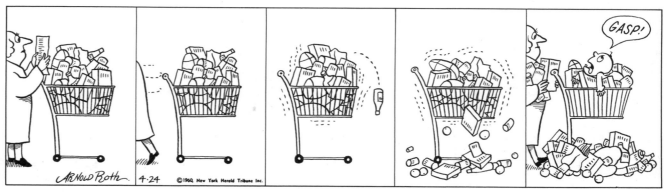

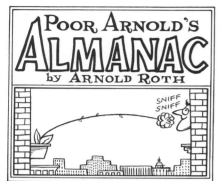

Poor Arnold's ALMANAC by ARNOLD ROTH

SNIFF SNIFF

FLOWERS

OH, ROMEO! A ROSE BY ANY OTHER NAME WOULD BE A JANE OR AN AGNES OR A...

FLOWERS CAN BE RAISED EASILY IN THE CITY...

...BUT THINGS CAN GET COMPLICATED IN THE SUBURBS!

5·1

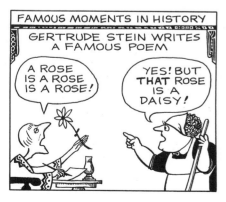

FAMOUS MOMENTS IN HISTORY

GERTRUDE STEIN WRITES A FAMOUS POEM

A ROSE IS A ROSE IS A ROSE!

YES! BUT **THAT** ROSE IS A DAISY!

A GIFT OF FLOWERS EXPRESSES LOVE & DEVOTION!

 1.

 2.

 3.

 4.

 5.

 6.

 7.

 8.

 9. BONG

ARNOLD ROTH.

49

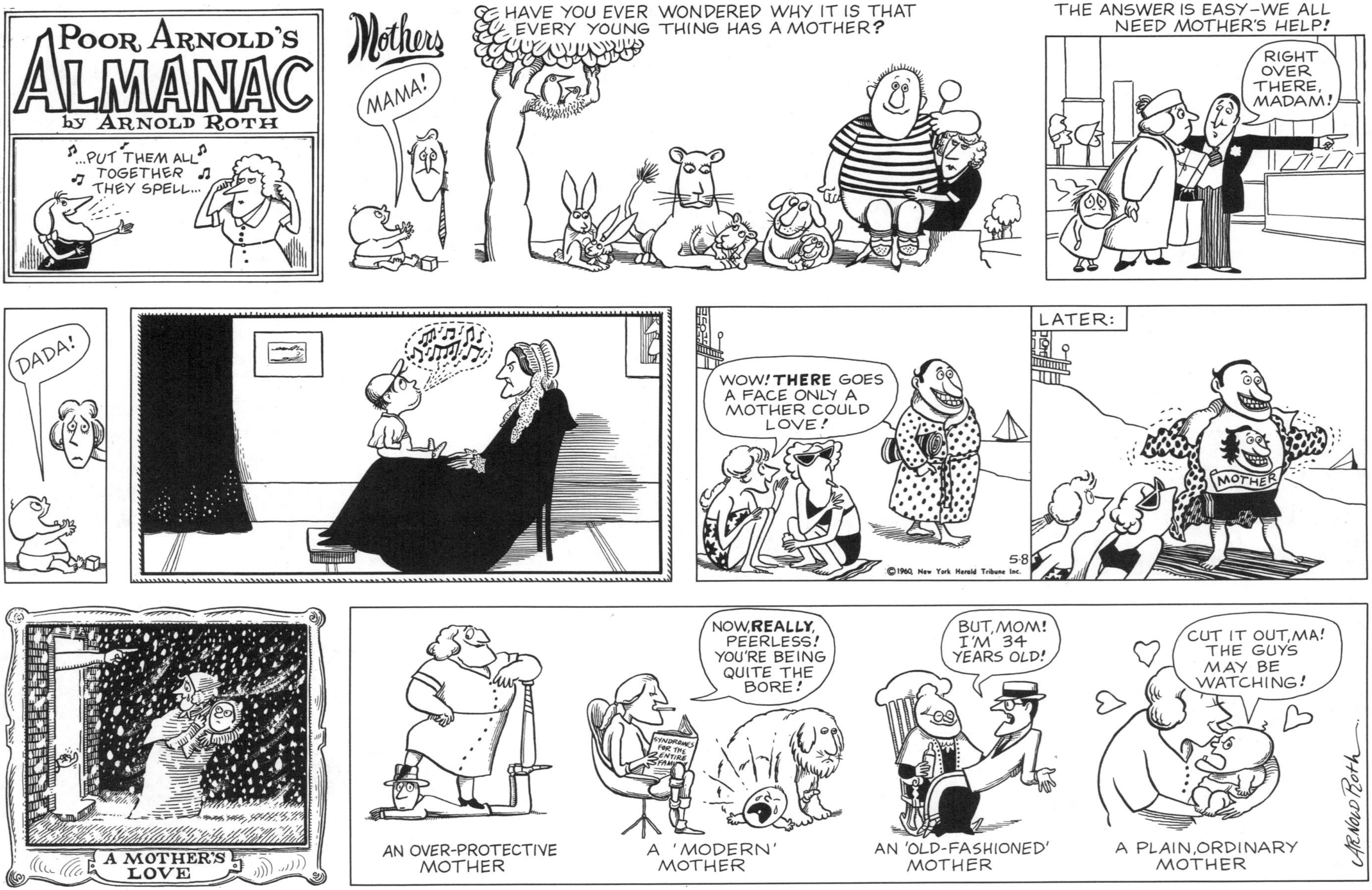
POOR ARNOLD'S
ALMANAC
by ARNOLD ROTH
...PUT THEM ALL TOGETHER THEY SPELL...
Mothers
MAMA!
HAVE YOU EVER WONDERED WHY IT IS THAT EVERY YOUNG THING HAS A MOTHER?
THE ANSWER IS EASY–WE ALL NEED MOTHER'S HELP!
RIGHT OVER THERE, MADAM!
DADA!
WOW! THERE GOES A FACE ONLY A MOTHER COULD LOVE!
5-8
©1960, New York Herald Tribune Inc.
LATER:
MOTHER
A MOTHER'S LOVE
AN OVER-PROTECTIVE MOTHER
NOW, REALLY, PEERLESS! YOU'RE BEING QUITE THE BORE!
SYNDROMES FOR THE ENTIRE FAMI
A 'MODERN' MOTHER
BUT, MOM! I'M 34 YEARS OLD!
AN 'OLD-FASHIONED' MOTHER
CUT IT OUT, MA! THE GUYS MAY BE WATCHING!
A PLAIN, ORDINARY MOTHER
ARNOLD ROTH

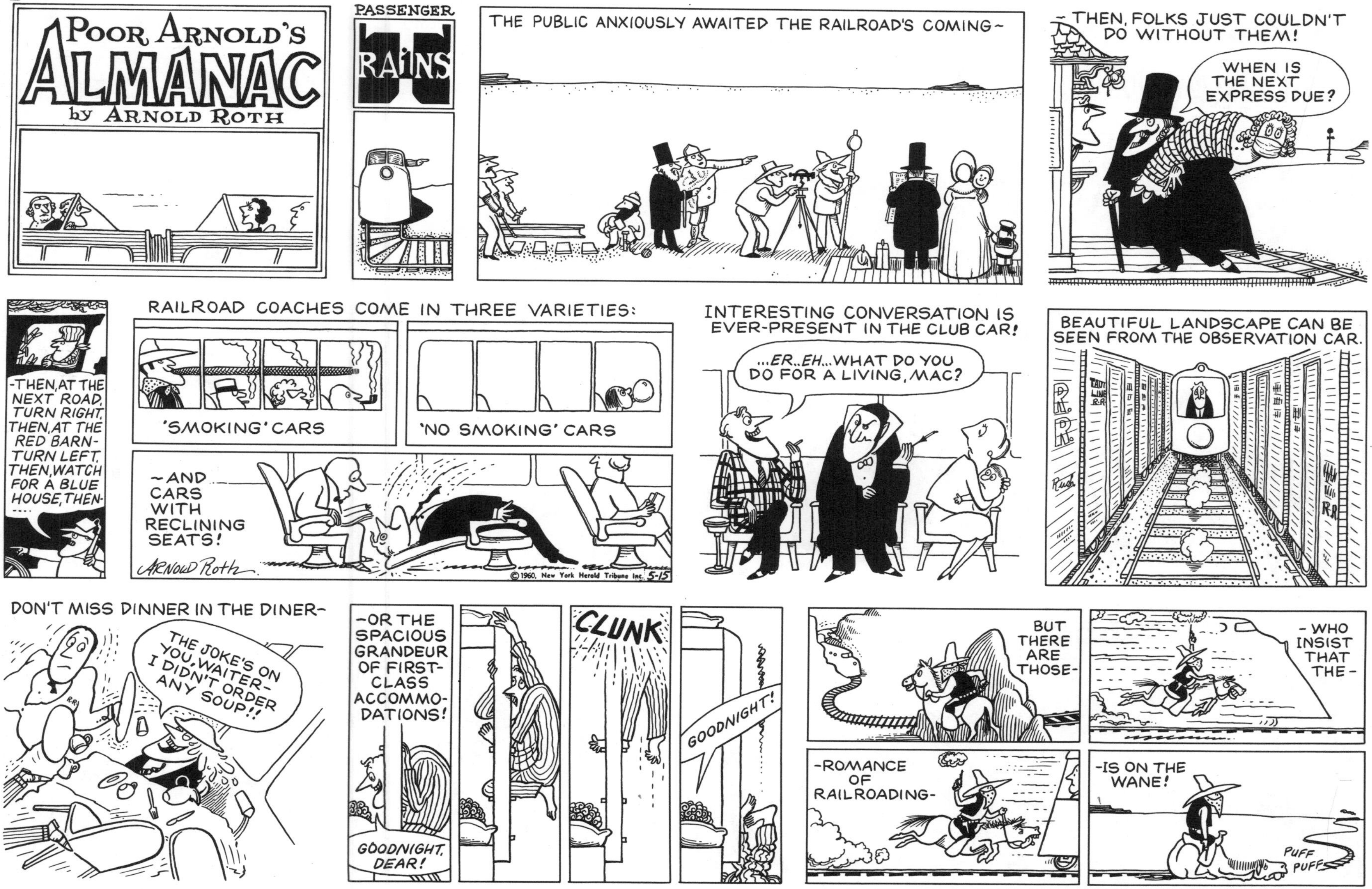

POOR ARNOLD'S ALMANAC
by ARNOLD ROTH
PASSENGER TRAINS
THE PUBLIC ANXIOUSLY AWAITED THE RAILROAD'S COMING~
~THEN, FOLKS JUST COULDN'T DO WITHOUT THEM!
WHEN IS THE NEXT EXPRESS DUE?
-THEN, AT THE NEXT ROAD, TURN RIGHT, THEN, AT THE RED BARN-TURN LEFT, THEN, WATCH FOR A BLUE HOUSE, THEN-....
RAILROAD COACHES COME IN THREE VARIETIES:
'SMOKING' CARS
'NO SMOKING' CARS
~AND CARS WITH RECLINING SEATS!
ARNOLD Roth
©1960, New York Herald Tribune Inc. 5-15
INTERESTING CONVERSATION IS EVER-PRESENT IN THE CLUB CAR!
...ER..EH...WHAT DO YOU DO FOR A LIVING, MAC?
BEAUTIFUL LANDSCAPE CAN BE SEEN FROM THE OBSERVATION CAR.
DON'T MISS DINNER IN THE DINER-
THE JOKE'S ON YOU, WAITER-I DIDN'T ORDER ANY SOUP!!
-OR THE SPACIOUS GRANDEUR OF FIRST-CLASS ACCOMMODATIONS!
GOODNIGHT, DEAR!
CLUNK
GOODNIGHT!
BUT THERE ARE THOSE-
-WHO INSIST THAT THE-
-ROMANCE OF RAILROADING-
-IS ON THE WANE!
PUFF PUFF

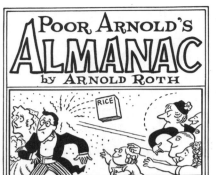

Poor Arnold's ALMANAC
by Arnold Roth

WE DD INGS

HE DOES!

WHAT IS MORE NATURAL FOR TWO YOUNG PEOPLE IN LOVE THAN—

— MARRIAGE?

MARRIAGE MEANS A WEDDING— —A WEDDING MEANS—

THE MOTHER-IN-LAW!

THERE ARE TWO BASIC 'STYLES' IN WEDDINGS—
STYLE 'A'—INFORMAL

I DO! I DO! BELIEVE ME, I DO-DO-DO-DO!

SOB! I ALWAYS CRY AT WEDDINGS —OR SHOOTINGS —OR BOTH!

5-22
© 1960, New York Herald Tribune Inc.
Trade Mark Reg. U. S. Pat. Off.

STYLE 'B'—FORMAL

SOB! I ALWAYS CRY AT MY WEDDINGS!

BECAUSE

MANY WONDERFUL TRADITIONS ARE CONNECTED TO WEDDINGS— 'TRADING RINGS'

'WEDDING PRESENTS'

'THE RECEPTION LINE'

'CUTTING THE CAKE'

GASP, DEAR!

ARNold Roth

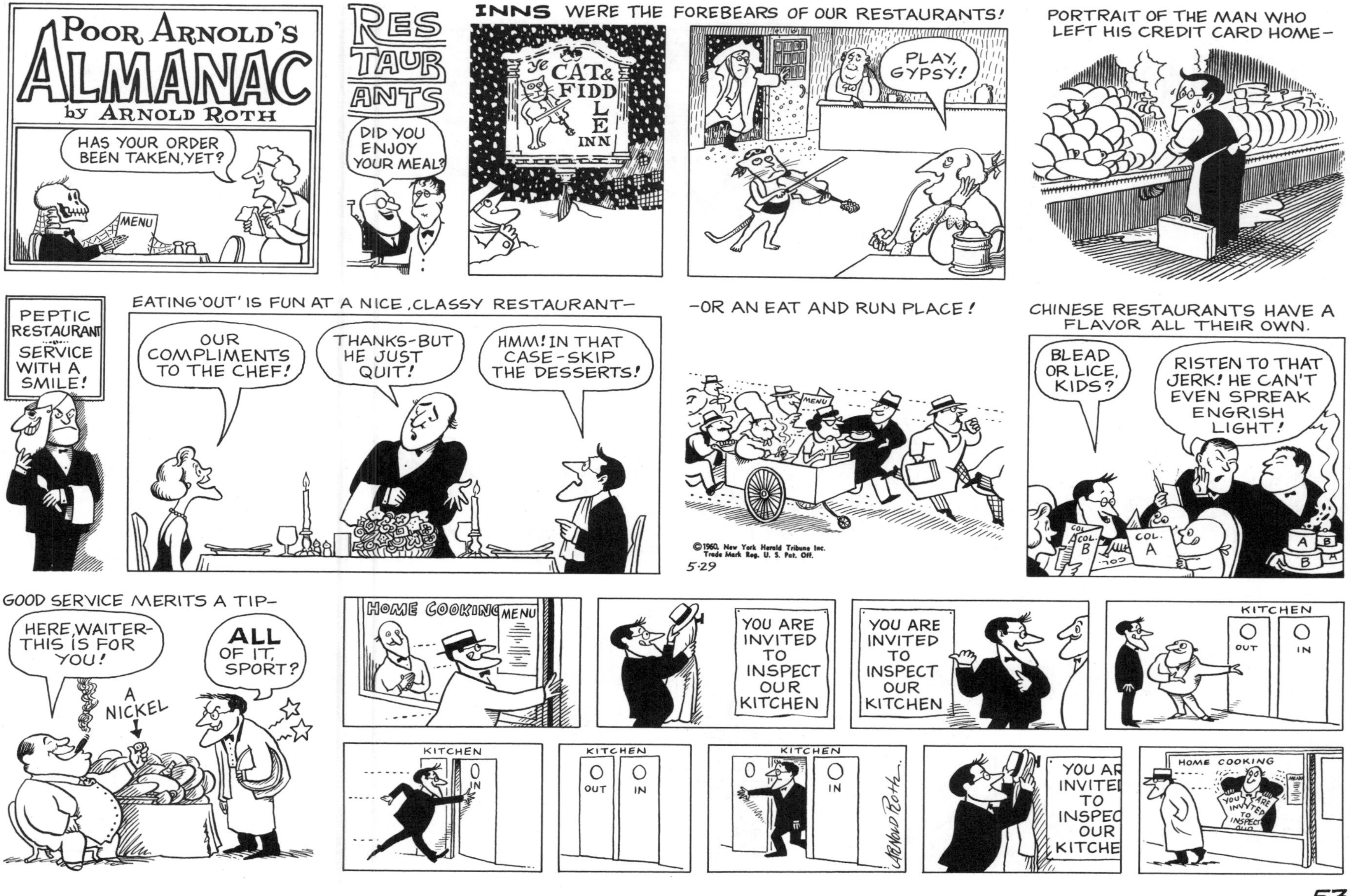

POOR ARNOLD'S
ALMANAC
by ARNOLD ROTH
HAS YOUR ORDER BEEN TAKEN, YET?
MENU
RES TAUR ANTS
DID YOU ENJOY YOUR MEAL?
INNS WERE THE FOREBEARS OF OUR RESTAURANTS!
Ye CAT & FIDD LE INN
PLAY, GYPSY!
PORTRAIT OF THE MAN WHO LEFT HIS CREDIT CARD HOME—
PEPTIC RESTAURANT
SERVICE WITH A SMILE!
EATING 'OUT' IS FUN AT A NICE, CLASSY RESTAURANT—
OUR COMPLIMENTS TO THE CHEF!
THANKS—BUT HE JUST QUIT!
HMM! IN THAT CASE—SKIP THE DESSERTS!
—OR AN EAT AND RUN PLACE!
MENU
©1960, New York Herald Tribune Inc.
Trade Mark Reg. U. S. Pat. Off.
5·29
CHINESE RESTAURANTS HAVE A FLAVOR ALL THEIR OWN.
BLEAD OR LICE, KIDS?
RISTEN TO THAT JERK! HE CAN'T EVEN SPREAK ENGRISH LIGHT!
COL. A
COL. B
A B
GOOD SERVICE MERITS A TIP—
HERE, WAITER—THIS IS FOR YOU!
A NICKEL
ALL OF IT, SPORT?
HOME COOKING
MENU
YOU ARE INVITED TO INSPECT OUR KITCHEN
YOU ARE INVITED TO INSPECT OUR KITCHEN
KITCHEN
OUT
IN
KITCHEN
IN
KITCHEN
OUT
IN
KITCHEN
IN
ARNOLD ROTH
YOU AR INVITE TO INSPEC OUR KITCHE
HOME COOKING

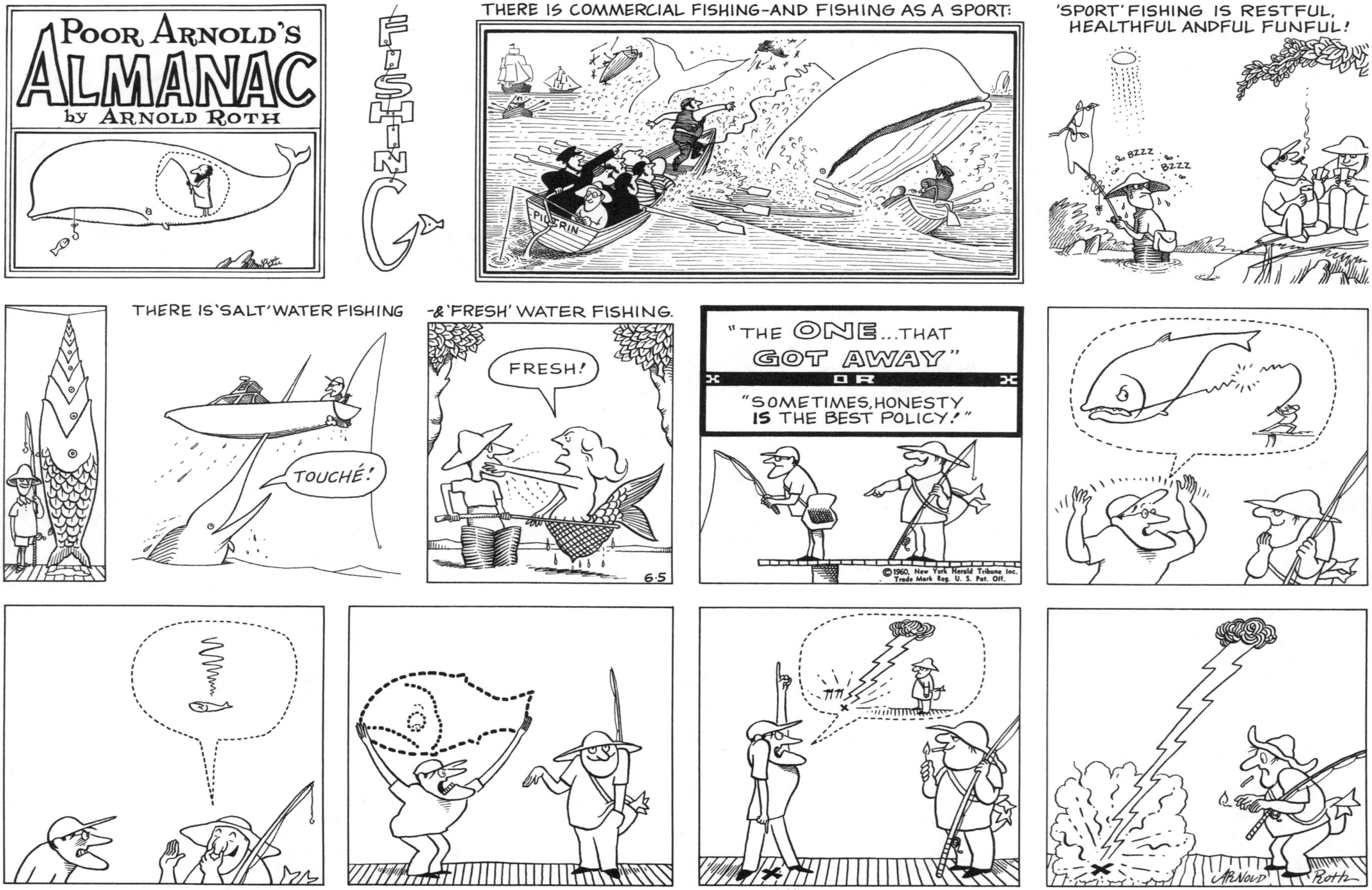
POOR ARNOLD'S
ALMANAC
by ARNOLD ROTH
FISHING
THERE IS COMMERCIAL FISHING-AND FISHING AS A SPORT:
PILGRIM
'SPORT' FISHING IS RESTFUL, HEALTHFUL ANDFUL FUNFUL!
BZZZ
BZZZ
THERE IS 'SALT' WATER FISHING
TOUCHÉ!
-&'FRESH' WATER FISHING.
FRESH!
6·5
"THE ONE...THAT GOT AWAY"
OR
"SOMETIMES, HONESTY IS THE BEST POLICY!"
©1960, New York Herald Tribune Inc.
Trade Mark Reg. U. S. Pat. Off.
ARNOLD Roth

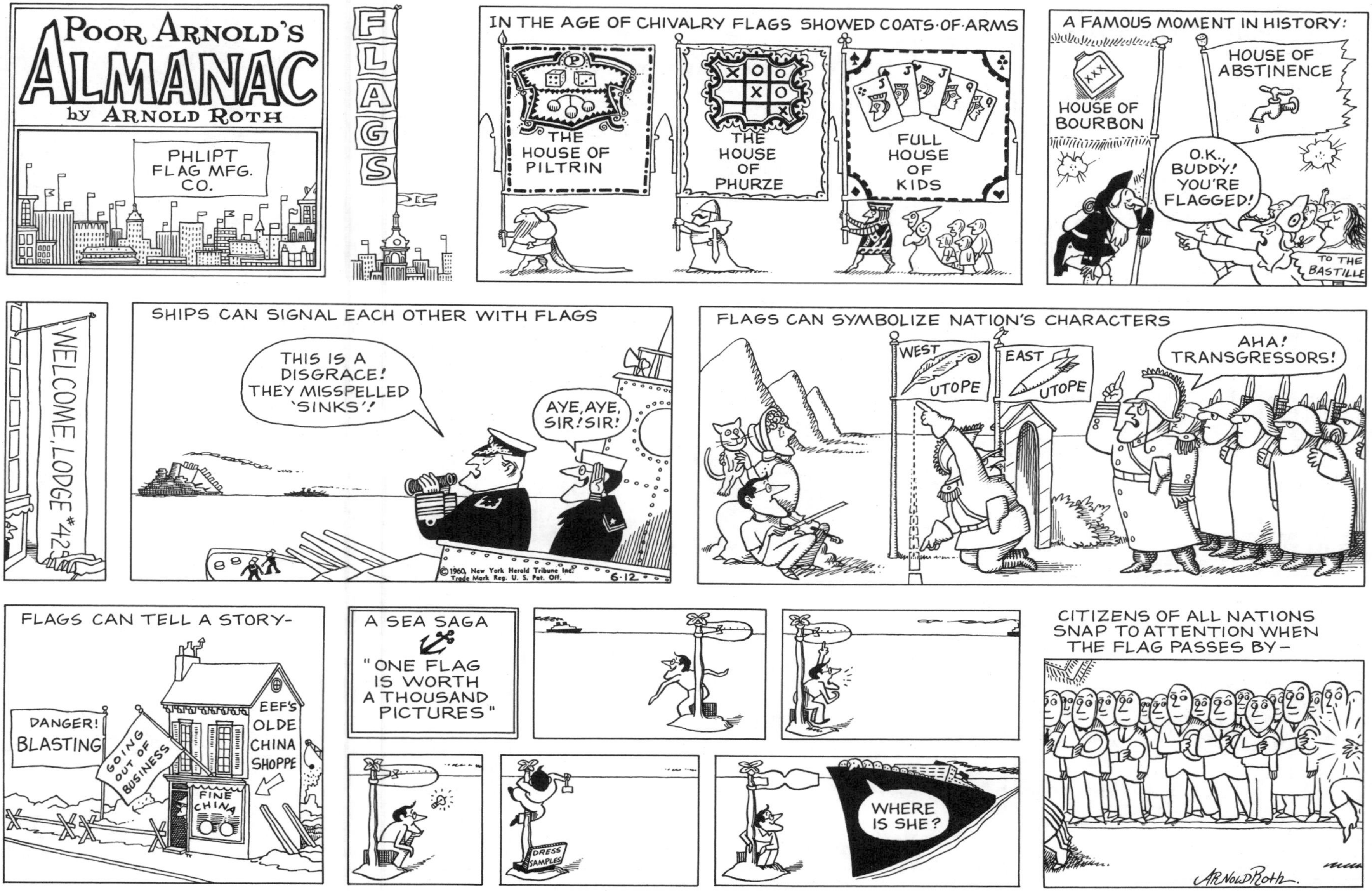
POOR ARNOLD'S ALMANAC
by ARNOLD ROTH
PHLIPT FLAG MFG. CO.
FLAGS
IN THE AGE OF CHIVALRY FLAGS SHOWED COATS·OF·ARMS
THE HOUSE OF PILTRIN
THE HOUSE OF PHURZE
FULL HOUSE OF KIDS
A FAMOUS MOMENT IN HISTORY:
HOUSE OF BOURBON
HOUSE OF ABSTINENCE
O.K., BUDDY! YOU'RE FLAGGED!
TO THE BASTILLE
WELCOME, LODGE #42
SHIPS CAN SIGNAL EACH OTHER WITH FLAGS
THIS IS A DISGRACE! THEY MISSPELLED 'SINKS'!
AYE, AYE, SIR! SIR!
©1960, New York Herald Tribune Inc. Trade Mark Reg. U. S. Pat. Off.
6·12
FLAGS CAN SYMBOLIZE NATION'S CHARACTERS
WEST UTOPE
EAST UTOPE
AHA! TRANSGRESSORS!
FLAGS CAN TELL A STORY-
DANGER! BLASTING
GOING OUT OF BUSINESS
EEF'S OLDE CHINA SHOPPE
FINE CHINA
A SEA SAGA
"ONE FLAG IS WORTH A THOUSAND PICTURES"
DRESS SAMPLES
WHERE IS SHE?
CITIZENS OF ALL NATIONS SNAP TO ATTENTION WHEN THE FLAG PASSES BY–
ARNOLD ROTH

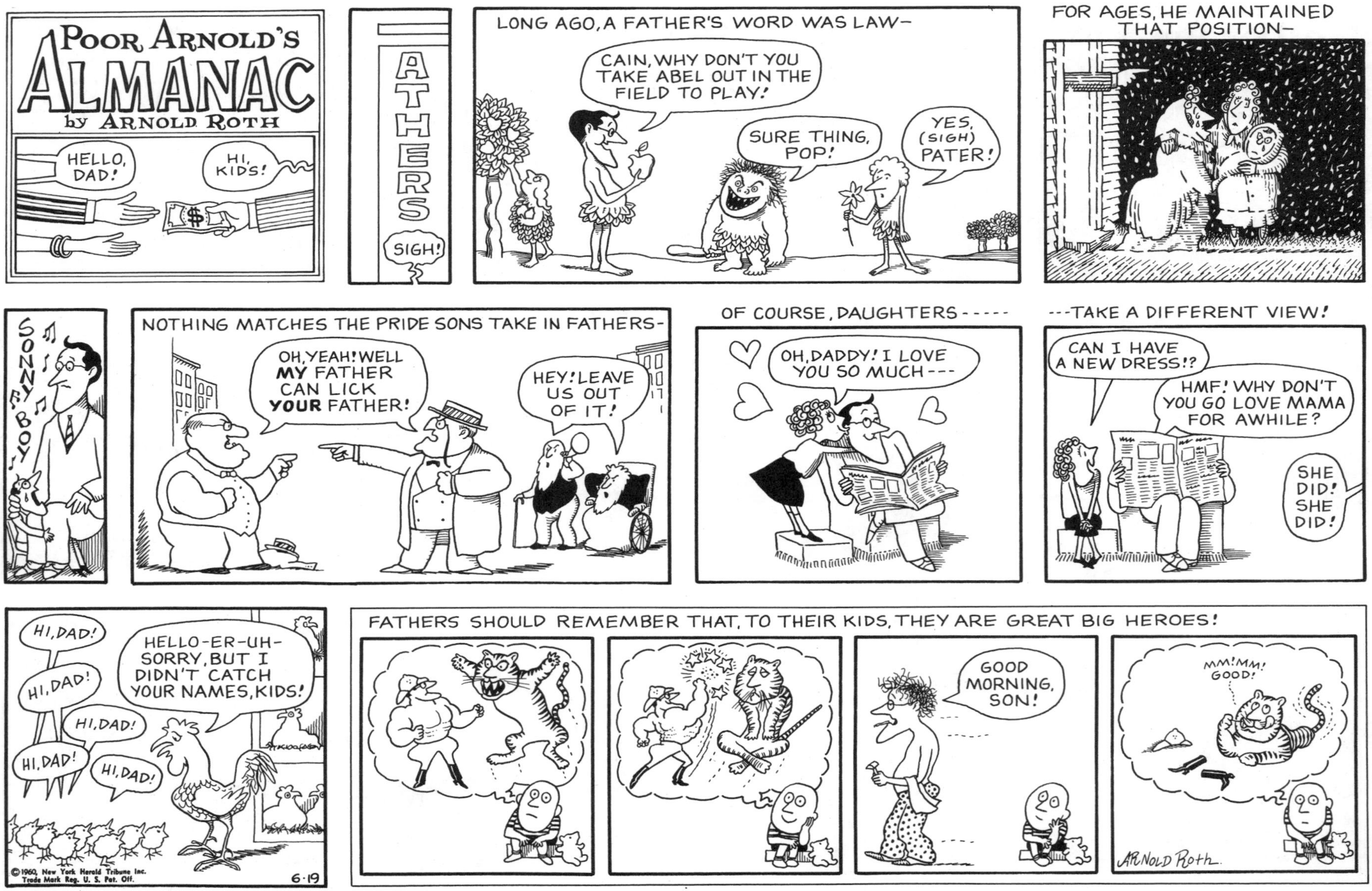

POOR ARNOLD'S ALMANAC
by ARNOLD ROTH
HELLO, DAD!
HI, KIDS!
FATHERS
SIGH!
LONG AGO, A FATHER'S WORD WAS LAW—
CAIN, WHY DON'T YOU TAKE ABEL OUT IN THE FIELD TO PLAY!
SURE THING, POP!
YES, (SIGH) PATER!
FOR AGES, HE MAINTAINED THAT POSITION—
SONNY BOY
NOTHING MATCHES THE PRIDE SONS TAKE IN FATHERS—
OH, YEAH! WELL MY FATHER CAN LICK YOUR FATHER!
HEY! LEAVE US OUT OF IT!
OF COURSE, DAUGHTERS - - - - -
OH, DADDY! I LOVE YOU SO MUCH - - -
- - -TAKE A DIFFERENT VIEW!
CAN I HAVE A NEW DRESS!?
HMF! WHY DON'T YOU GO LOVE MAMA FOR AWHILE?
SHE DID! SHE DID!
HI, DAD!
HI, DAD!
HI, DAD!
HI, DAD!
HI, DAD!
HELLO-ER-UH- SORRY, BUT I DIDN'T CATCH YOUR NAMES, KIDS!
©1960, New York Herald Tribune Inc. Trade Mark Reg. U. S. Pat. Off.
6·19
FATHERS SHOULD REMEMBER THAT, TO THEIR KIDS, THEY ARE GREAT BIG HEROES!
GOOD MORNING, SON!
MM! MM! GOOD!
ARNOLD ROTH

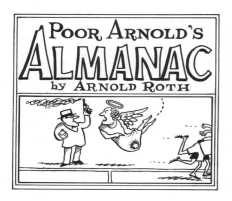

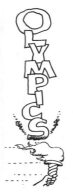

POOR ARNOLD'S ALMANAC
by ARNOLD ROTH
OLYMPICS
EVERY FOUR YEARS COUNTRIES TAKE TIME OUT FROM THEIR USUAL OCCUPATIONS-
WE'RE GONNA GET YOU GUYS!
XXX
OOO
-TO ENTER INTO REAL COMPETITION AT THE OLYMPICS-
WE'RE GONNA GET YOU GUYS!
3
2nd
FIRST
THE OLYMPICS ARE STARTED BY A RUNNER WITH A TORCH-
AHA! BREAKING TRAINING!
WE OUGHTA GET THAT GUY!
COACH
I SMOKE
CIGGIE
SAYS
SOME OLYMPIC HIGHLIGHTS-
SWIMMING-
-HURDLES-
-JAVELIN THROW-
-RELAYS-
-HIGH JUMP-
-POLE VAULT!
SOME WIN, SOME LOSE- BUT THE GAMES ARE ALL THAT MATTER-
WE'RE GONNA GET YOU GUYS!
1ST
2nd
3rd
XXX
OOO
THE TRUE OLYMPIC SPIRIT-
©1960, New York Herald Tribune Inc.
Trade Mark Reg. U. S. Pat. Off.
6·26
ARNOLD ROTH

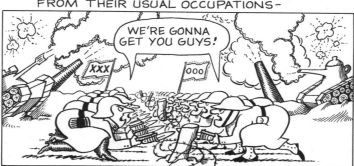

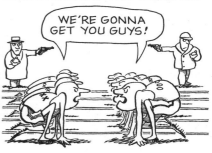

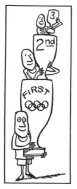

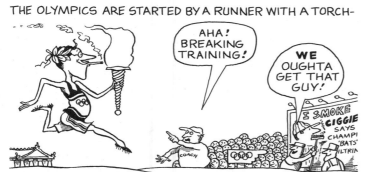

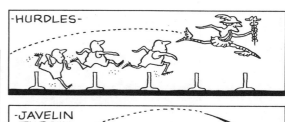

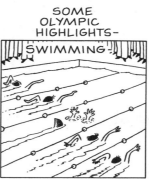

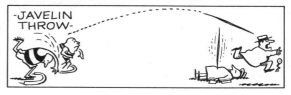

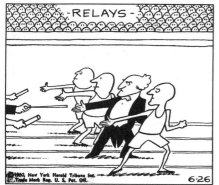

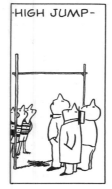

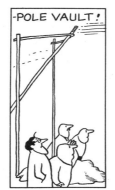

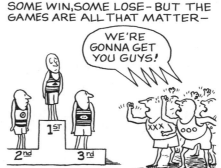

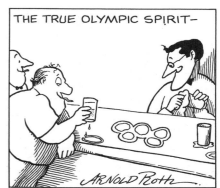

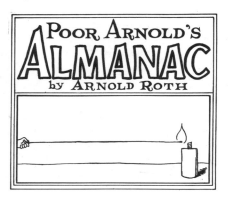

POOR ARNOLD'S ALMANAC
by ARNOLD ROTH

FIREWORKS FIREWORKS FIREWORKS

'UNSUNG HEROES' NO.1: THE INVENTOR OF FIREWORKS!

BOOM

WHAT'S FOR DINNER?

ONE FROM COLUMN 'A' TWO FROM....

THE CHINESE MADE GREAT ADVANCES—

HONORABLE BANG

HONORABLE BOOM

HONORABLEVOOM

NORABL POP

HONORABLE KRM

BOOM

THERE IS NO LIMIT AS TO WHAT CAN BE DONE TODAY—

YEAR AFTER YEAR— THE SAME OLD CORN!

FIREWORKS (OR 'PYROTECHNICS') BECAME POPULAR IN SIXTEENTH CENTURY EUROPE—

—AND, **I**, SÉNOR RUGGIERI, WILL GIVE YOU A SHOW WITHOUT EQUAL!

RUGGIERI 'PYRO-TECHNICS'

COUNT BOLOGNA DIED OF 'OVER-EATING'

LUIGI PASTO DIED OF POVERTY ('UNDER-EATING')

FAVORITE FORMS OF FIREWORKS:

ROMAN CANDLES—

III! II! I! ZERO, NERO!

SAY! THAT GIVES ME AN IDEA——

—PINWHEELS—

—LEAKS IN GAS PIPES—

GAD! I WONDER HOW THEY **DO** THAT!

7-3 © 1960, New York Herald Tribune Inc.
Trade Mark Reg. U.S. Pat. Off.

—AND ROCKETS!

10!9!8!7!6!5! 4!3!2!1!ZERO!— ZERO——ZERO
—10!9!8!7!6!5!——

CAPE CANAVERAL

ARNOLD Roth

58

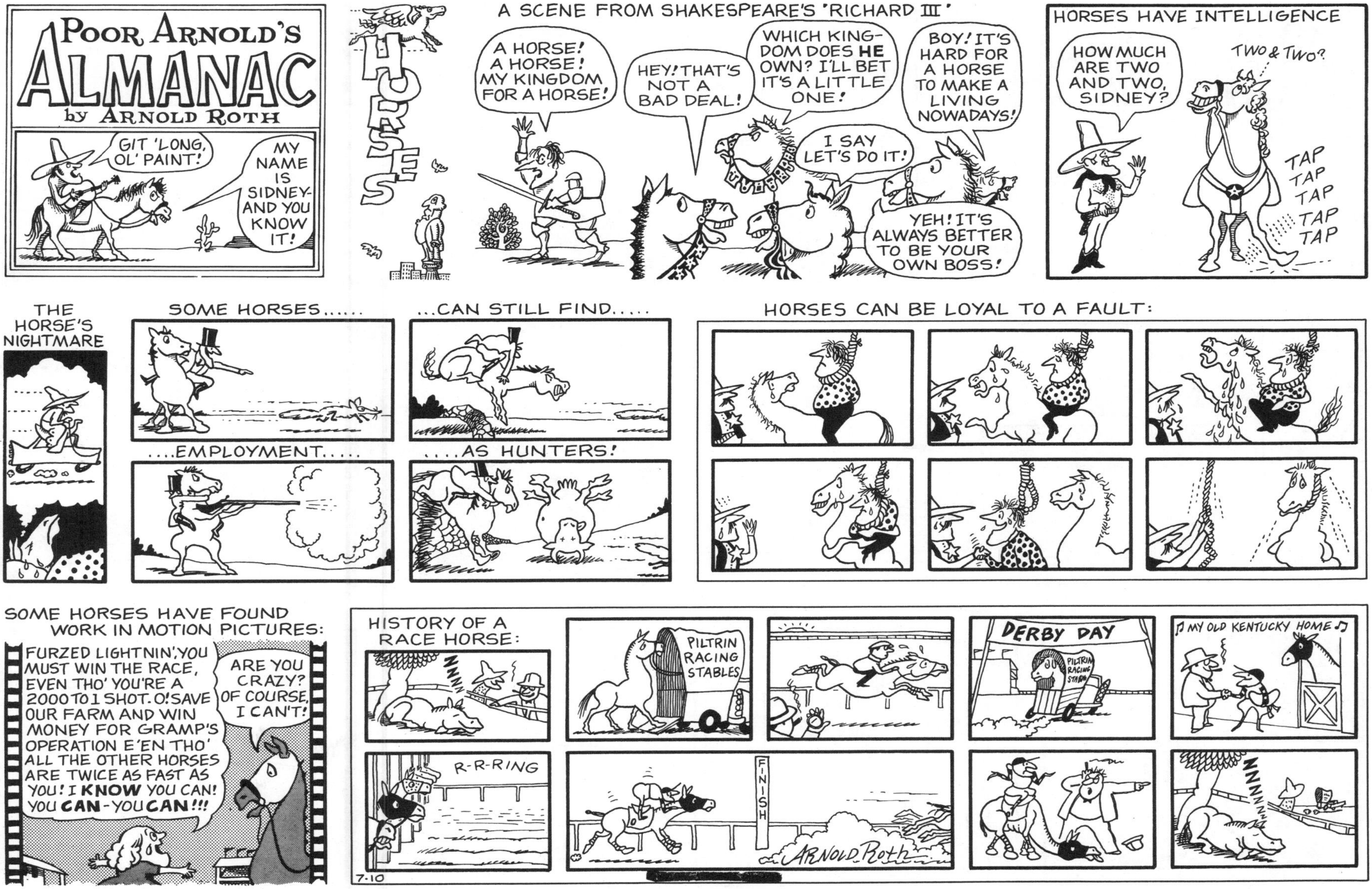
POOR ARNOLD'S
ALMANAC
by ARNOLD ROTH
GIT 'LONG, OL' PAINT!
MY NAME IS SIDNEY- AND YOU KNOW IT!
HORSES
A SCENE FROM SHAKESPEARE'S 'RICHARD III'
A HORSE! A HORSE! MY KINGDOM FOR A HORSE!
HEY! THAT'S NOT A BAD DEAL!
WHICH KING-DOM DOES HE OWN? I'LL BET IT'S A LITTLE ONE!
I SAY LET'S DO IT!
BOY! IT'S HARD FOR A HORSE TO MAKE A LIVING NOWADAYS!
YEH! IT'S ALWAYS BETTER TO BE YOUR OWN BOSS!
HORSES HAVE INTELLIGENCE
HOW MUCH ARE TWO AND TWO, SIDNEY?
TWO & TWO?
TAP TAP TAP TAP TAP
THE HORSE'S NIGHTMARE
SOME HORSES......
...CAN STILL FIND.....
....EMPLOYMENT.....
....AS HUNTERS!
HORSES CAN BE LOYAL TO A FAULT:
SOME HORSES HAVE FOUND WORK IN MOTION PICTURES:
FURZED LIGHTNIN', YOU MUST WIN THE RACE, EVEN THO' YOU'RE A 2000 TO 1 SHOT. O! SAVE OUR FARM AND WIN MONEY FOR GRAMP'S OPERATION E'EN THO' ALL THE OTHER HORSES ARE TWICE AS FAST AS YOU! I KNOW YOU CAN! YOU CAN - YOU CAN!!!
ARE YOU CRAZY? OF COURSE, I CAN'T!
HISTORY OF A RACE HORSE:
ZZZ
PILTRIN RACING STABLES
DERBY DAY
PILTRIN RACING STABLES
♫ MY OLD KENTUCKY HOME ♫
R-R-RING
FINISH
ARNOLD ROTH
ZZZZZ
7-10
[redacted]

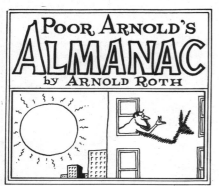

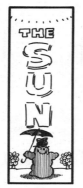

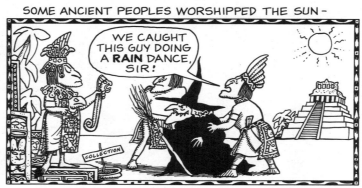

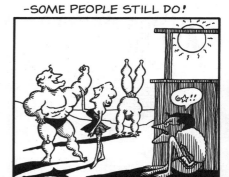

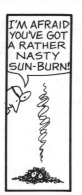

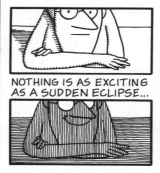

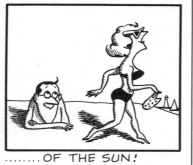

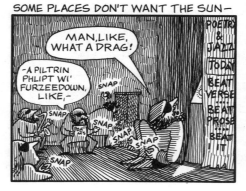

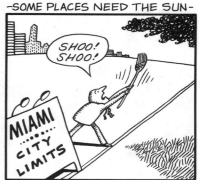

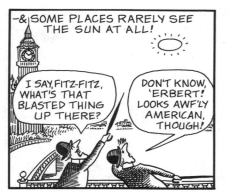

POOR ARNOLD'S
ALMANAC
by ARNOLD ROTH
THE SUN
SOME ANCIENT PEOPLES WORSHIPPED THE SUN-
WE CAUGHT THIS GUY DOING A **RAIN** DANCE, SIR!
COLLECTION
-SOME PEOPLE STILL DO!
I'M AFRAID YOU'VE GOT A RATHER NASTY SUN-BURN!
NOTHING IS AS EXCITING AS A SUDDEN ECLIPSE...
........OF THE SUN!
SOME PLACES DON'T WANT THE SUN-
MAN, LIKE, WHAT A DRAG!
-A PILTRIN PHLIPT WI' FURZEEDOWN, LIKE,-
SNAP
POETRY & JAZZ TODAY BEAT VERSE .... BEAT PROSE .... BEAT IT
-SOME PLACES NEED THE SUN-
SHOO! SHOO!
MIAMI CITY LIMITS
-& SOME PLACES RARELY SEE THE SUN AT ALL!
I SAY, FITZ-FITZ, WHAT'S THAT BLASTED THING UP THERE?
DON'T KNOW, 'ERBERT! LOOKS AWF'LY AMERICAN, THOUGH!
THERE ARE BEAUTIFUL SUNRISES-
-AND, OF COURSE, SUNSETS!
GEE! ISN'T IT BEAUTIFUL!
ISN'T **WHAT** BEAUTIFUL?
7.17 © 1960, New York Herald Tribune Inc.
ARNOLD ROTH

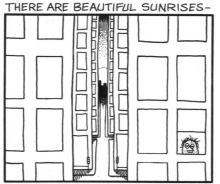

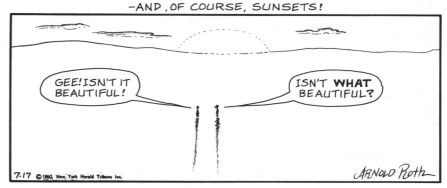

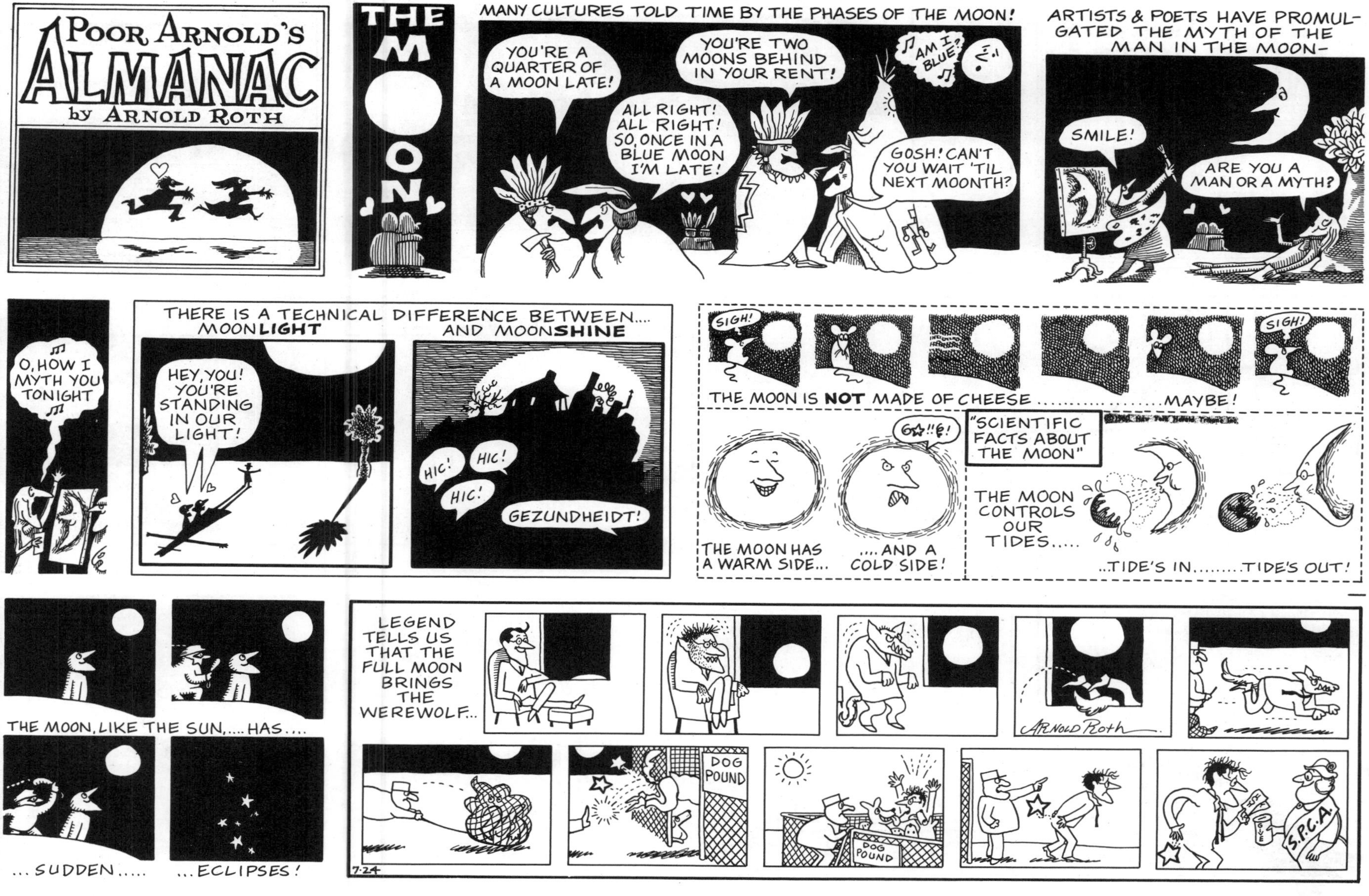
POOR ARNOLD'S
ALMANAC
by ARNOLD ROTH
THE MOON
MANY CULTURES TOLD TIME BY THE PHASES OF THE MOON!
YOU'RE A QUARTER OF A MOON LATE!
ALL RIGHT! ALL RIGHT! SO, ONCE IN A BLUE MOON I'M LATE!
YOU'RE TWO MOONS BEHIND IN YOUR RENT!
AM I BLUE?
GOSH! CAN'T YOU WAIT 'TIL NEXT MOONTH?
ARTISTS & POETS HAVE PROMULGATED THE MYTH OF THE MAN IN THE MOON–
SMILE!
ARE YOU A MAN OR A MYTH?
O, HOW I MYTH YOU TONIGHT
THERE IS A TECHNICAL DIFFERENCE BETWEEN.... MOONLIGHT AND MOONSHINE
HEY, YOU! YOU'RE STANDING IN OUR LIGHT!
HIC!
HIC!
HIC!
GEZUNDHEIDT!
SIGH!
SIGH!
THE MOON IS NOT MADE OF CHEESE ....MAYBE!
THE MOON HAS A WARM SIDE...
....AND A COLD SIDE!
"SCIENTIFIC FACTS ABOUT THE MOON"
THE MOON CONTROLS OUR TIDES.....
..TIDE'S IN.........TIDE'S OUT!
THE MOON, LIKE THE SUN,.... HAS....
... SUDDEN.....
...ECLIPSES!
LEGEND TELLS US THAT THE FULL MOON BRINGS THE WEREWOLF...
ARNOLD ROTH
DOG POUND
DOG POUND
S.P.C.A.
7·24

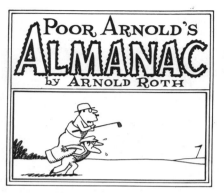

POOR ARNOLD'S
ALMANAC
by ARNOLD ROTH
OLF
THE SCOTS DEVELOPED.....
....GOLF.....
...AND SKIN-DIVING!
THE OBJECT OF THE GAME
NIP
IS TO KNOCK THE BALL
NIP
INTO THE CUP WITH AS FEW
NIP
STROKES AS ARE
NIP
NECESSARY!
AH!
FORE!
HE MISSED!
THOUGH GOLF IS NOT NECESSARILLY A RICH MAN'S GAME - IT **IS** MOST POPULAR DURING TIMES OF PROSPERITY!
FORE!
1927
1931
1960
DOC, ALL I EVER THINK ABOUT IS **GOLF**! MORNING, NOON AND NIGHT IT'S **GOLF**! **GOLF**! **GOLF**! NOTHING ELSE INTERESTS ME!
HMM! HAVE YOU EVER HEARD OF **GIRLS?**
7·31
"GOLFER'S LANGUAGE FOR THE BEGINNER" (EXPLAINED IN TERMS OF GOOD & BAD)
FORE!
"HOLE-IN-ONE" (GOOD)
VERY FUNNY! VERY FUNNY!
"BUNKER"= SAND TRAP (BAD)
"EAGLE"- 2 UNDER PAR (VERY GOOD)!
"BIRDIE"- 1 UNDER PAR (GOOD)!
"BOGEY"-1 OVER PAR (GOOD & BAD)!
SURE! I KNOW **WHAT** IT IS - I'M JUST **NOT** SURE IT'S ONE OF **OURS**!
ARNOLD ROTH

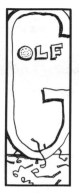

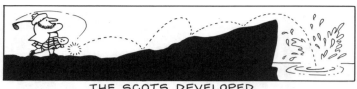

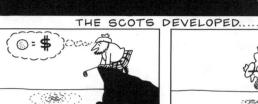

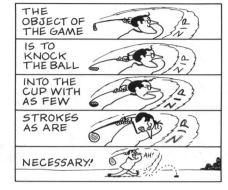

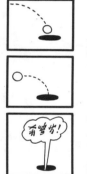

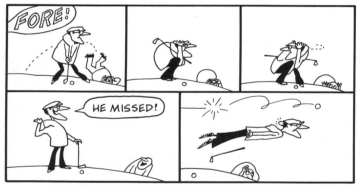

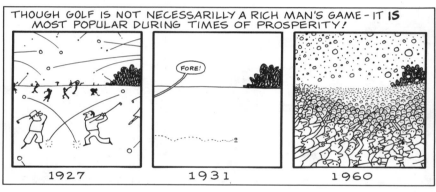

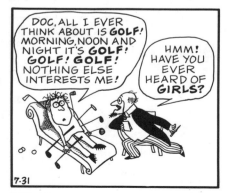

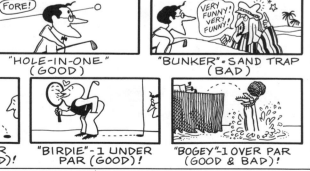

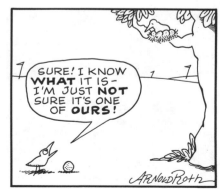

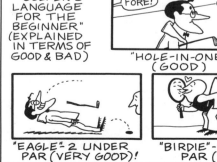

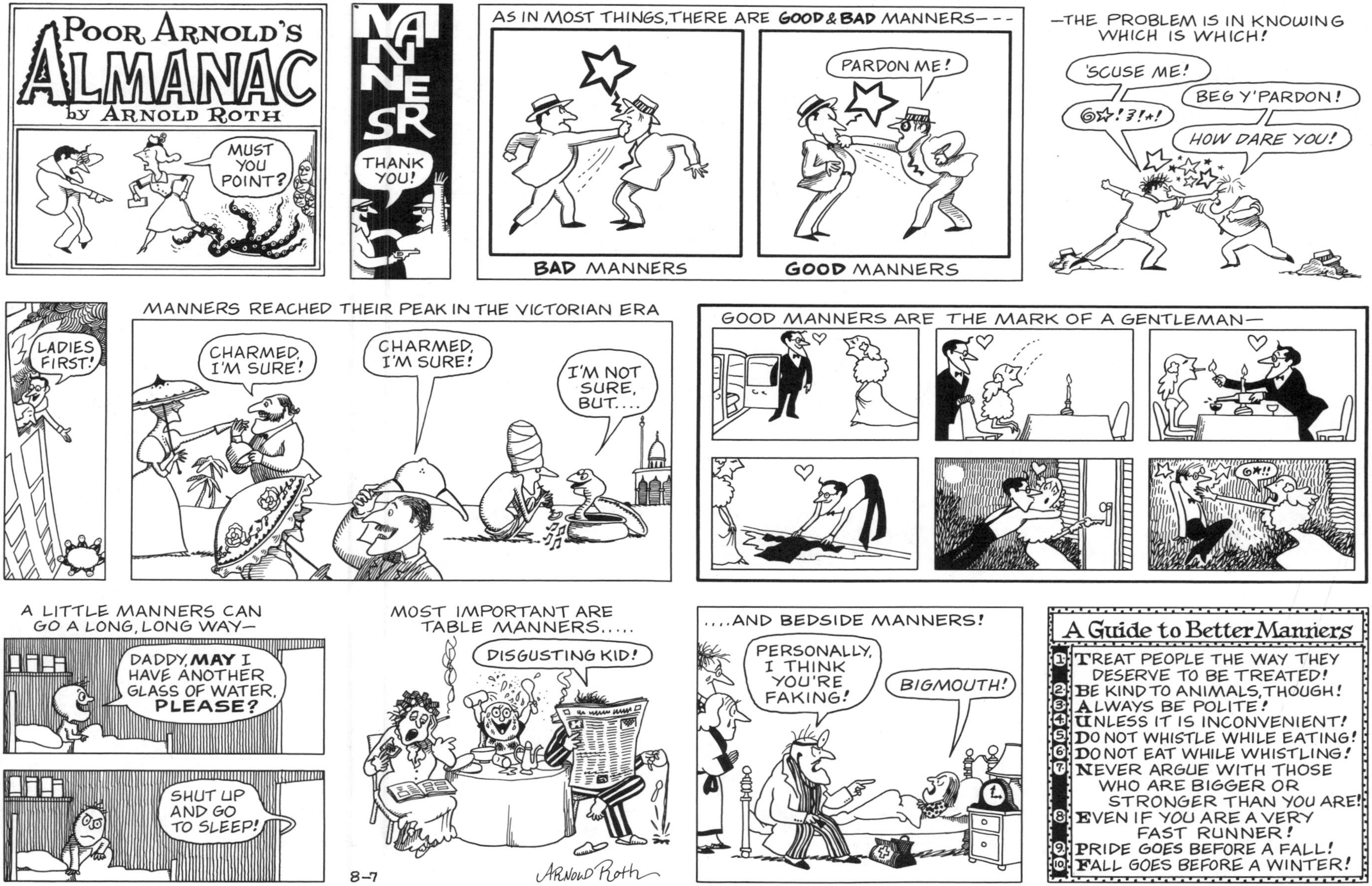
POOR ARNOLD'S
ALMANAC
by ARNOLD ROTH
MUST YOU POINT?
MANNERS
THANK YOU!
AS IN MOST THINGS, THERE ARE GOOD & BAD MANNERS---
BAD MANNERS
PARDON ME!
GOOD MANNERS
—THE PROBLEM IS IN KNOWING WHICH IS WHICH!
'SCUSE ME!
BEG Y'PARDON!
HOW DARE YOU!
LADIES FIRST!
MANNERS REACHED THEIR PEAK IN THE VICTORIAN ERA
CHARMED, I'M SURE!
CHARMED, I'M SURE!
I'M NOT SURE, BUT....
GOOD MANNERS ARE THE MARK OF A GENTLEMAN—
A LITTLE MANNERS CAN GO A LONG, LONG WAY—
DADDY, MAY I HAVE ANOTHER GLASS OF WATER, PLEASE?
SHUT UP AND GO TO SLEEP!
MOST IMPORTANT ARE TABLE MANNERS.....
DISGUSTING KID!
8-7
ARNOLD ROTH
....AND BEDSIDE MANNERS!
PERSONALLY, I THINK YOU'RE FAKING!
BIGMOUTH!
A Guide to Better Manners
1. TREAT PEOPLE THE WAY THEY DESERVE TO BE TREATED!
2. BE KIND TO ANIMALS, THOUGH!
3. ALWAYS BE POLITE!
4. UNLESS IT IS INCONVENIENT!
5. DO NOT WHISTLE WHILE EATING!
6. DO NOT EAT WHILE WHISTLING!
7. NEVER ARGUE WITH THOSE WHO ARE BIGGER OR STRONGER THAN YOU ARE!
8. EVEN IF YOU ARE A VERY FAST RUNNER!
9. PRIDE GOES BEFORE A FALL!
10. FALL GOES BEFORE A WINTER!

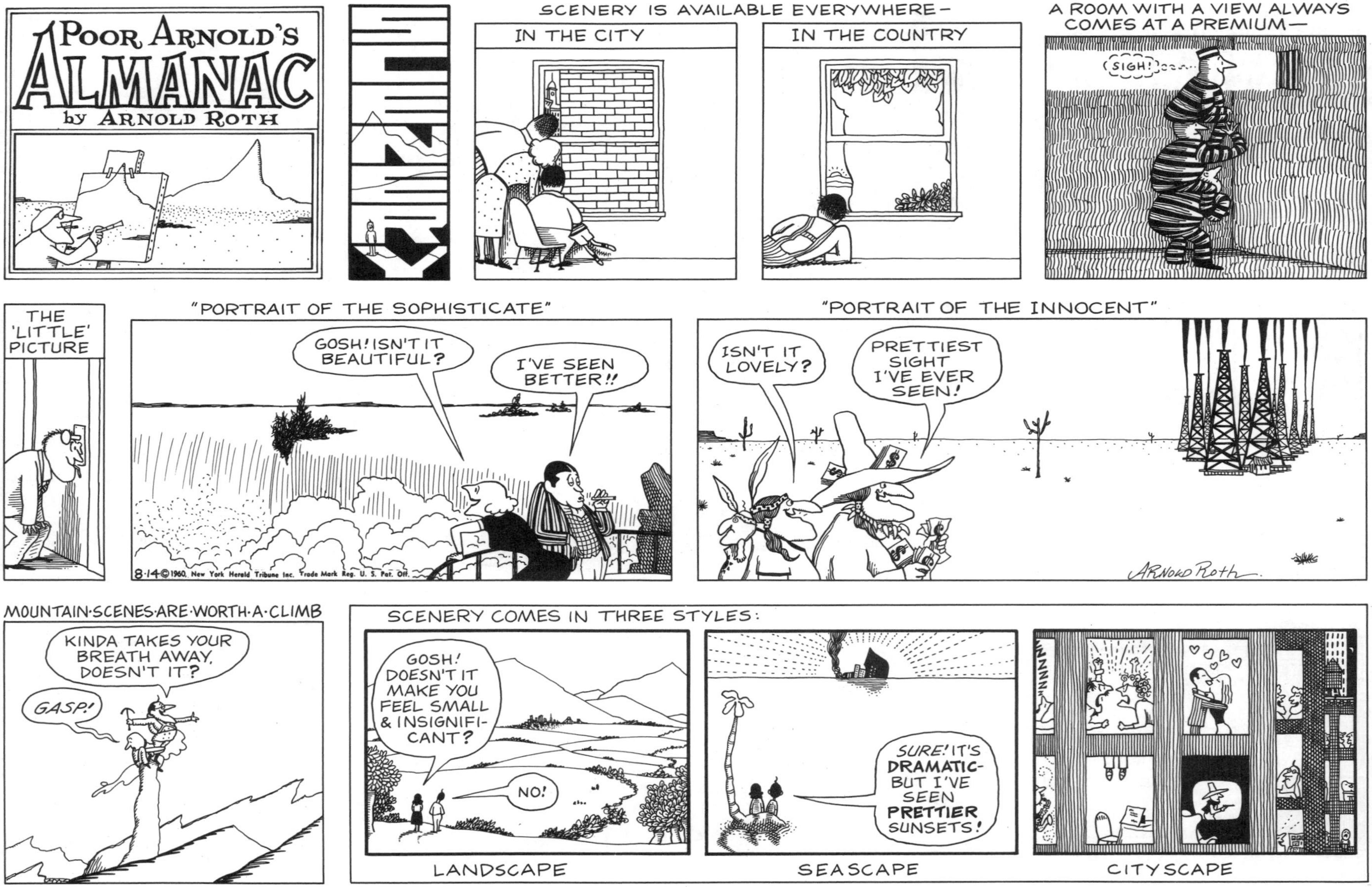

POOR ARNOLD'S
ALMANAC
by ARNOLD ROTH
SCENERY IS AVAILABLE EVERYWHERE—
IN THE CITY
IN THE COUNTRY
A ROOM WITH A VIEW ALWAYS COMES AT A PREMIUM—
SIGH!
THE 'LITTLE' PICTURE
"PORTRAIT OF THE SOPHISTICATE"
GOSH! ISN'T IT BEAUTIFUL?
I'VE SEEN BETTER!!
8·14 © 1960, New York Herald Tribune Inc. Trade Mark Reg. U. S. Pat. Off.
"PORTRAIT OF THE INNOCENT"
ISN'T IT LOVELY?
PRETTIEST SIGHT I'VE EVER SEEN!
ARNOLD ROTH
MOUNTAIN·SCENES·ARE·WORTH·A·CLIMB
KINDA TAKES YOUR BREATH AWAY, DOESN'T IT?
GASP!
SCENERY COMES IN THREE STYLES:
GOSH! DOESN'T IT MAKE YOU FEEL SMALL & INSIGNIFICANT?
NO!
LANDSCAPE
SURE! IT'S DRAMATIC- BUT I'VE SEEN PRETTIER SUNSETS!
SEASCAPE
CITYSCAPE

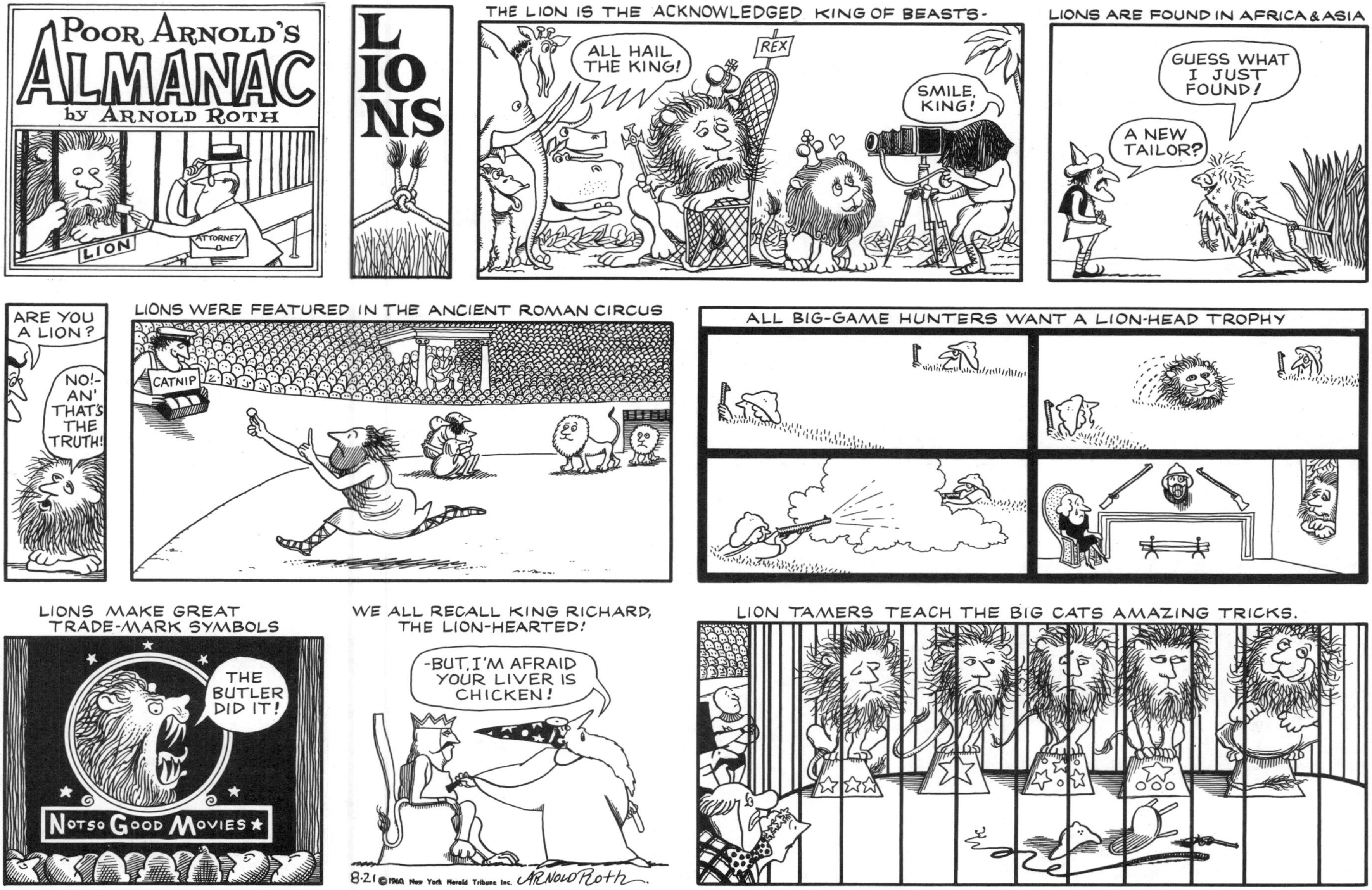
POOR ARNOLD'S
ALMANAC
by ARNOLD ROTH
LION
ATTORNEY
LIONS
THE LION IS THE ACKNOWLEDGED KING OF BEASTS-
ALL HAIL THE KING!
REX
SMILE, KING!
LIONS ARE FOUND IN AFRICA & ASIA
GUESS WHAT I JUST FOUND!
A NEW TAILOR?
ARE YOU A LION?
NO!- AN' THAT'S THE TRUTH!
LIONS WERE FEATURED IN THE ANCIENT ROMAN CIRCUS
CATNIP
ALL BIG-GAME HUNTERS WANT A LION-HEAD TROPHY
LIONS MAKE GREAT TRADE-MARK SYMBOLS
THE BUTLER DID IT!
NOTSO GOOD MOVIES
WE ALL RECALL KING RICHARD, THE LION-HEARTED!
-BUT, I'M AFRAID YOUR LIVER IS CHICKEN!
8·21 ©1960 New York Herald Tribune Inc. ARNOLD ROTH
LION TAMERS TEACH THE BIG CATS AMAZING TRICKS.

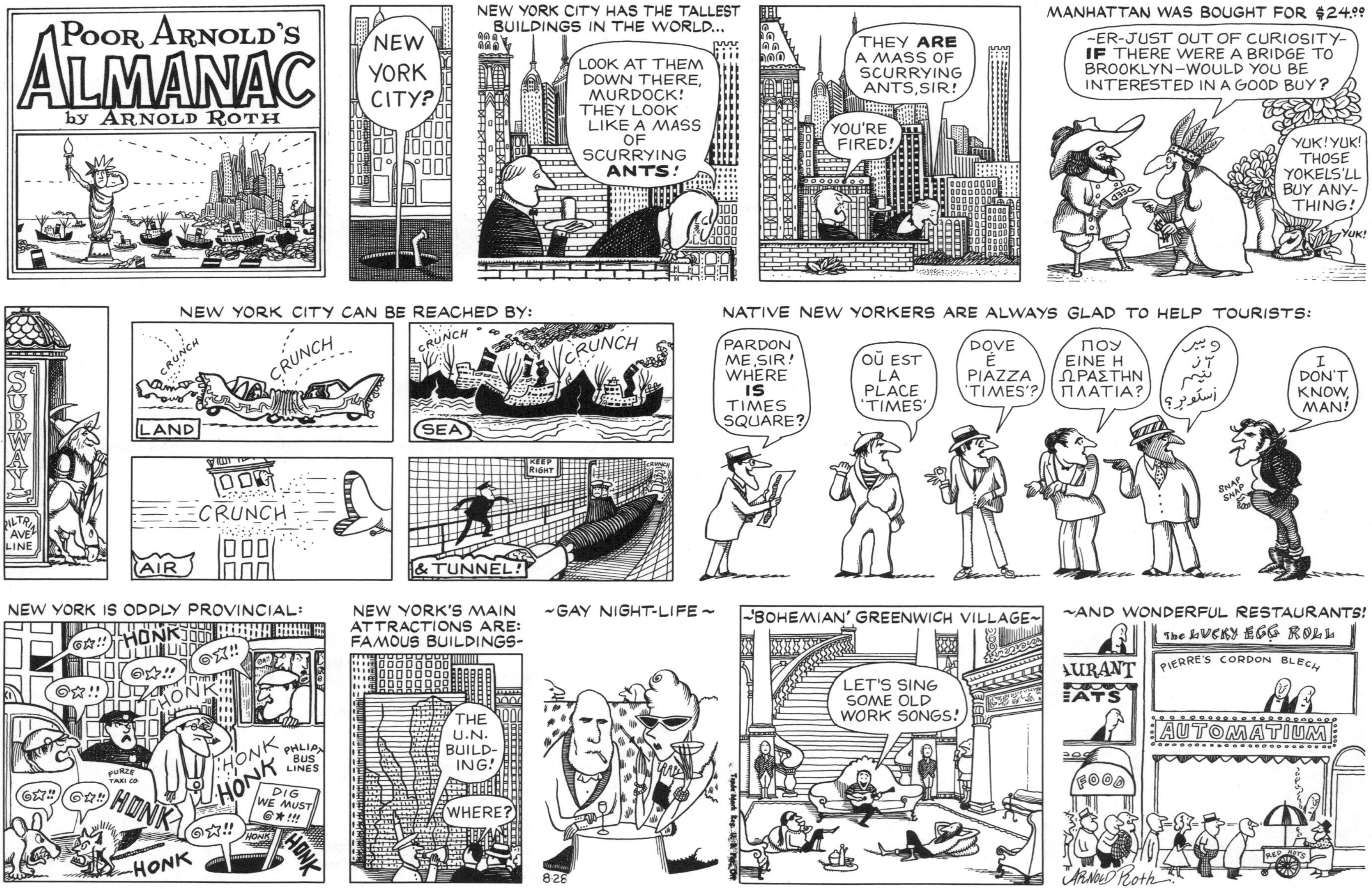

POOR ARNOLD'S
ALMANAC
by ARNOLD ROTH
NEW YORK CITY?
NEW YORK CITY HAS THE TALLEST BUILDINGS IN THE WORLD...
LOOK AT THEM DOWN THERE, MURDOCK! THEY LOOK LIKE A MASS OF SCURRYING **ANTS**!
THEY **ARE** A MASS OF SCURRYING ANTS, SIR!
YOU'RE FIRED!
MANHATTAN WAS BOUGHT FOR $24.00
-ER-JUST OUT OF CURIOSITY- **IF** THERE WERE A BRIDGE TO BROOKLYN-WOULD YOU BE INTERESTED IN A GOOD BUY?
DEED
YUK! YUK! THOSE YOKELS'LL BUY ANY-THING!
YUK!
SUBWAY
PILTRIN AVE LINE
NEW YORK CITY CAN BE REACHED BY:
CRUNCH
CRUNCH
LAND
CRUNCH
CRUNCH
SEA
CRUNCH
AIR
KEEP RIGHT
CRUNCH
& TUNNEL!
NATIVE NEW YORKERS ARE ALWAYS GLAD TO HELP TOURISTS:
PARDON ME, SIR! WHERE **IS** TIMES SQUARE?
OÙ EST LA PLACE 'TIMES'
DOVE É PIAZZA 'TIMES'?
ΠΟΥ ΕΙΝΕ Η ΩΡΑΣΤΗΝ ΠΛΑΤΙΑ?
SNAP SNAP
I DON'T KNOW, MAN!
NEW YORK IS ODDLY PROVINCIAL:
HONK
HONK
HONK
HONK
HONK
HONK
HONK
HONK
FURZE TAXI CO.
PHLIPT BUS LINES
DIG WE MUST
NEW YORK'S MAIN ATTRACTIONS ARE: FAMOUS BUILDINGS-
THE U.N. BUILD-ING!
WHERE?
~GAY NIGHT-LIFE~
8·28
~'BOHEMIAN' GREENWICH VILLAGE~
LET'S SING SOME OLD WORK SONGS!
~AND WONDERFUL RESTAURANTS!
The LUCKY EGG ROLL
AURANT
EATS
PIERRE'S CORDON BLECH
AUTOMATIUM
FOOD
RED HOTS
ARNOLD Roth

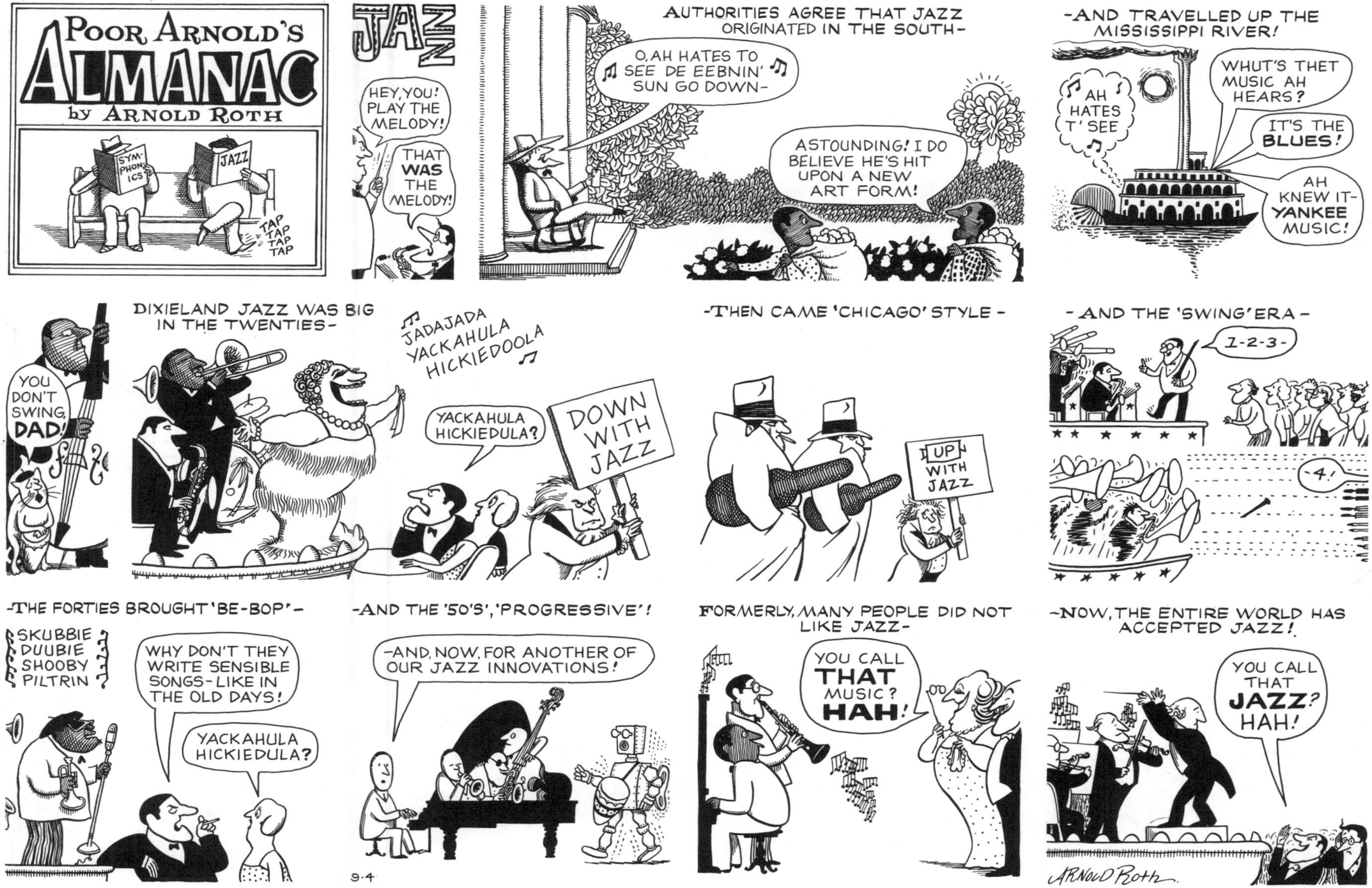
POOR ARNOLD'S
ALMANAC
by ARNOLD ROTH
SYMPHONICS
JAZZ
TAP TAP TAP TAP
JAZZ
HEY, YOU! PLAY THE MELODY!
THAT WAS THE MELODY!
AUTHORITIES AGREE THAT JAZZ ORIGINATED IN THE SOUTH–
O, AH HATES TO SEE DE EEBNIN' SUN GO DOWN–
ASTOUNDING! I DO BELIEVE HE'S HIT UPON A NEW ART FORM!
–AND TRAVELLED UP THE MISSISSIPPI RIVER!
AH HATES T' SEE
WHUT'S THET MUSIC AH HEARS?
IT'S THE BLUES!
AH KNEW IT– YANKEE MUSIC!
YOU DON'T SWING, DAD!
DIXIELAND JAZZ WAS BIG IN THE TWENTIES–
JADAJADA YACKAHULA HICKIEDOOLA
YACKAHULA HICKIEDULA?
DOWN WITH JAZZ
–THEN CAME 'CHICAGO' STYLE–
UP WITH JAZZ
–AND THE 'SWING' ERA–
1-2-3-
-4!
–THE FORTIES BROUGHT 'BE-BOP'–
SKUBBIE DUUBIE SHOOBY PILTRIN
WHY DON'T THEY WRITE SENSIBLE SONGS–LIKE IN THE OLD DAYS!
YACKAHULA HICKIEDULA?
–AND THE '50'S', 'PROGRESSIVE'!
–AND, NOW, FOR ANOTHER OF OUR JAZZ INNOVATIONS!
9·4
FORMERLY, MANY PEOPLE DID NOT LIKE JAZZ–
YOU CALL THAT MUSIC? HAH!
–NOW, THE ENTIRE WORLD HAS ACCEPTED JAZZ!
YOU CALL THAT JAZZ? HAH!
ARNOLD ROTH

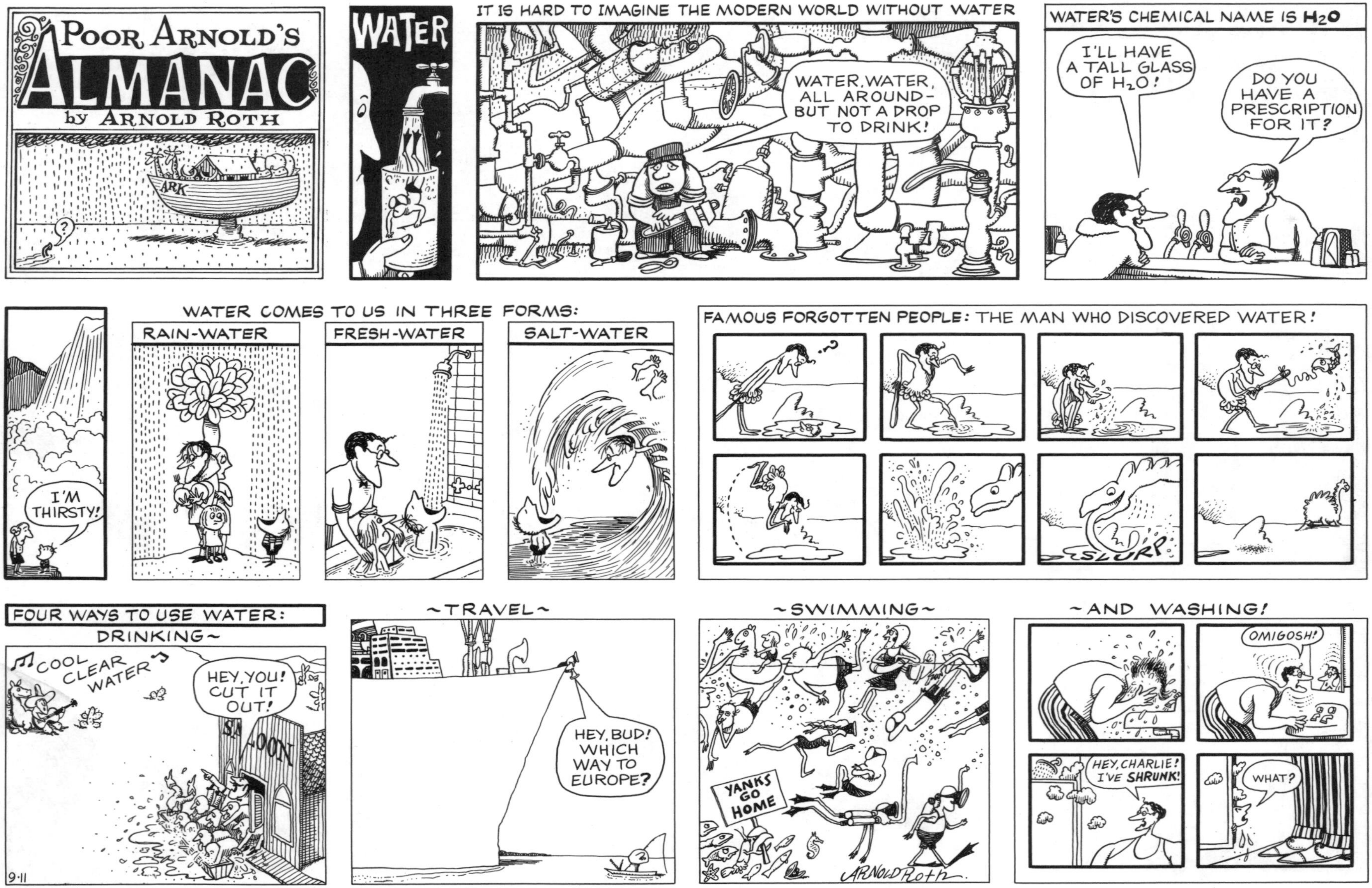

POOR ARNOLD'S
ALMANAC
by ARNOLD ROTH
ARK
?
WATER
IT IS HARD TO IMAGINE THE MODERN WORLD WITHOUT WATER
WATER, WATER, ALL AROUND– BUT NOT A DROP TO DRINK!
WATER'S CHEMICAL NAME IS H2O
I'LL HAVE A TALL GLASS OF H2O!
DO YOU HAVE A PRESCRIPTION FOR IT?
I'M THIRSTY!
WATER COMES TO US IN THREE FORMS:
RAIN-WATER
FRESH-WATER
SALT-WATER
FAMOUS FORGOTTEN PEOPLE: THE MAN WHO DISCOVERED WATER!
SLURP
FOUR WAYS TO USE WATER:
DRINKING~
COOL CLEAR WATER
HEY, YOU! CUT IT OUT!
SALOON
9·11
~TRAVEL~
HEY, BUD! WHICH WAY TO EUROPE?
~SWIMMING~
YANKS GO HOME
ARNOLD ROTH
~AND WASHING!
OMIGOSH!
HEY, CHARLIE! I'VE SHRUNK!
WHAT?

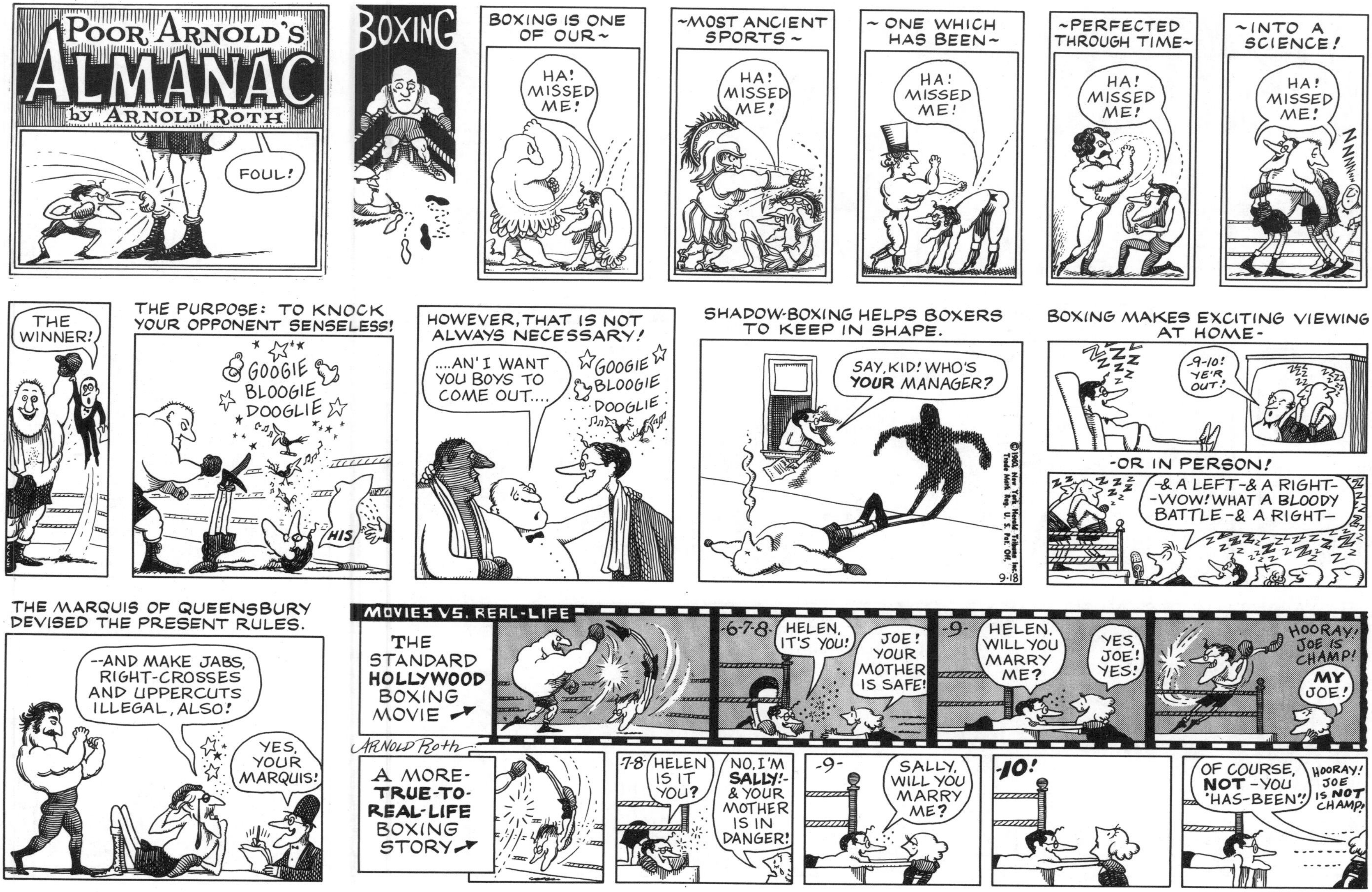
POOR ARNOLD'S ALMANAC
by ARNOLD ROTH
FOUL!
BOXING
BOXING IS ONE OF OUR~
HA! MISSED ME!
~MOST ANCIENT SPORTS~
HA! MISSED ME!
~ONE WHICH HAS BEEN~
HA! MISSED ME!
~PERFECTED THROUGH TIME~
HA! MISSED ME!
~INTO A SCIENCE!
HA! MISSED ME!
ZZZ
THE WINNER!
THE PURPOSE: TO KNOCK YOUR OPPONENT SENSELESS!
GOOGIE BLOOGIE DOOGLIE
HIS
HOWEVER, THAT IS NOT ALWAYS NECESSARY!
....AN' I WANT YOU BOYS TO COME OUT....
GOOGIE BLOOGIE DOOGLIE
SHADOW-BOXING HELPS BOXERS TO KEEP IN SHAPE.
SAY, KID! WHO'S **YOUR** MANAGER?
© 1960, New York Herald Tribune Inc. Trade Mark Reg. U. S. Pat. Off.
9·18
BOXING MAKES EXCITING VIEWING AT HOME-
-9-10! YE'R OUT!
-OR IN PERSON!
-& A LEFT-& A RIGHT- -WOW! WHAT A BLOODY BATTLE-& A RIGHT-
THE MARQUIS OF QUEENSBURY DEVISED THE PRESENT RULES.
--AND MAKE JABS, RIGHT-CROSSES AND UPPERCUTS ILLEGAL, ALSO!
YES, YOUR MARQUIS!
MOVIES VS. REAL-LIFE
THE STANDARD **HOLLYWOOD** BOXING MOVIE
-6-7-8-
HELEN, IT'S YOU!
JOE! YOUR MOTHER IS SAFE!
-9-
HELEN, WILL YOU MARRY ME?
YES, JOE! YES!
HOORAY! JOE IS CHAMP!
MY JOE!
ARNOLD Roth
A MORE-**TRUE-TO-REAL-LIFE** BOXING STORY
-7-8-
HELEN IS IT YOU?
NO, I'M **SALLY!**- & YOUR MOTHER IS IN DANGER!
-9-
SALLY, WILL YOU MARRY ME?
-10!
OF COURSE, **NOT** -YOU 'HAS-BEEN'!
HOORAY! JOE IS **NOT** CHAMP!

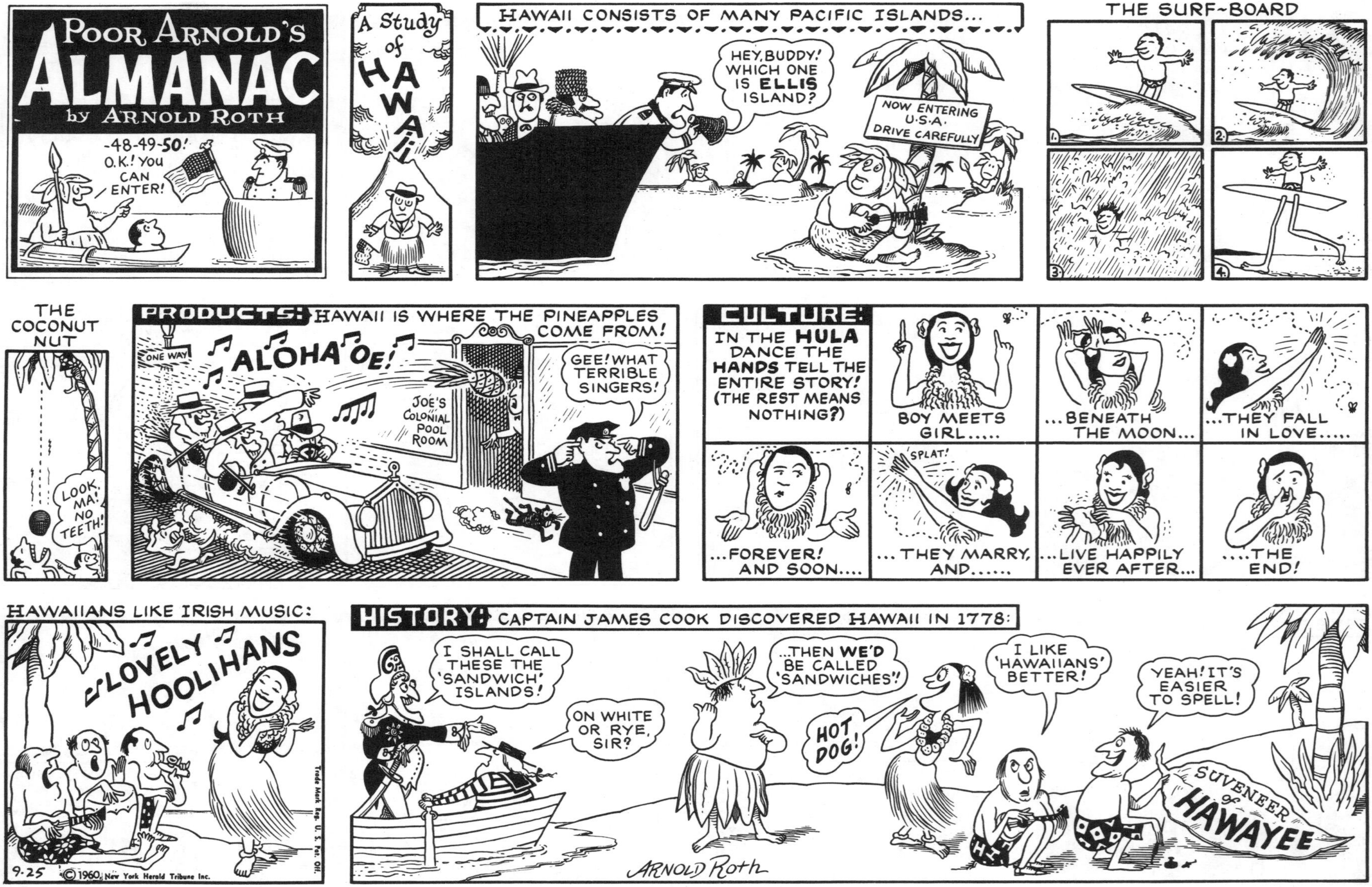

POOR ARNOLD'S
ALMANAC
by ARNOLD ROTH
-48-49-50! O.K.! YOU CAN ENTER!
A Study of HAWAii
HAWAII CONSISTS OF MANY PACIFIC ISLANDS...
HEY, BUDDY! WHICH ONE IS ELLIS ISLAND?
NOW ENTERING U.S.A. DRIVE CAREFULLY
THE SURF~BOARD
1.
2.
3.
4.
THE COCONUT NUT
LOOK, MA! NO TEETH!
PRODUCTS: HAWAII IS WHERE THE PINEAPPLES COME FROM!
ONE WAY
ALOHA OE!
JOE'S COLONIAL POOL ROOM
GEE! WHAT TERRIBLE SINGERS!
CULTURE: IN THE HULA DANCE THE HANDS TELL THE ENTIRE STORY! (THE REST MEANS NOTHING?)
BOY MEETS GIRL.....
...BENEATH THE MOON...
...THEY FALL IN LOVE.....
...FOREVER! AND SOON....
SPLAT!
... THEY MARRY, AND......
...LIVE HAPPILY EVER AFTER...
....THE END!
HAWAIIANS LIKE IRISH MUSIC:
LOVELY HOOLIHANS
9-25
© 1960, New York Herald Tribune Inc.
Trade Mark Reg. U. S. Pat. Off.
HISTORY: CAPTAIN JAMES COOK DISCOVERED HAWAII IN 1778:
I SHALL CALL THESE THE 'SANDWICH' ISLANDS!
ON WHITE OR RYE, SIR?
...THEN WE'D BE CALLED 'SANDWICHES'!
HOT DOG!
I LIKE 'HAWAIIANS' BETTER!
YEAH! IT'S EASIER TO SPELL!
SUVENEER of HAWAYEE
ARNOLD Roth

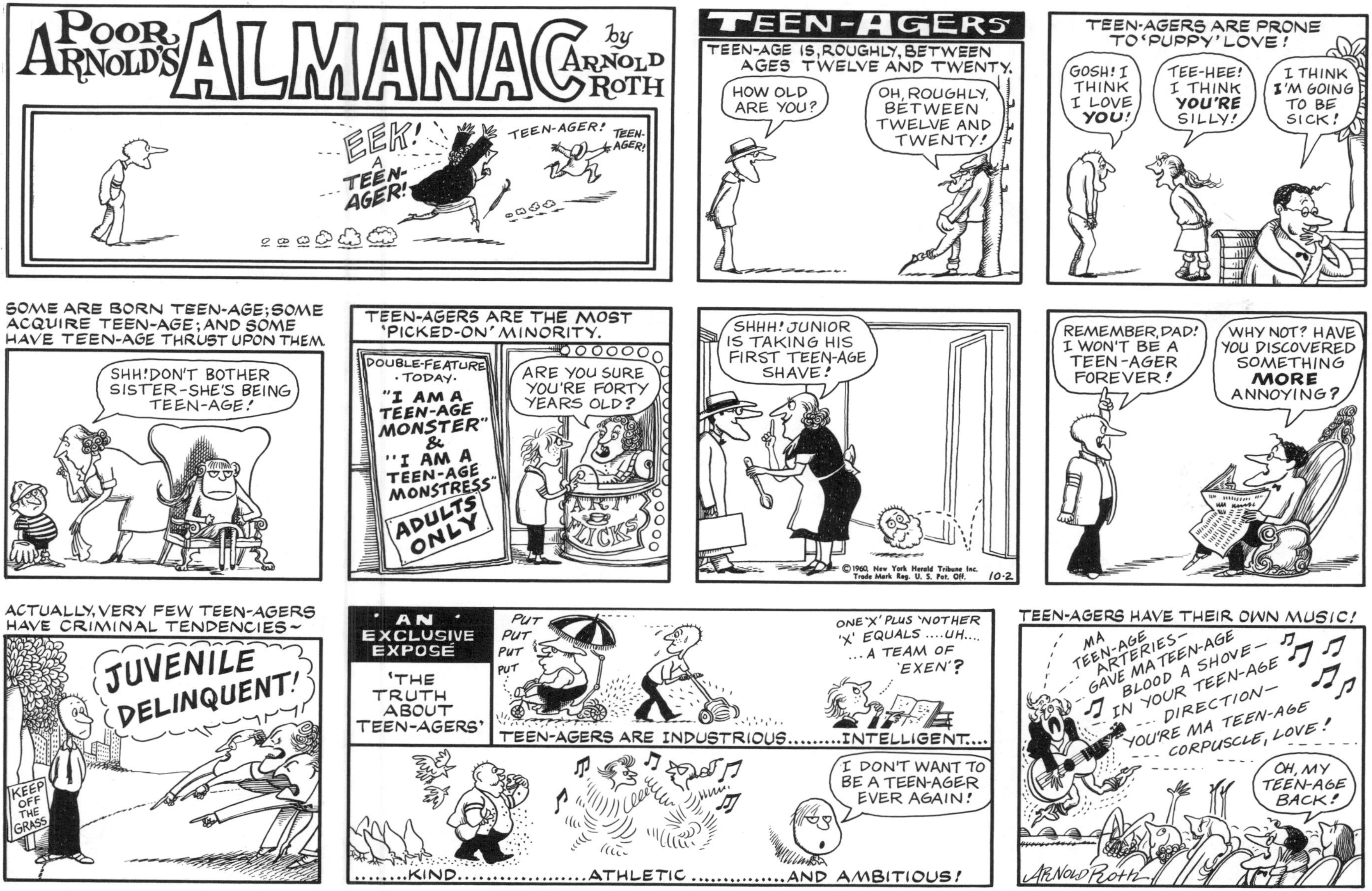
POOR ARNOLD'S ALMANAC by ARNOLD ROTH
EEK! A TEEN-AGER!
TEEN-AGER!
TEEN-AGER!
TEEN-AGERS
TEEN-AGE IS, ROUGHLY, BETWEEN AGES TWELVE AND TWENTY.
HOW OLD ARE YOU?
OH, ROUGHLY, BETWEEN TWELVE AND TWENTY!
TEEN-AGERS ARE PRONE TO 'PUPPY' LOVE!
GOSH! I THINK I LOVE YOU!
TEE-HEE! I THINK YOU'RE SILLY!
I THINK I'M GOING TO BE SICK!
SOME ARE BORN TEEN-AGE; SOME ACQUIRE TEEN-AGE; AND SOME HAVE TEEN-AGE THRUST UPON THEM.
SHH! DON'T BOTHER SISTER-SHE'S BEING TEEN-AGE!
TEEN-AGERS ARE THE MOST 'PICKED-ON' MINORITY.
DOUBLE-FEATURE ·TODAY·
"I AM A TEEN-AGE MONSTER" & "I AM A TEEN-AGE MONSTRESS"
ADULTS ONLY
ARE YOU SURE YOU'RE FORTY YEARS OLD?
ART FLICKS
SHHH! JUNIOR IS TAKING HIS FIRST TEEN-AGE SHAVE!
© 1960, New York Herald Tribune Inc. Trade Mark Reg. U. S. Pat. Off.
10-2
REMEMBER, DAD! I WON'T BE A TEEN-AGER FOREVER!
WHY NOT? HAVE YOU DISCOVERED SOMETHING MORE ANNOYING?
ACTUALLY, VERY FEW TEEN-AGERS HAVE CRIMINAL TENDENCIES~
JUVENILE DELINQUENT!
KEEP OFF THE GRASS
AN EXCLUSIVE EXPOSÉ
'THE TRUTH ABOUT TEEN-AGERS'
PUT PUT PUT PUT
ONE 'X' PLUS 'NOTHER 'X' EQUALS ....UH.... ...A TEAM OF 'EXEN'?
TEEN-AGERS ARE INDUSTRIOUS.........INTELLIGENT....
I DON'T WANT TO BE A TEEN-AGER EVER AGAIN!
........KIND..................ATHLETIC ....AND AMBITIOUS!
TEEN-AGERS HAVE THEIR OWN MUSIC!
MA TEEN-AGE ARTERIES- GAVE MA TEEN-AGE BLOOD A SHOVE- IN YOUR TEEN-AGE DIRECTION- YOU'RE MA TEEN-AGE CORPUSCLE, LOVE!
OH, MY TEEN-AGE BACK!
ARNOLD ROTH

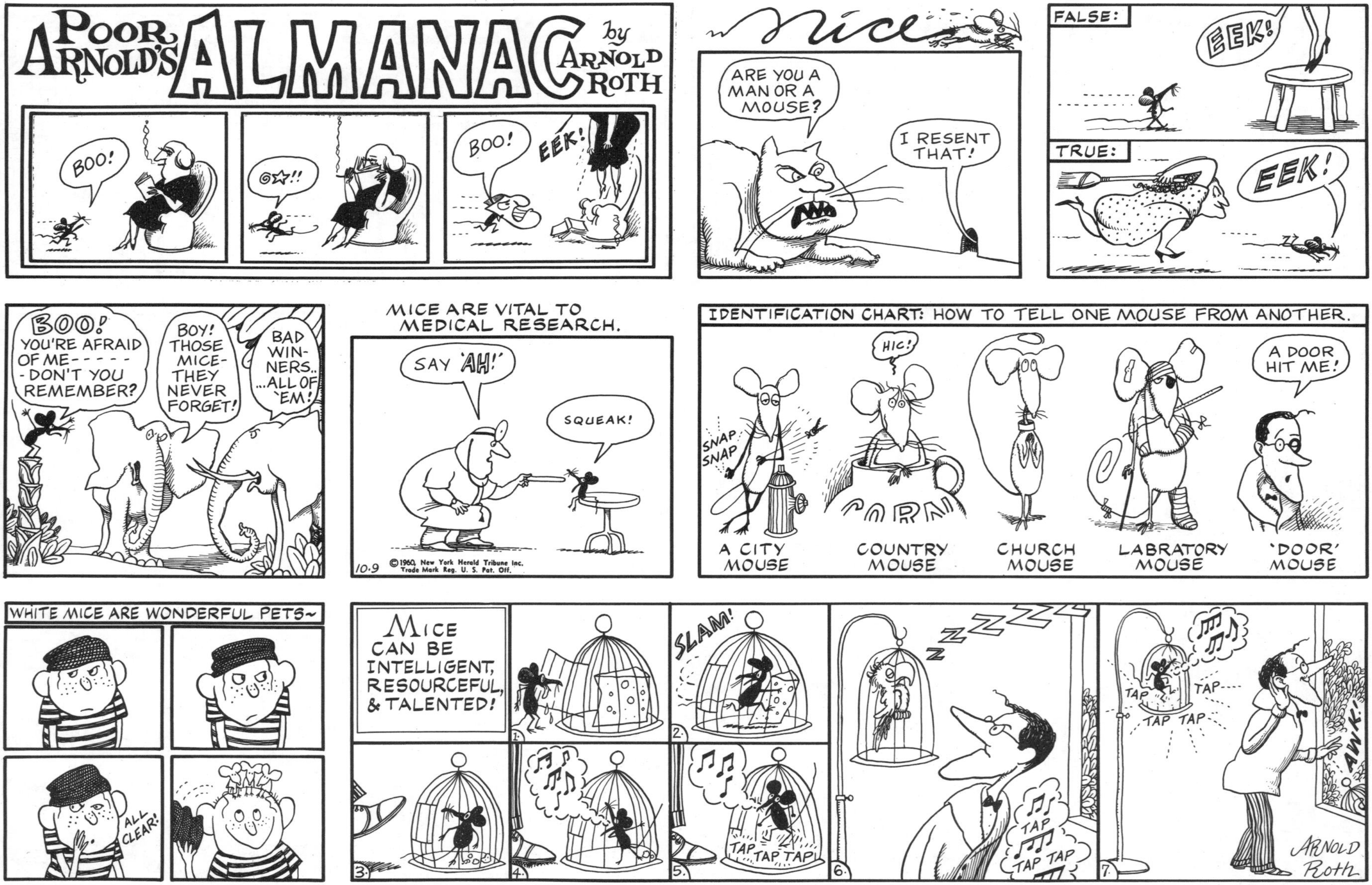
POOR ARNOLD'S ALMANAC
by ARNOLD ROTH
BOO!
@☆!!
BOO!
EEK!
MICE
ARE YOU A MAN OR A MOUSE?
I RESENT THAT!
FALSE:
EEK!
TRUE:
EEK!
BOO! YOU'RE AFRAID OF ME- - - - - - DON'T YOU REMEMBER?
BOY! THOSE MICE- THEY NEVER FORGET!
BAD WIN-NERS.. ...ALL OF 'EM!
MICE ARE VITAL TO MEDICAL RESEARCH.
SAY 'AH!'
SQUEAK!
10·9
© 1960, New York Herald Tribune Inc. Trade Mark Reg. U. S. Pat. Off.
IDENTIFICATION CHART: HOW TO TELL ONE MOUSE FROM ANOTHER.
SNAP SNAP
HIC!
CORN
A DOOR HIT ME!
A CITY MOUSE
COUNTRY MOUSE
CHURCH MOUSE
LABRATORY MOUSE
'DOOR' MOUSE
WHITE MICE ARE WONDERFUL PETS~
ALL CLEAR!
MICE CAN BE INTELLIGENT, RESOURCEFUL, & TALENTED!
1.
SLAM!
2.
3.
4.
5.
TAP TAP TAP
6.
TAP
TAP TAP
7.
TAP TAP
TAP TAP
AWK!
ARNOLD Roth

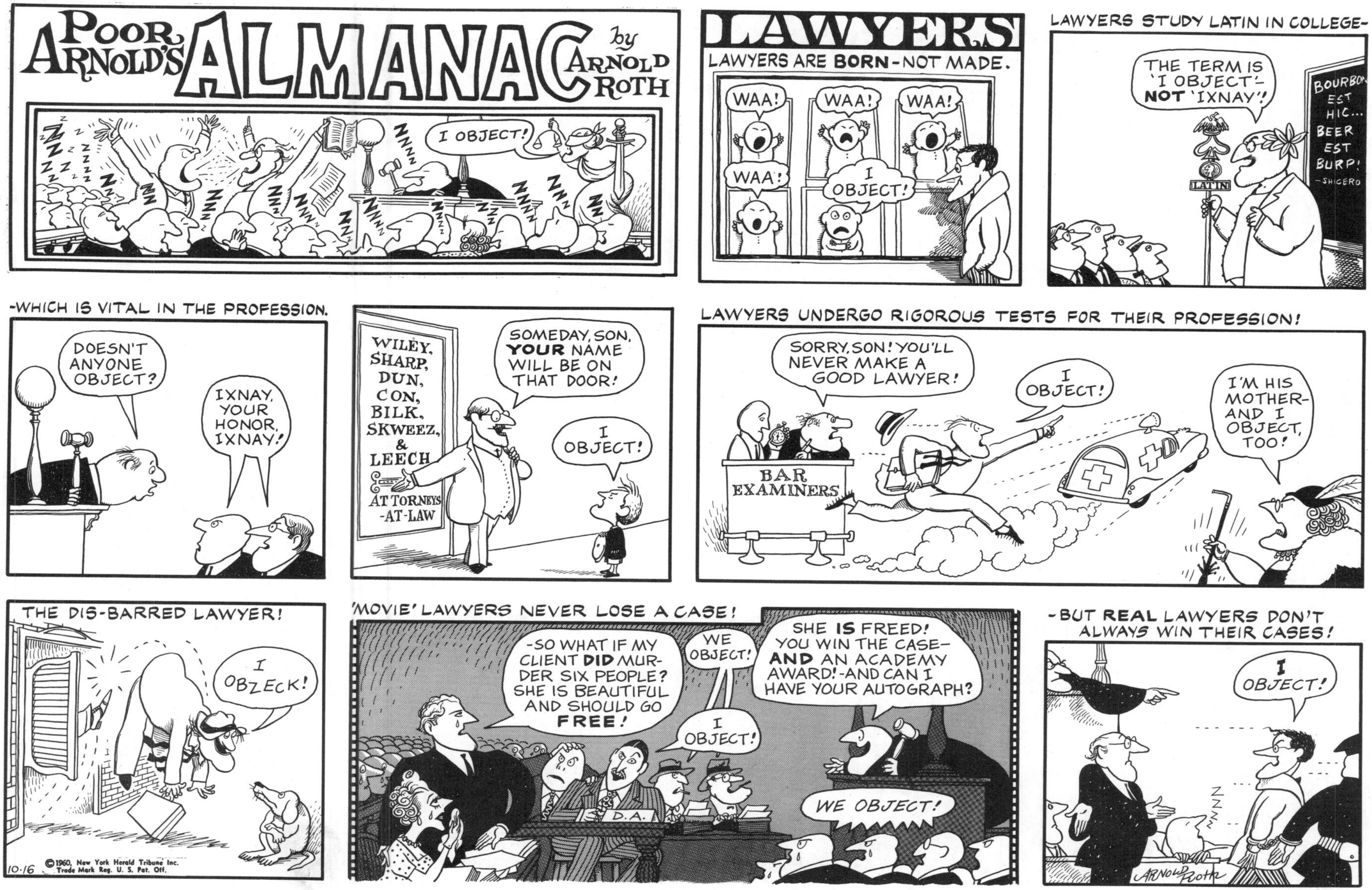
POOR ARNOLD'S ALMANAC
by ARNOLD ROTH
I OBJECT!
LAWYERS
LAWYERS ARE BORN - NOT MADE.
WAA!
WAA!
WAA!
WAA!
I OBJECT!
LAWYERS STUDY LATIN IN COLLEGE-
THE TERM IS 'I OBJECT'- NOT 'IXNAY'!
BOURBON EST HIC... BEER EST BURP! -SHICERO
LATIN
-WHICH IS VITAL IN THE PROFESSION.
DOESN'T ANYONE OBJECT?
IXNAY, YOUR HONOR, IXNAY!
WILEY, SHARP, DUN, CON, BILK, SKWEEZ, & LEECH
ATTORNEYS-AT-LAW
SOMEDAY, SON, YOUR NAME WILL BE ON THAT DOOR!
I OBJECT!
LAWYERS UNDERGO RIGOROUS TESTS FOR THEIR PROFESSION!
SORRY, SON! YOU'LL NEVER MAKE A GOOD LAWYER!
BAR EXAMINERS
I OBJECT!
I'M HIS MOTHER- AND I OBJECT, TOO!
THE DIS-BARRED LAWYER!
I OBZECK!
'MOVIE' LAWYERS NEVER LOSE A CASE!
-SO WHAT IF MY CLIENT DID MURDER SIX PEOPLE? SHE IS BEAUTIFUL AND SHOULD GO FREE!
WE OBJECT!
SHE IS FREED! YOU WIN THE CASE- AND AN ACADEMY AWARD!-AND CAN I HAVE YOUR AUTOGRAPH?
I OBJECT!
D.A.
WE OBJECT!
-BUT REAL LAWYERS DON'T ALWAYS WIN THEIR CASES!
I OBJECT!
10-16
©1960, New York Herald Tribune Inc. Trade Mark Reg. U. S. Pat. Off.
ARNOLD ROTH

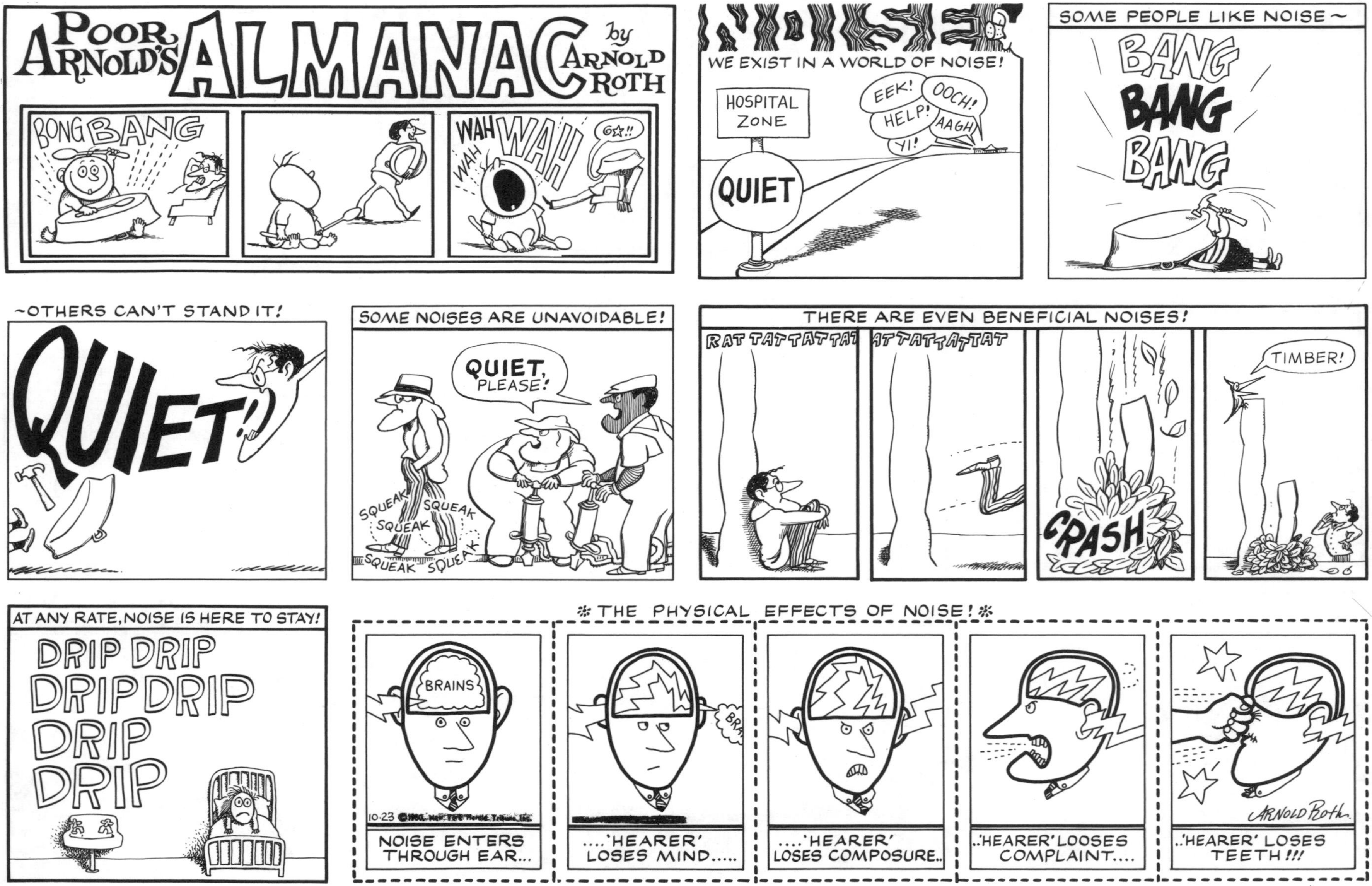

POOR ARNOLD'S ALMANAC
by ARNOLD ROTH
BONG BANG
WAH WAH WAH WAH
G☆!!
NOISE
WE EXIST IN A WORLD OF NOISE!
HOSPITAL ZONE
QUIET
EEK!
OOCH!
HELP!
AAGH
YI!
SOME PEOPLE LIKE NOISE ~
BANG
BANG
BANG
~OTHERS CAN'T STAND IT!
QUIET!
SOME NOISES ARE UNAVOIDABLE!
QUIET, PLEASE!
SQUEAK SQUEAK SQUEAK SQUEAK SQUEAK
THERE ARE EVEN BENEFICIAL NOISES!
RAT TAT TAT TAT TAT
AT TAT TAT TAT
CRASH
TIMBER!
AT ANY RATE, NOISE IS HERE TO STAY!
DRIP DRIP
DRIP DRIP
DRIP
DRIP
✲ THE PHYSICAL EFFECTS OF NOISE! ✲
BRAINS
NOISE ENTERS THROUGH EAR...
10·23
....'HEARER' LOSES MIND.....
....'HEARER' LOSES COMPOSURE..
..'HEARER' LOOSES COMPLAINT....
..'HEARER' LOSES TEETH!!!
ARNOLD ROTH

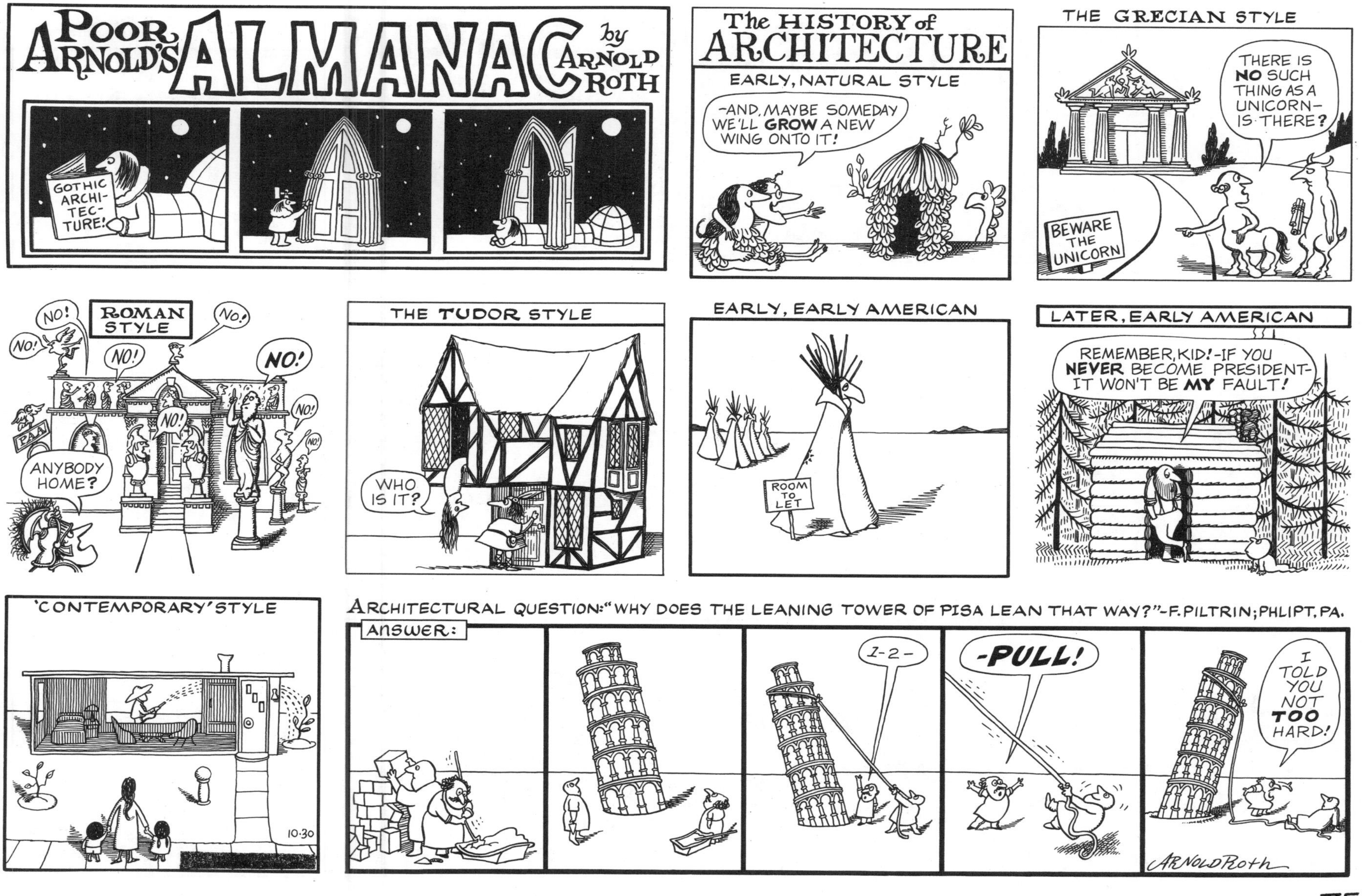
POOR ARNOLD'S ALMANAC
by ARNOLD ROTH
GOTHIC ARCHI- TEC- TURE!
The HISTORY of ARCHITECTURE
EARLY, NATURAL STYLE
-AND, MAYBE SOMEDAY WE'LL GROW A NEW WING ONTO IT!
THE GRECIAN STYLE
THERE IS NO SUCH THING AS A UNICORN- IS THERE?
BEWARE THE UNICORN
ROMAN STYLE
NO!
NO!
NO!
NO!
NO!
NO!
NO!
NO!
ANYBODY HOME?
THE TUDOR STYLE
WHO IS IT?
EARLY, EARLY AMERICAN
ROOM TO LET
LATER, EARLY AMERICAN
REMEMBER, KID!-IF YOU NEVER BECOME PRESIDENT- IT WON'T BE MY FAULT!
'CONTEMPORARY' STYLE
10·30
ARCHITECTURAL QUESTION: "WHY DOES THE LEANING TOWER OF PISA LEAN THAT WAY?"-F. PILTRIN; PHLIPT, PA.
ANSWER:
1-2-
-PULL!
I TOLD YOU NOT TOO HARD!
ARNOLD ROTH

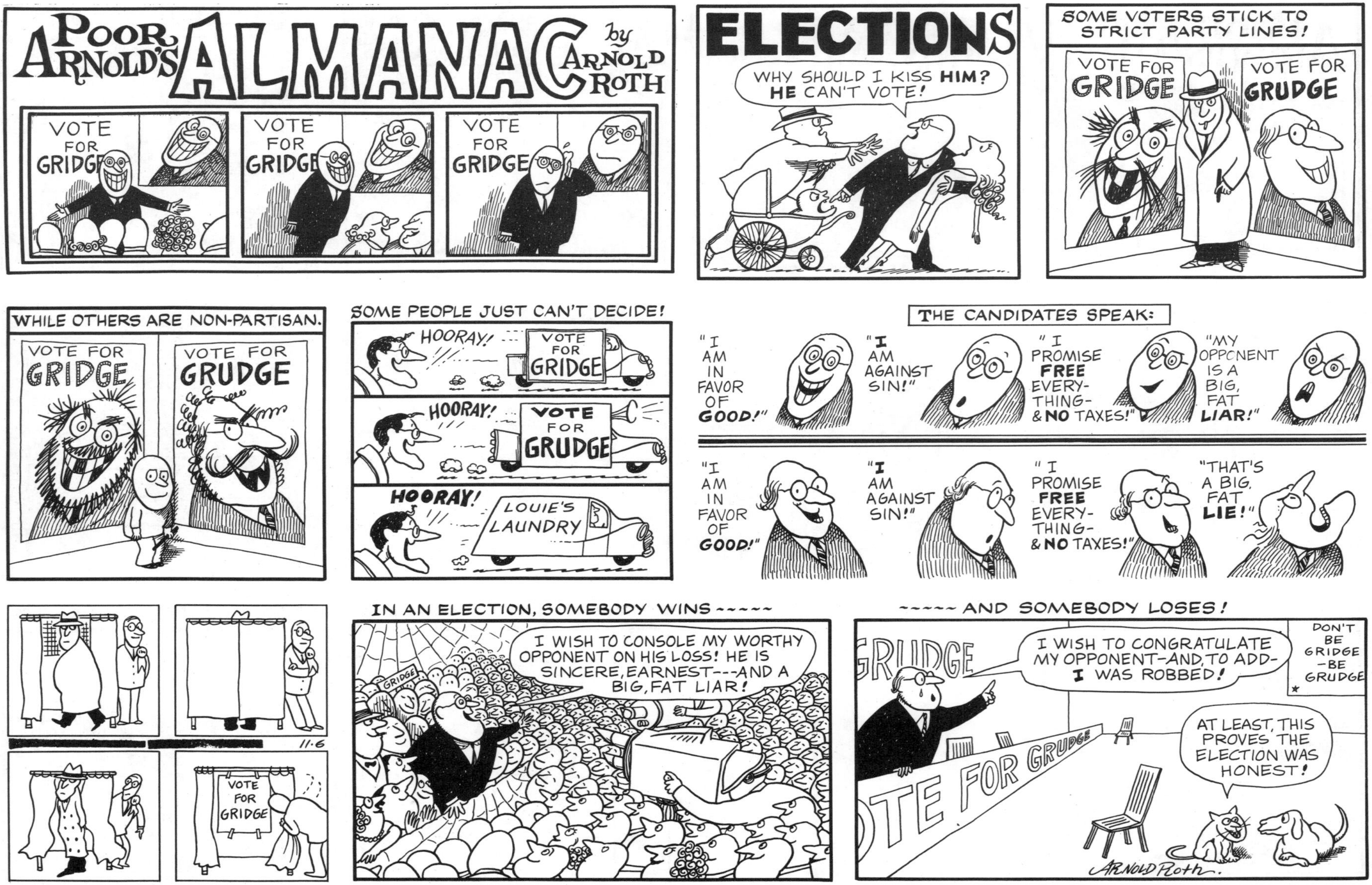
POOR ARNOLD'S ALMANAC
by ARNOLD ROTH
VOTE FOR GRIDGE
VOTE FOR GRIDGE
VOTE FOR GRIDGE
ELECTIONS
WHY SHOULD I KISS HIM? HE CAN'T VOTE!
SOME VOTERS STICK TO STRICT PARTY LINES!
VOTE FOR GRIDGE
VOTE FOR GRUDGE
WHILE OTHERS ARE NON-PARTISAN.
VOTE FOR GRIDGE
VOTE FOR GRUDGE
SOME PEOPLE JUST CAN'T DECIDE!
HOORAY!
VOTE FOR GRIDGE
HOORAY!
VOTE FOR GRUDGE
HOORAY!
LOUIE'S LAUNDRY
THE CANDIDATES SPEAK:
"I AM IN FAVOR OF GOOD!"
"I AM AGAINST SIN!"
"I PROMISE FREE EVERY-THING- & NO TAXES!"
"MY OPPONENT IS A BIG, FAT LIAR!"
"I AM IN FAVOR OF GOOD!"
"I AM AGAINST SIN!"
"I PROMISE FREE EVERY-THING- & NO TAXES!"
"THAT'S A BIG, FAT LIE!"
11-6
VOTE FOR GRIDGE
IN AN ELECTION, SOMEBODY WINS ------
GRIDGE
I WISH TO CONSOLE MY WORTHY OPPONENT ON HIS LOSS! HE IS SINCERE, EARNEST---AND A BIG, FAT LIAR!
------ AND SOMEBODY LOSES!
GRUDGE
I WISH TO CONGRATULATE MY OPPONENT-AND, TO ADD- I WAS ROBBED!
DON'T BE GRIDGE -BE GRUDGE
VOTE FOR GRUDGE
AT LEAST, THIS PROVES THE ELECTION WAS HONEST!
ARNOLD ROTH.

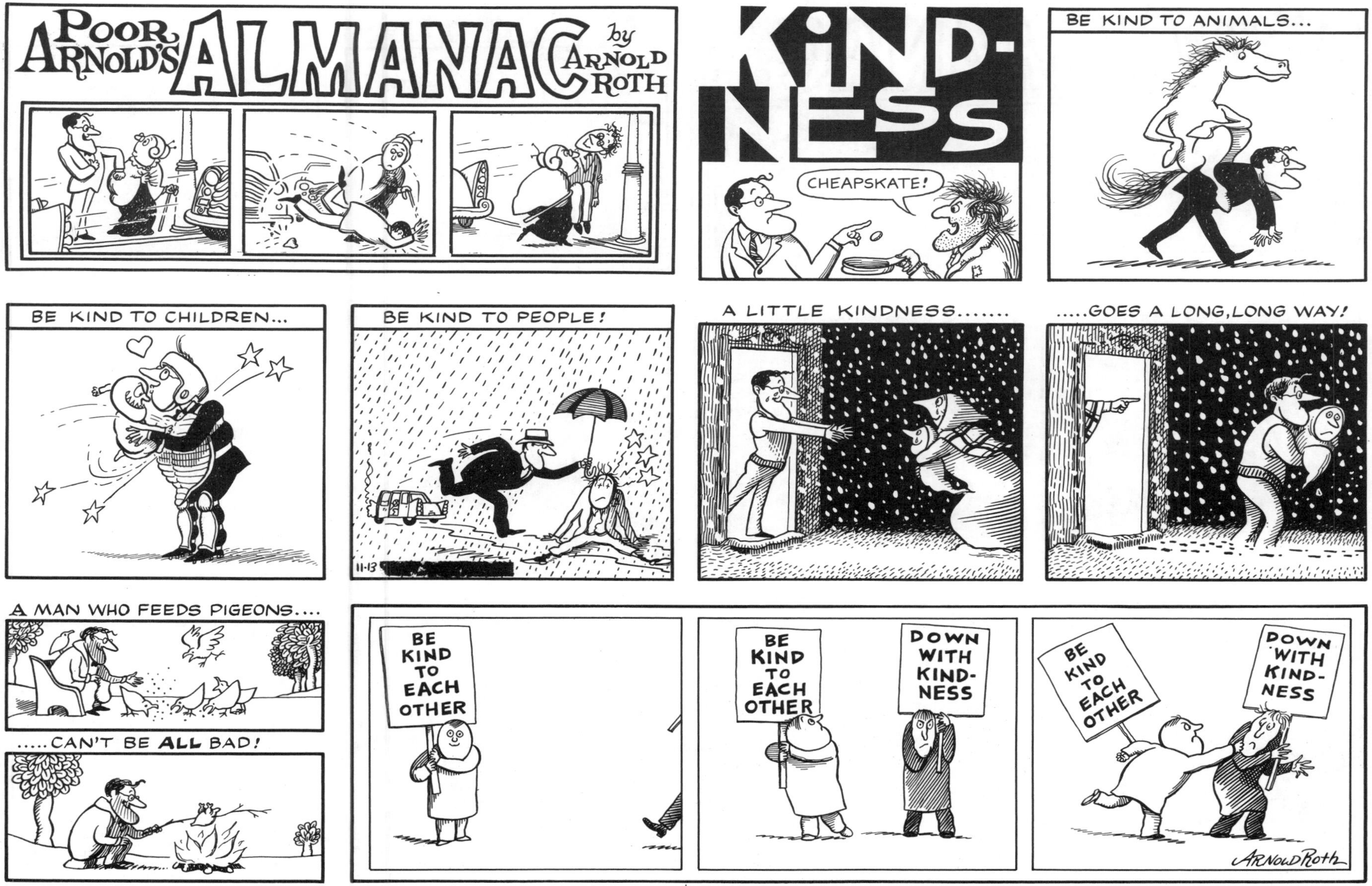
POOR ARNOLD'S ALMANAC by ARNOLD ROTH
KIND-NESS
CHEAPSKATE!
BE KIND TO ANIMALS...
BE KIND TO CHILDREN...
BE KIND TO PEOPLE!
11-13 [redacted]
A LITTLE KINDNESS.......
.....GOES A LONG, LONG WAY!
A MAN WHO FEEDS PIGEONS....
.....CAN'T BE **ALL** BAD!
BE KIND TO EACH OTHER
BE KIND TO EACH OTHER
DOWN WITH KIND-NESS
BE KIND TO EACH OTHER
DOWN WITH KIND-NESS
ARNOLD ROTH

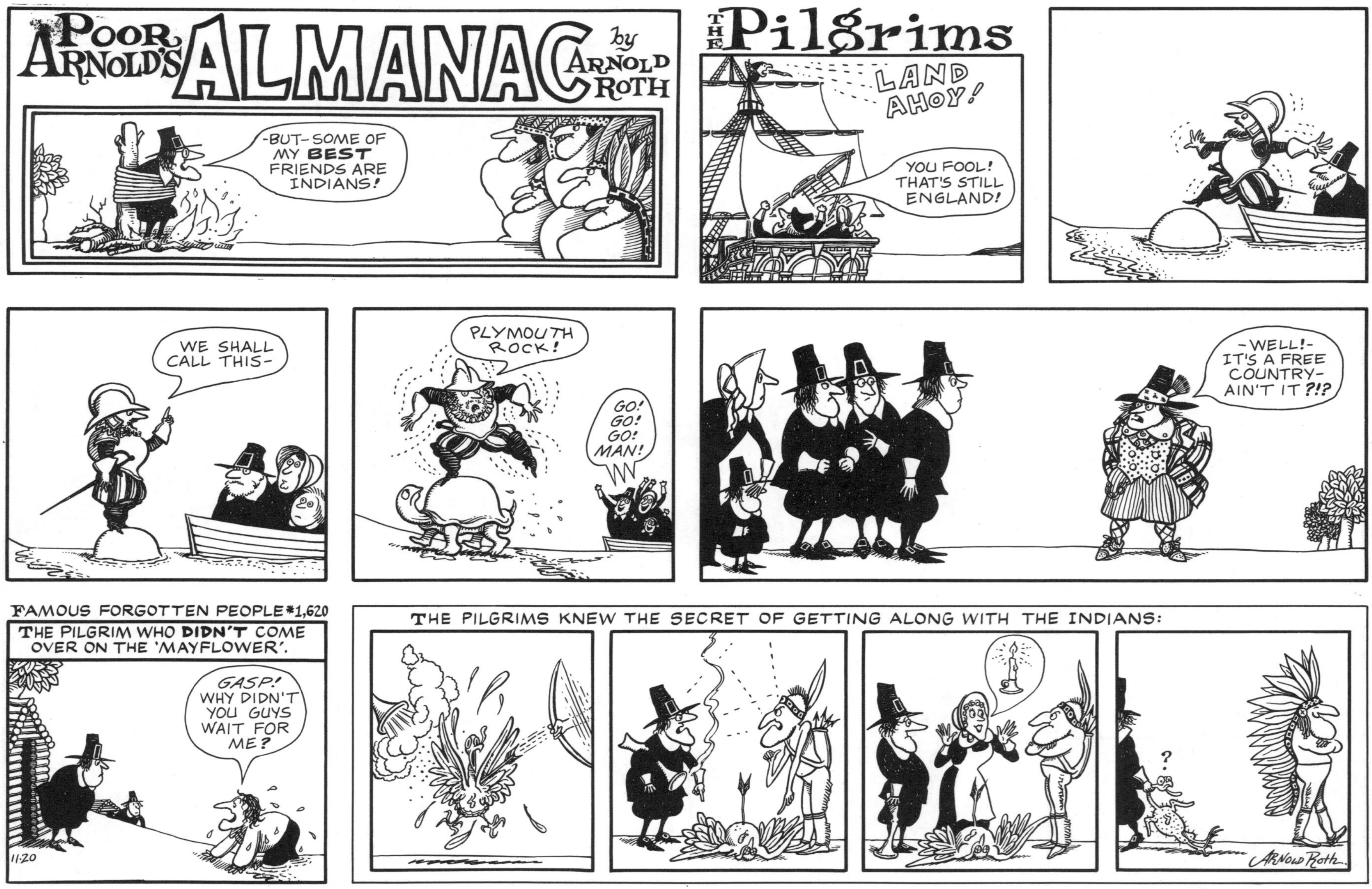
POOR ARNOLD'S ALMANAC by ARNOLD ROTH
-BUT- SOME OF MY BEST FRIENDS ARE INDIANS!
THE Pilgrims
LAND AHOY!
YOU FOOL! THAT'S STILL ENGLAND!
WE SHALL CALL THIS-
PLYMOUTH ROCK!
GO! GO! GO! MAN!
-WELL!- IT'S A FREE COUNTRY- AIN'T IT ?!?
FAMOUS FORGOTTEN PEOPLE #1,620
THE PILGRIM WHO DIDN'T COME OVER ON THE 'MAYFLOWER'.
GASP! WHY DIDN'T YOU GUYS WAIT FOR ME?
11·20
THE PILGRIMS KNEW THE SECRET OF GETTING ALONG WITH THE INDIANS:
?
ARNOLD ROTH

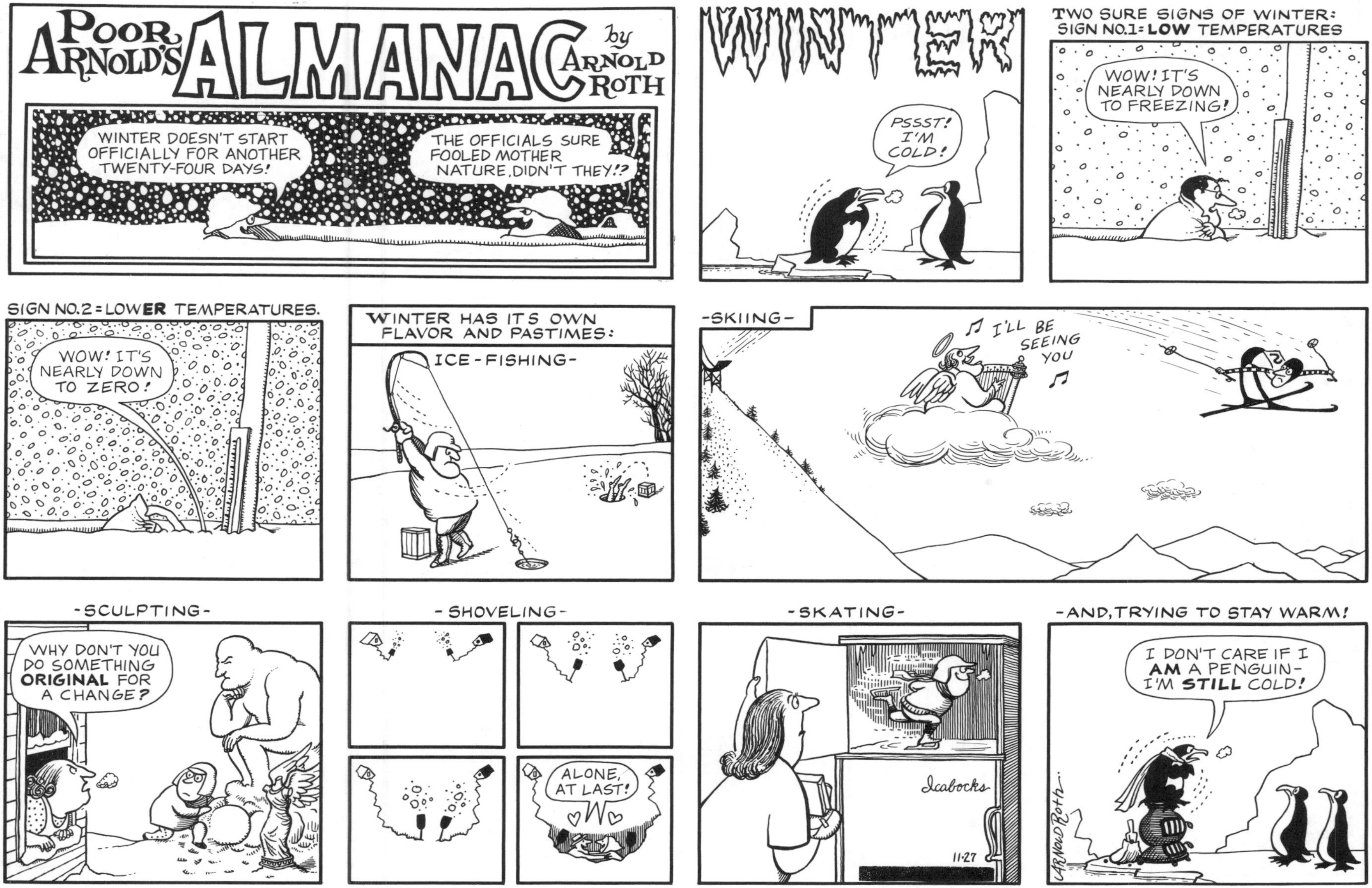
POOR ARNOLD'S ALMANAC by ARNOLD ROTH
WINTER DOESN'T START OFFICIALLY FOR ANOTHER TWENTY-FOUR DAYS!
THE OFFICIALS SURE FOOLED MOTHER NATURE, DIDN'T THEY!?
WINTER
PSSST! I'M COLD!
TWO SURE SIGNS OF WINTER: SIGN NO.1 = LOW TEMPERATURES
WOW! IT'S NEARLY DOWN TO FREEZING!
SIGN NO.2 = LOWER TEMPERATURES.
WOW! IT'S NEARLY DOWN TO ZERO!
WINTER HAS ITS OWN FLAVOR AND PASTIMES:
-ICE-FISHING-
-SKIING-
I'LL BE SEEING YOU
-SCULPTING-
WHY DON'T YOU DO SOMETHING ORIGINAL FOR A CHANGE?
-SHOVELING-
ALONE, AT LAST!
-SKATING-
Icabocks
11-27
-AND, TRYING TO STAY WARM!
I DON'T CARE IF I AM A PENGUIN- I'M STILL COLD!
ARNOLD ROTH

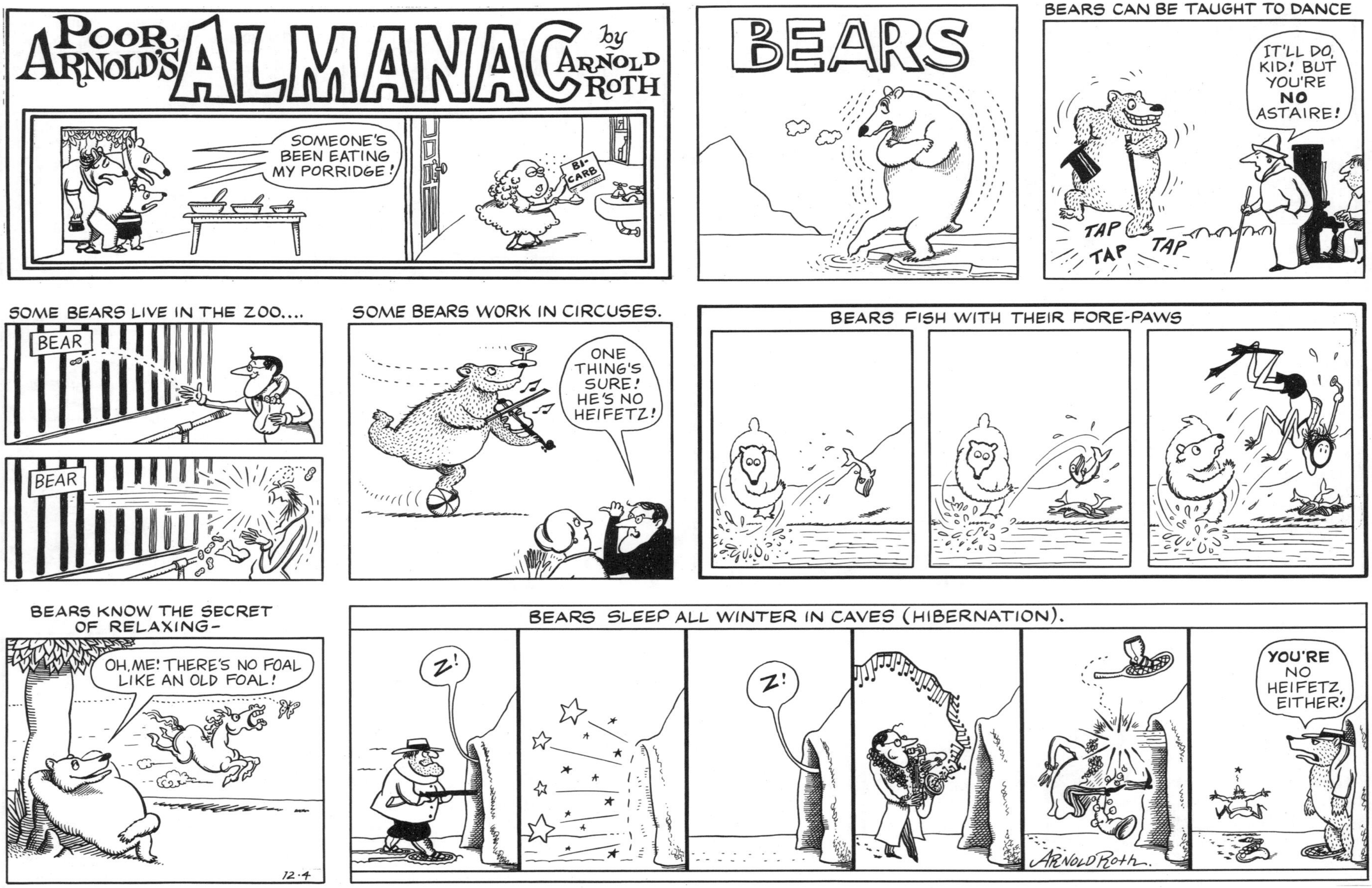
POOR ARNOLD'S ALMANAC by ARNOLD ROTH
SOMEONE'S BEEN EATING MY PORRIDGE!
BI-CARB
BEARS
BEARS CAN BE TAUGHT TO DANCE
IT'LL DO, KID! BUT YOU'RE NO ASTAIRE!
TAP TAP TAP
SOME BEARS LIVE IN THE ZOO....
BEAR
BEAR
SOME BEARS WORK IN CIRCUSES.
ONE THING'S SURE! HE'S NO HEIFETZ!
BEARS FISH WITH THEIR FORE-PAWS
BEARS KNOW THE SECRET OF RELAXING-
OH, ME! THERE'S NO FOAL LIKE AN OLD FOAL!
12·4
BEARS SLEEP ALL WINTER IN CAVES (HIBERNATION).
Z!
Z!
YOU'RE NO HEIFETZ, EITHER!
ARNOLD ROTH.

POOR ARNOLD'S ALMANAC by ARNOLD ROTH
OUR TEAM
BASKETBALL
A BASKETBALL TEAM CONSISTS OF FIVE PLAYERS.
I CAN'T TELL IF IT'S FIVE... WITH A ONE-LEGGED PLAYER.....OR FOUR WITH A THREE-LEGGED PLAYER!
TWO REFEREES ARE NEEDED:
TWEET! FOUL! FOR WEARING UNSHINED SNEAKERS!
TWEET! FOUL! FOR HAVING BOWED LEGS!
BASIC BASKETBALL TECHNIQUES:
1. DRIBBLING
ICH!
TWEET! FOUL! FOR SAYING 'ICH'!
2. PASSING
OOF!
TWEET! FOUL! FOR NAME CALLING!
3. REBOUNDING
TWEET! FOUL! FOR DOING THE 'CHARLESTON'!
4. SHOOTING
TWEET! FOUL! - JUST PLAIN FOUL!
12-11
ALTHOUGH IT ISN'T VITAL-
- IT IS AN ASSET -
-FOR A PLAYER TO BE -
ARNOLD ROTH
-TALL!

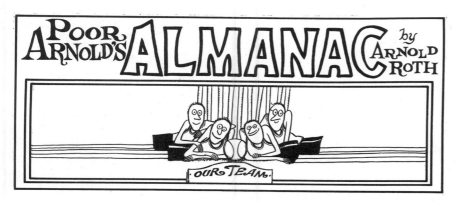

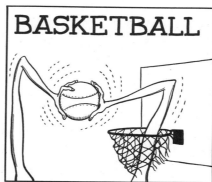

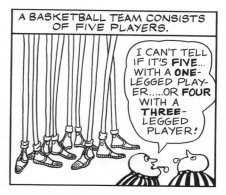

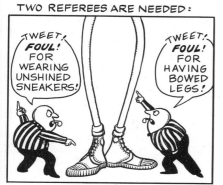

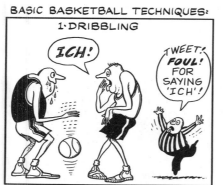

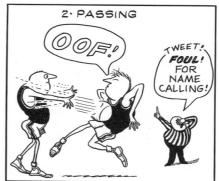

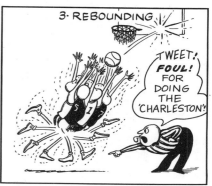

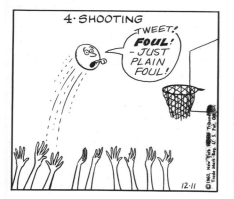

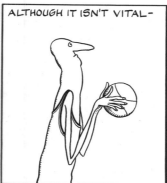

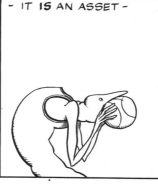

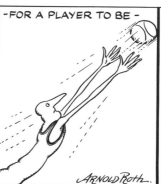

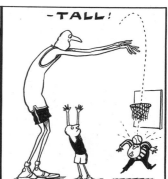

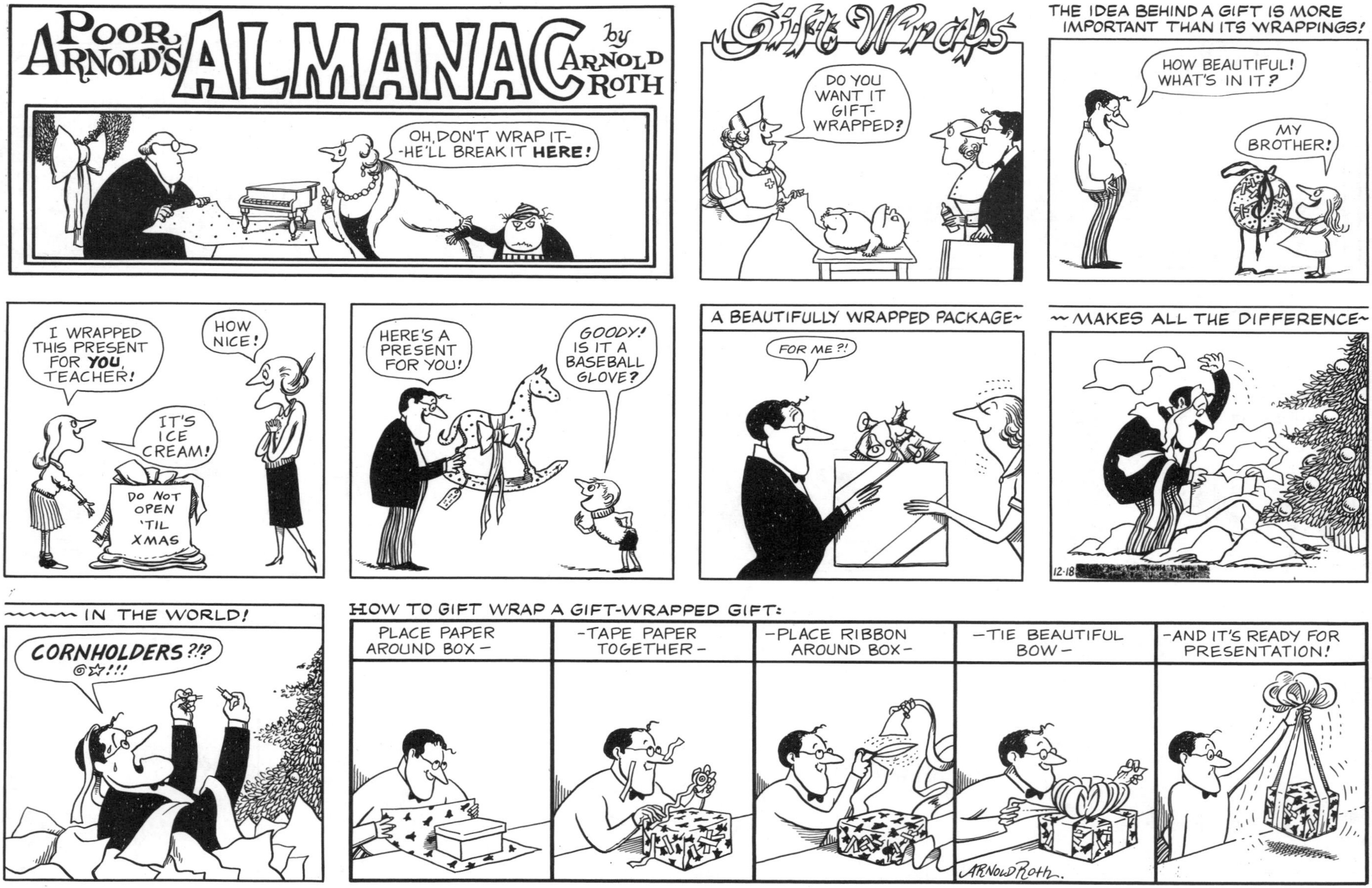
POOR ARNOLD'S ALMANAC
by ARNOLD ROTH
OH, DON'T WRAP IT- -HE'LL BREAK IT HERE!
Gift Wraps
DO YOU WANT IT GIFT-WRAPPED?
THE IDEA BEHIND A GIFT IS MORE IMPORTANT THAN ITS WRAPPINGS!
HOW BEAUTIFUL! WHAT'S IN IT?
MY BROTHER!
I WRAPPED THIS PRESENT FOR YOU, TEACHER!
HOW NICE!
IT'S ICE CREAM!
DO NOT OPEN 'TIL XMAS
HERE'S A PRESENT FOR YOU!
GOODY! IS IT A BASEBALL GLOVE?
A BEAUTIFULLY WRAPPED PACKAGE~
FOR ME?!
~MAKES ALL THE DIFFERENCE~
12-18 [redacted]
~~~~ IN THE WORLD!
CORNHOLDERS?!? ©☆!!!
HOW TO GIFT WRAP A GIFT-WRAPPED GIFT:
PLACE PAPER AROUND BOX-
-TAPE PAPER TOGETHER-
-PLACE RIBBON AROUND BOX-
-TIE BEAUTIFUL BOW-
-AND IT'S READY FOR PRESENTATION!
ARNOLD ROTH.
~~~~

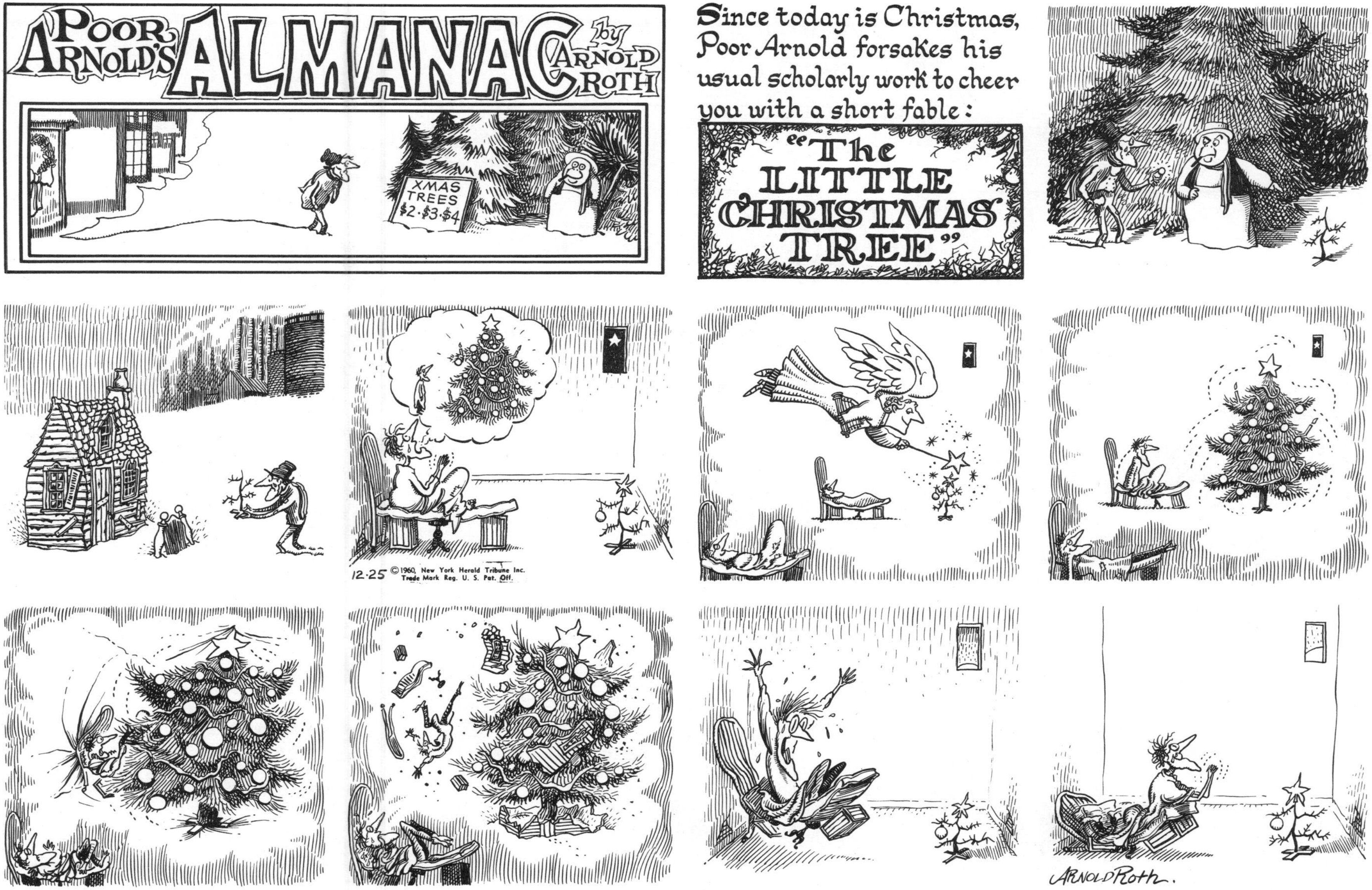
Poor Arnold's ALMANAC by Arnold Roth
XMAS TREES $2·$3·$4
Since today is Christmas, Poor Arnold forsakes his usual scholarly work to cheer you with a short fable:
"The LITTLE CHRISTMAS TREE"
12·25
© 1960, New York Herald Tribune Inc.
Trade Mark Reg. U. S. Pat. Off.
ARNOLD ROTH.

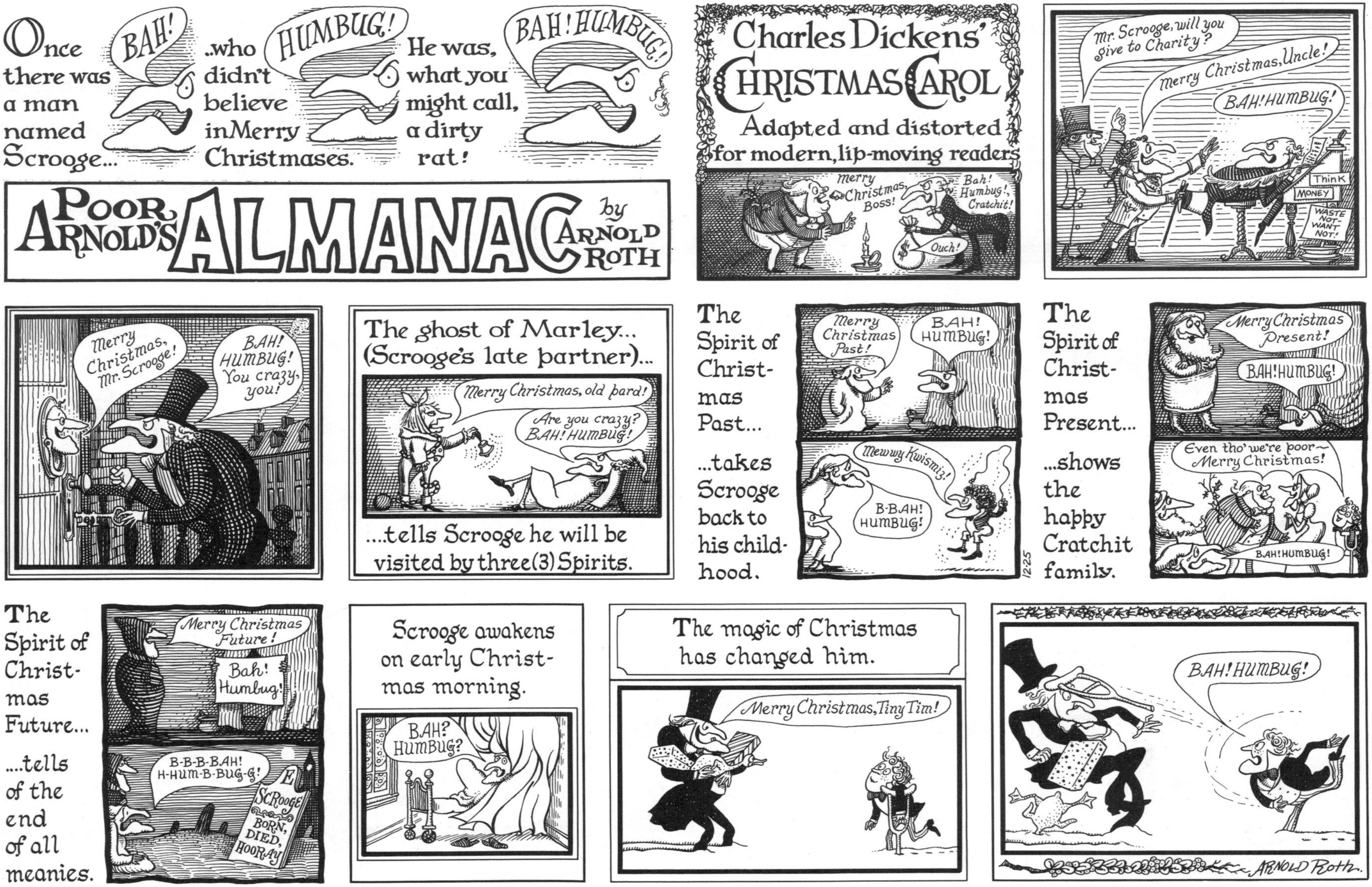
Once there was a man named Scrooge...
BAH!
..who didn't believe in Merry Christmases.
HUMBUG!
He was, what you might call, a dirty rat!
BAH! HUMBUG!
POOR ARNOLD'S ALMANAC by ARNOLD ROTH
Charles Dickens' CHRISTMAS CAROL
Adapted and distorted for modern, lip-moving readers
Merry Christmas, Boss!
Bah! Humbug!, Cratchit!
Ouch!
Mr. Scrooge, will you give to Charity?
Merry Christmas, Uncle!
BAH! HUMBUG!
Think
MONEY
WASTE NOT-WANT NOT!
Merry Christmas, Mr. Scrooge!
BAH! HUMBUG! You crazy, you!
The ghost of Marley... (Scrooge's late partner)...
Merry Christmas, old pard!
Are you crazy? BAH! HUMBUG!
...tells Scrooge he will be visited by three (3) Spirits.
The Spirit of Christmas Past...
Merry Christmas Past!
BAH! HUMBUG!
...takes Scrooge back to his childhood.
Mewwy Kwismiz!
B-BAH! HUMBUG!
12-25
The Spirit of Christmas Present...
Merry Christmas Present!
BAH! HUMBUG!
...shows the happy Cratchit family.
Even tho' we're poor~ Merry Christmas!
BAH! HUMBUG!
The Spirit of Christmas Future...
Merry Christmas Future!
Bah! Humbug!
....tells of the end of all meanies.
B-B-B-BAH! H-HUM-B-BUG-G!
E
SCROOGE BORN, DIED, HOORAY
Scrooge awakens on early Christmas morning.
BAH? HUMBUG?
The magic of Christmas has changed him.
Merry Christmas, Tiny Tim!
BAH! HUMBUG!
ARNOLD ROTH

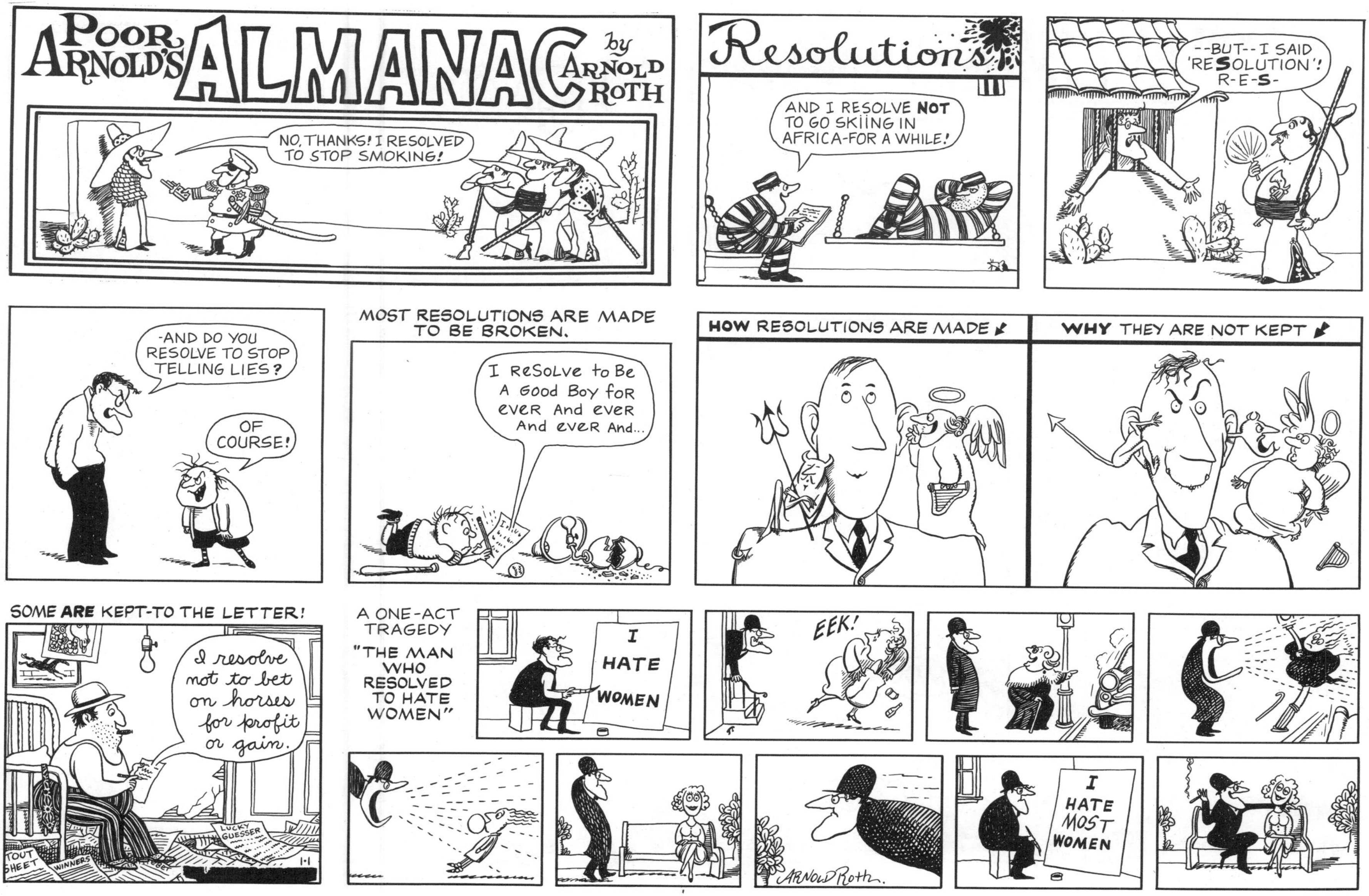
POOR ARNOLD'S ALMANAC by ARNOLD ROTH
NO, THANKS! I RESOLVED TO STOP SMOKING!
Resolutions
AND I RESOLVE NOT TO GO SKIING IN AFRICA-FOR A WHILE!
--BUT--I SAID 'RESOLUTION'! R-E-S-
-AND DO YOU RESOLVE TO STOP TELLING LIES?
OF COURSE!
MOST RESOLUTIONS ARE MADE TO BE BROKEN.
I ReSoLve to Be A Good Boy for ever And ever And ever And...
HOW RESOLUTIONS ARE MADE
WHY THEY ARE NOT KEPT
SOME ARE KEPT-TO THE LETTER!
I resolve not to bet on horses for profit or gain.
LUCKY GUESSER
TOUT SHEET
WINNERS
1-1
[redacted]
A ONE-ACT TRAGEDY "THE MAN WHO RESOLVED TO HATE WOMEN"
I HATE WOMEN
EEK!
I HATE MOST WOMEN
ARNOLD Roth

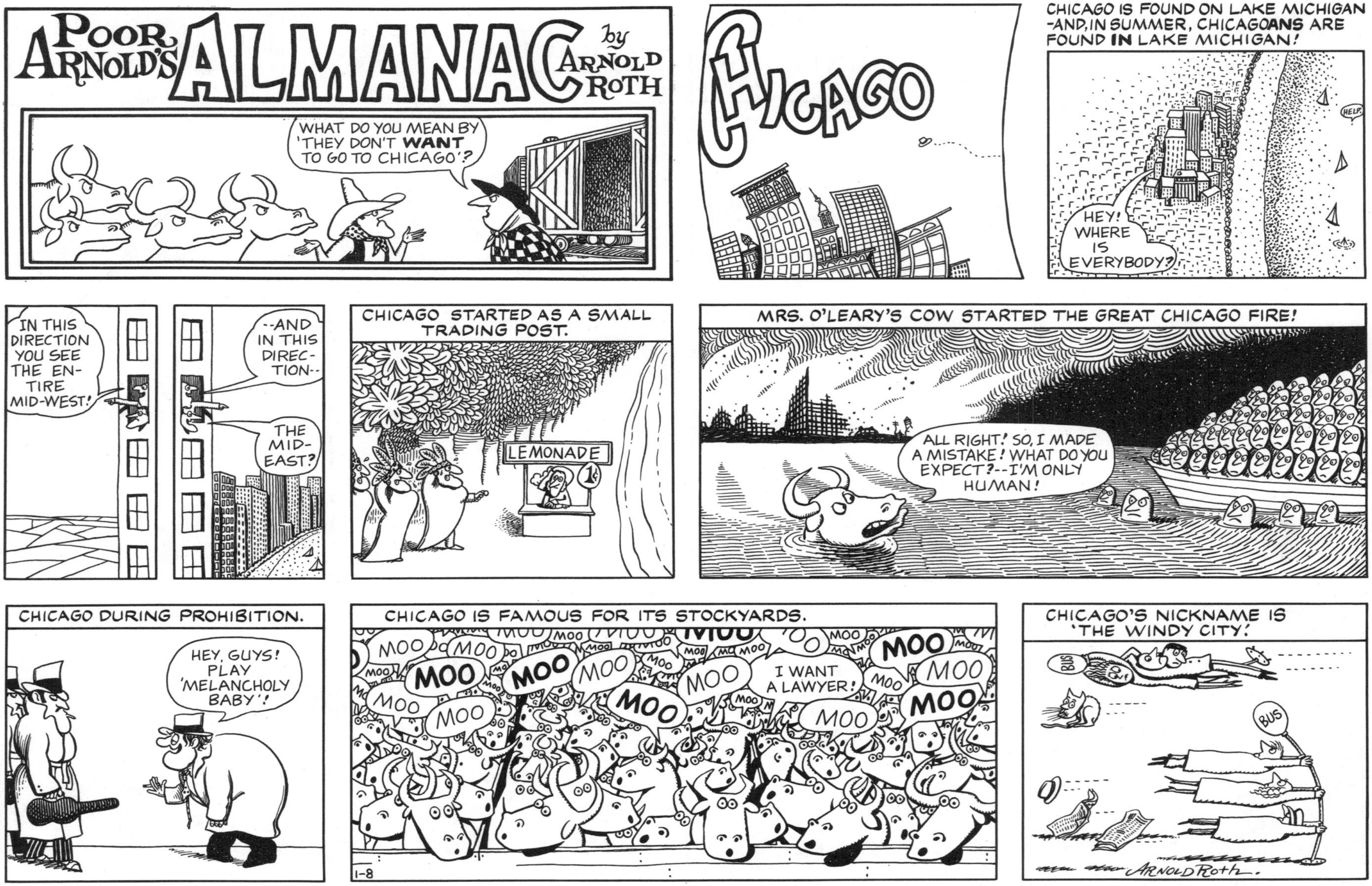

POOR ARNOLD'S ALMANAC
by ARNOLD ROTH
WHAT DO YOU MEAN BY 'THEY DON'T **WANT** TO GO TO CHICAGO'?
CHICAGO
CHICAGO IS FOUND ON LAKE MICHIGAN -AND, IN SUMMER, CHICAGO**ANS** ARE FOUND **IN** LAKE MICHIGAN!
HELP
HEY! WHERE IS EVERYBODY?
IN THIS DIRECTION YOU SEE THE ENTIRE MID-WEST!
--AND IN THIS DIRECTION--
THE MID-EAST?
CHICAGO STARTED AS A SMALL TRADING POST.
LEMONADE
1¢
MRS. O'LEARY'S COW STARTED THE GREAT CHICAGO FIRE!
ALL RIGHT! SO, I MADE A MISTAKE! WHAT DO YOU EXPECT?--I'M ONLY HUMAN!
CHICAGO DURING PROHIBITION.
HEY, GUYS! PLAY 'MELANCHOLY BABY'!
CHICAGO IS FAMOUS FOR ITS STOCKYARDS.
MOO
I WANT A LAWYER!
1-8
CHICAGO'S NICKNAME IS 'THE WINDY CITY'.
BUS
ARNOLD ROTH

POOR ARNOLD'S ALMANAC by ARNOLD ROTH

SCHOOL of ENGINEERING

GOOD MORNING, TEACHER!

GOOD MORNING, CLASS!

ENGINEERS

WE CAME TO ANSWER YOUR AD FOR ENGINEERS!

MISSILE PROJECT A NO·1

ENGINEERS DESIGN EVERYTHING IN MODERN USE!

-WELL- NEARLY EVERYTHING!

ENGINEERS MAKE DISCOVERIES.

I'VE JUST PROVED WE CAN GO TO THE MOON!

WHAT DO YOU MEAN BY WE?

ENGINEERS DO WONDERS WITH ELECTRONIC BUSINESS MACHINES!

THIS MACHINE CAN OUT-THINK ANY EXECUTIVE!

YES!—AND YOU'RE FIRED!

© 1961, New York Herald Tribune Inc.
Trade Mark Reg. U.S. Pat. Off.
1-15

ENGINEERS ARE RESPONSIBLE FOR OUR ROCKET SUCCESSES.

PLAN

NEW PLAN

NEW PLAN

NEW, NEW PLAN

YIPPEE!

NEW, NEW PLAN CASE SOLVED!

ENGINEERING APTITUDE TEST:

	YES	NO
1· ARE YOU INCLINED TO 'LET GEORGE DO IT'?		
2· IS 'GEORGE' AN ENGINEER?		
3· ARE YOU 'HANDY' AROUND THE HOUSE?		
4· ARE YOU 'HARDLY' AROUND THE HOUSE?		
5· WHERE DO YOU HANG OUT, THEN?		

ANALYSIS:
IF YOU ANSWERED 'NO' TO ANY QUESTION—MAKE ENGINEERING YOUR CAREER. IF YOU ANSWERED 'YES'—MAKE BELIEVE YOU ANSWERED 'NO' AND BECOME AN ENGINEER, ANYWAY!

FAMOUS FORGOTTEN PEOPLE: "THE WORLD'S FIRST ENGINEER"

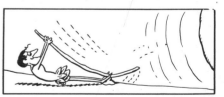

CLAP! CLAP! CLAP!

ARNOLD ROTH.

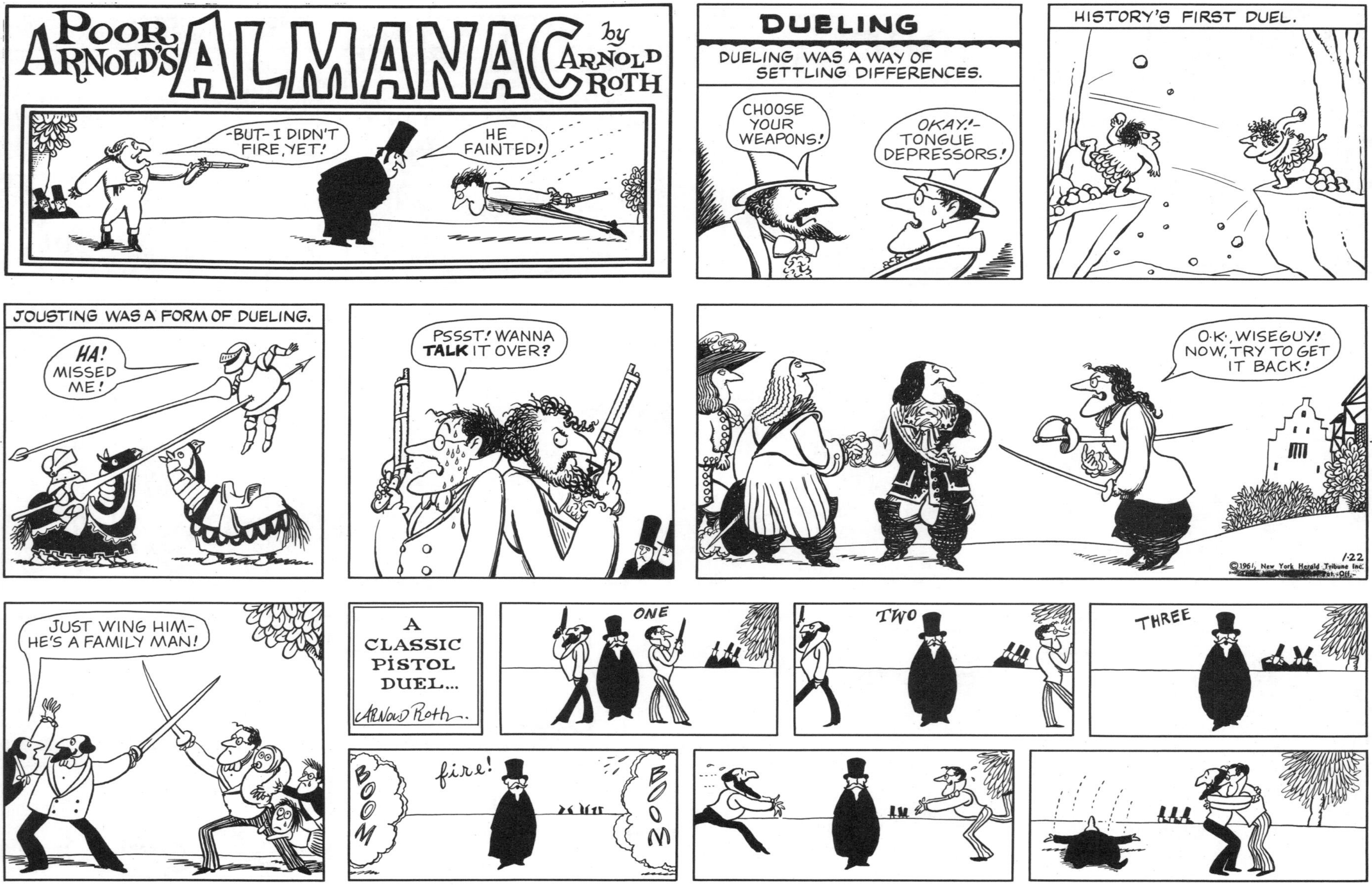

POOR ARNOLD'S ALMANAC by ARNOLD ROTH
-BUT- I DIDN'T FIRE, YET!
HE FAINTED!
DUELING
DUELING WAS A WAY OF SETTLING DIFFERENCES.
CHOOSE YOUR WEAPONS!
OKAY!- TONGUE DEPRESSORS!
HISTORY'S FIRST DUEL.
JOUSTING WAS A FORM OF DUELING.
HA! MISSED ME!
PSSST! WANNA TALK IT OVER?
O.K., WISEGUY! NOW, TRY TO GET IT BACK!
1-22
©1961, New York Herald Tribune Inc.
JUST WING HIM- HE'S A FAMILY MAN!
A CLASSIC PISTOL DUEL...
ARNOLD ROTH
ONE
TWO
THREE
BOOM
fire!
BOOM

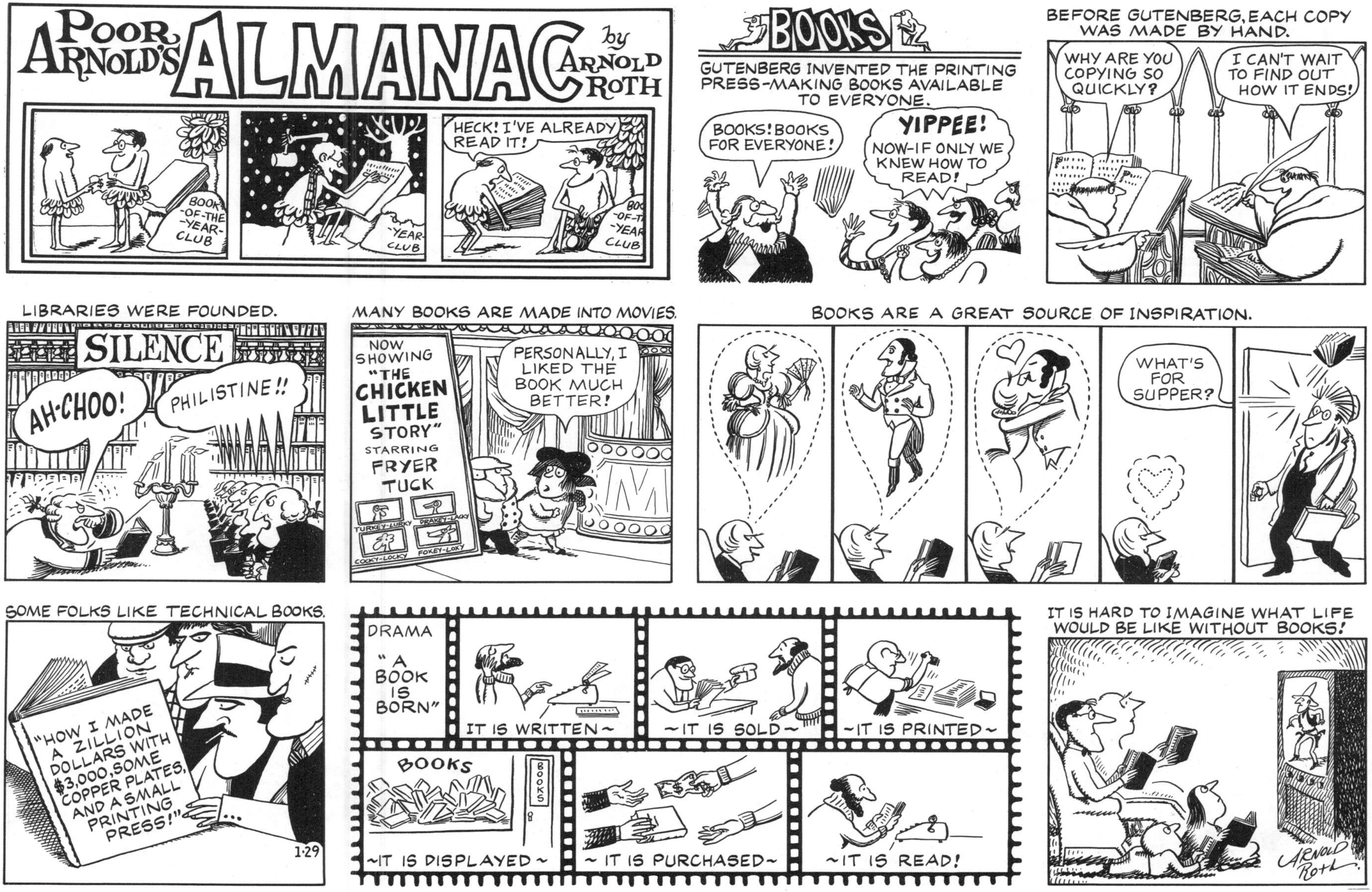

POOR ARNOLD'S ALMANAC by ARNOLD ROTH
BOOK-OF-THE-YEAR-CLUB
-YEAR-CLUB
HECK! I'VE ALREADY READ IT!
BOOKS
GUTENBERG INVENTED THE PRINTING PRESS-MAKING BOOKS AVAILABLE TO EVERYONE.
BOOKS! BOOKS FOR EVERYONE!
YIPPEE! NOW-IF ONLY WE KNEW HOW TO READ!
BEFORE GUTENBERG, EACH COPY WAS MADE BY HAND.
WHY ARE YOU COPYING SO QUICKLY?
I CAN'T WAIT TO FIND OUT HOW IT ENDS!
LIBRARIES WERE FOUNDED.
SILENCE
AH-CHOO!
PHILISTINE!!
MANY BOOKS ARE MADE INTO MOVIES.
NOW SHOWING "THE CHICKEN LITTLE STORY" STARRING FRYER TUCK
TURKEY-LURKY
DRAKEY-LACKY
COCKY-LOCKY
FOXEY-LOXY
PERSONALLY, I LIKED THE BOOK MUCH BETTER!
BOOKS ARE A GREAT SOURCE OF INSPIRATION.
WHAT'S FOR SUPPER?
SOME FOLKS LIKE TECHNICAL BOOKS.
"HOW I MADE A ZILLION DOLLARS WITH $3,000, SOME COPPER PLATES, AND A SMALL PRINTING PRESS!"
1·29
DRAMA "A BOOK IS BORN"
~IT IS WRITTEN~
~IT IS SOLD~
~IT IS PRINTED~
BOOKS
BOOKS
~IT IS DISPLAYED~
~IT IS PURCHASED~
~IT IS READ!
IT IS HARD TO IMAGINE WHAT LIFE WOULD BE LIKE WITHOUT BOOKS!
ARNOLD ROTH

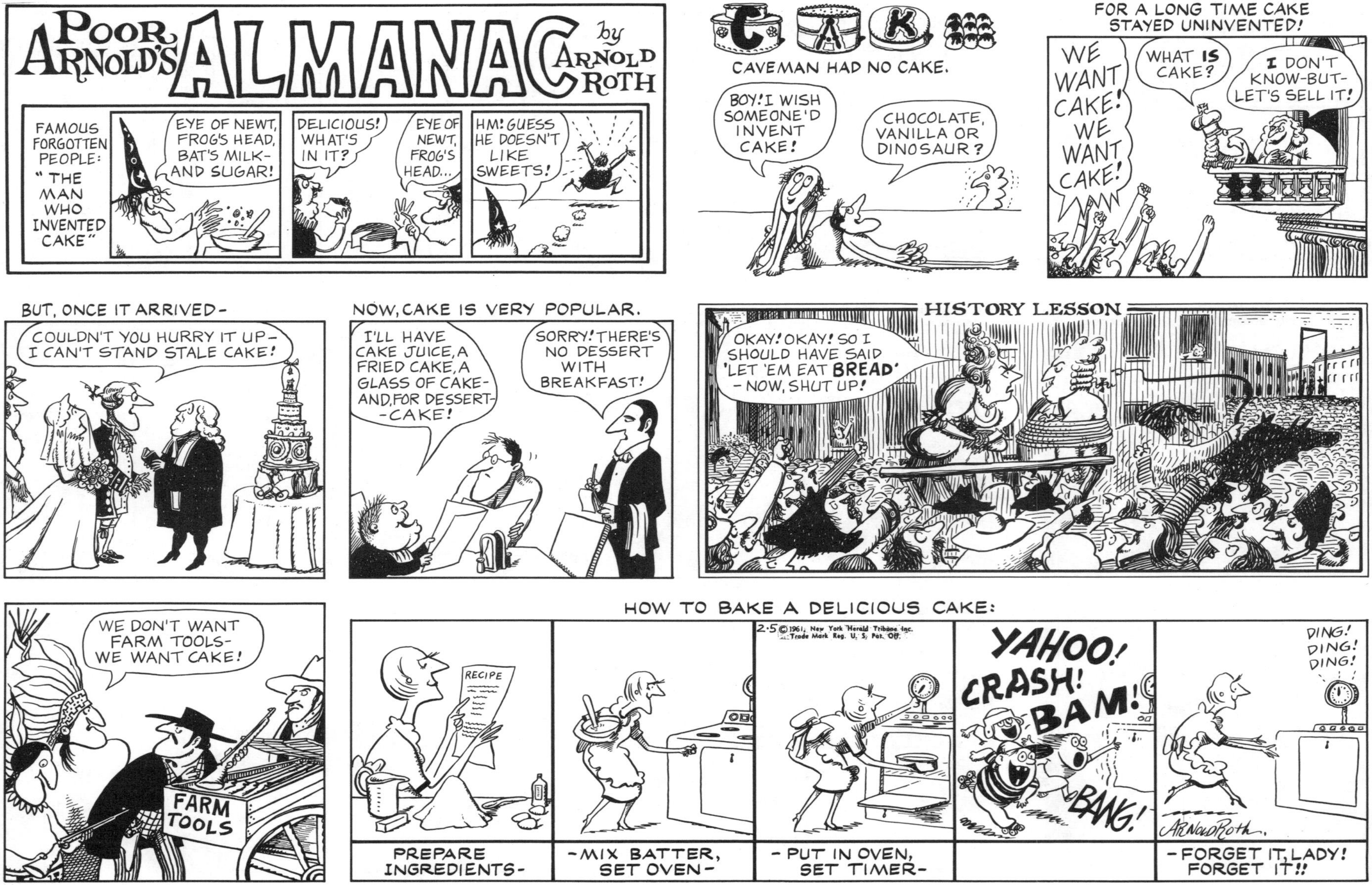
POOR ARNOLD'S ALMANAC by ARNOLD ROTH
FAMOUS FORGOTTEN PEOPLE: "THE MAN WHO INVENTED CAKE"
EYE OF NEWT, FROG'S HEAD, BAT'S MILK-AND SUGAR!
DELICIOUS! WHAT'S IN IT?
EYE OF NEWT, FROG'S HEAD...
HM! GUESS HE DOESN'T LIKE SWEETS!
CAKE
CAVEMAN HAD NO CAKE.
BOY! I WISH SOMEONE'D INVENT CAKE!
CHOCOLATE, VANILLA OR DINOSAUR?
FOR A LONG TIME CAKE STAYED UNINVENTED!
WE WANT CAKE! WE WANT CAKE!
WHAT IS CAKE?
I DON'T KNOW-BUT-LET'S SELL IT!
BUT, ONCE IT ARRIVED-
COULDN'T YOU HURRY IT UP-I CAN'T STAND STALE CAKE!
NOW, CAKE IS VERY POPULAR.
I'LL HAVE CAKE JUICE, A FRIED CAKE, A GLASS OF CAKE-AND, FOR DESSERT--CAKE!
SORRY! THERE'S NO DESSERT WITH BREAKFAST!
HISTORY LESSON
OKAY! OKAY! SO I SHOULD HAVE SAID 'LET 'EM EAT BREAD' - NOW, SHUT UP!
WE DON'T WANT FARM TOOLS-WE WANT CAKE!
FARM TOOLS
HOW TO BAKE A DELICIOUS CAKE:
RECIPE
PREPARE INGREDIENTS-
-MIX BATTER, SET OVEN-
2·5 © 1961, New York Herald Tribune Inc. Trade Mark Reg. U. S. Pat. Off.
-PUT IN OVEN, SET TIMER-
YAHOO! CRASH! BAM! BANG!
DING! DING! DING!
ARNOLD ROTH
-FORGET IT, LADY! FORGET IT!!

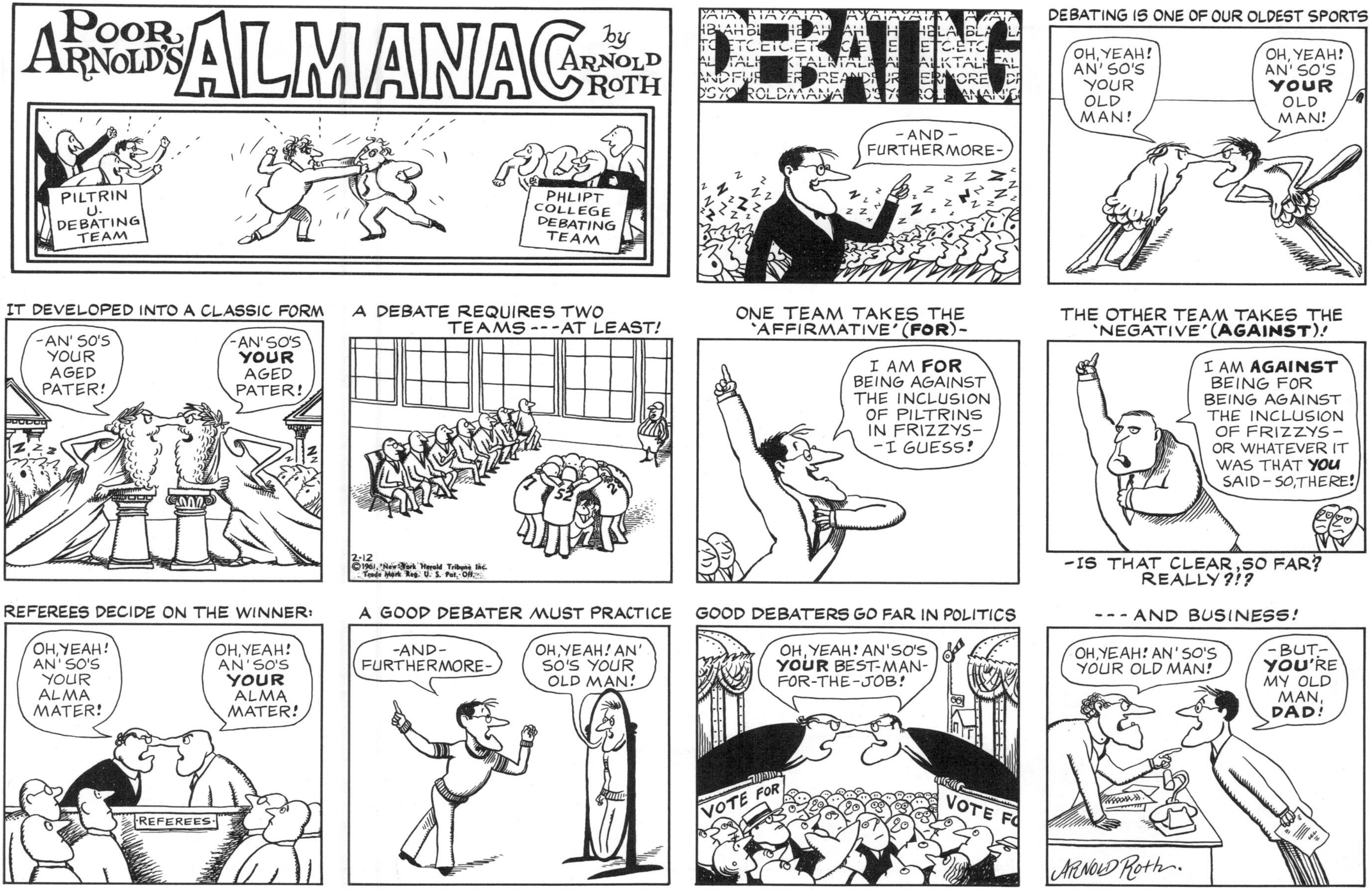
POOR ARNOLD'S ALMANAC by ARNOLD ROTH
PILTRIN U. DEBATING TEAM
PHLIPT COLLEGE DEBATING TEAM
DEBATING
-AND- FURTHERMORE-
DEBATING IS ONE OF OUR OLDEST SPORTS
OH, YEAH! AN' SO'S YOUR OLD MAN!
OH, YEAH! AN' SO'S YOUR OLD MAN!
IT DEVELOPED INTO A CLASSIC FORM
-AN' SO'S YOUR AGED PATER!
-AN' SO'S YOUR AGED PATER!
A DEBATE REQUIRES TWO TEAMS---AT LEAST!
2-12 ©1961, New York Herald Tribune Inc. Trade Mark Reg. U. S. Pat. Off.
ONE TEAM TAKES THE 'AFFIRMATIVE' (FOR)-
I AM FOR BEING AGAINST THE INCLUSION OF PILTRINS IN FRIZZYS- -I GUESS!
THE OTHER TEAM TAKES THE 'NEGATIVE' (AGAINST)!
I AM AGAINST BEING FOR BEING AGAINST THE INCLUSION OF FRIZZYS- OR WHATEVER IT WAS THAT YOU SAID-SO, THERE!
-IS THAT CLEAR, SO FAR? REALLY?!?
REFEREES DECIDE ON THE WINNER:
OH, YEAH! AN' SO'S YOUR ALMA MATER!
OH, YEAH! AN' SO'S YOUR ALMA MATER!
REFEREES
A GOOD DEBATER MUST PRACTICE
-AND- FURTHERMORE-
OH, YEAH! AN' SO'S YOUR OLD MAN!
GOOD DEBATERS GO FAR IN POLITICS
OH, YEAH! AN' SO'S YOUR BEST-MAN-FOR-THE-JOB!
VOTE FOR
VOTE FO
---AND BUSINESS!
OH, YEAH! AN' SO'S YOUR OLD MAN!
-BUT- YOU'RE MY OLD MAN, DAD!
ARNOLD Roth

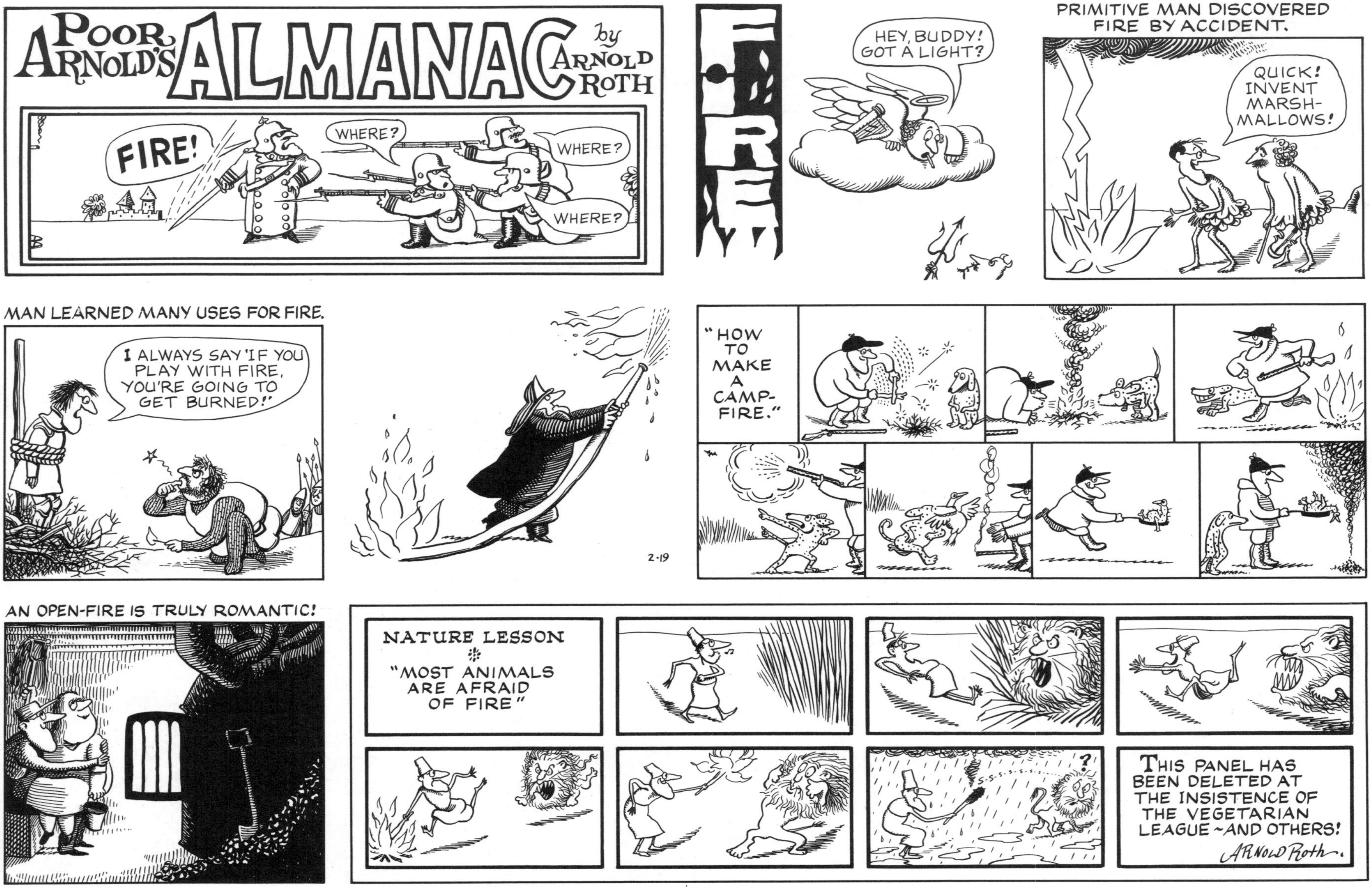
POOR ARNOLD'S ALMANAC
by ARNOLD ROTH
FIRE!
WHERE?
WHERE?
WHERE?
FIRE
HEY, BUDDY! GOT A LIGHT?
PRIMITIVE MAN DISCOVERED FIRE BY ACCIDENT.
QUICK! INVENT MARSH-MALLOWS!
MAN LEARNED MANY USES FOR FIRE.
I ALWAYS SAY 'IF YOU PLAY WITH FIRE, YOU'RE GOING TO GET BURNED!'
2-19
"HOW TO MAKE A CAMP-FIRE."
AN OPEN-FIRE IS TRULY ROMANTIC!
NATURE LESSON
"MOST ANIMALS ARE AFRAID OF FIRE"
THIS PANEL HAS BEEN DELETED AT THE INSISTENCE OF THE VEGETARIAN LEAGUE ~ AND OTHERS!
ARNOLD ROTH.

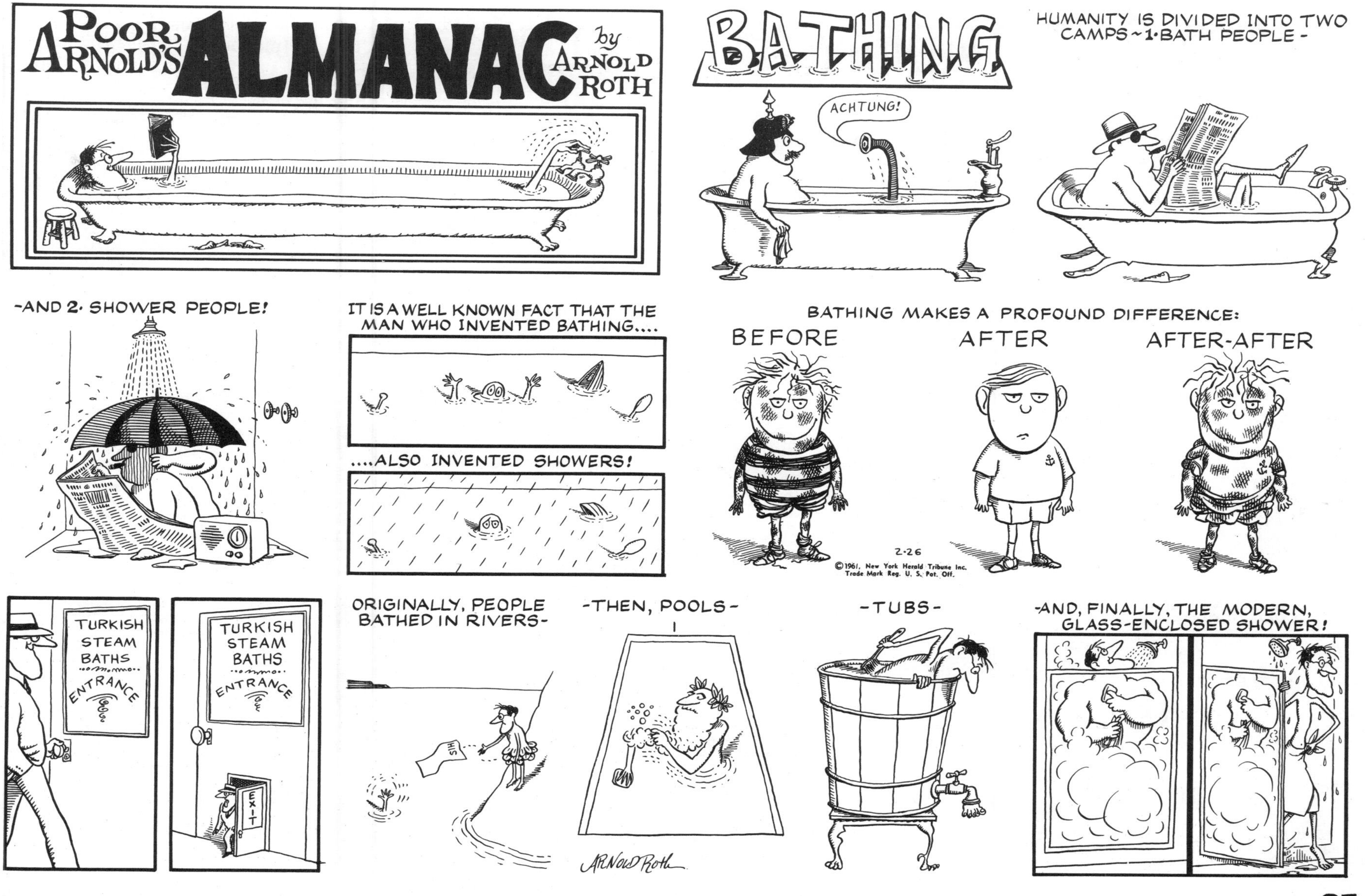
POOR ARNOLD'S ALMANAC by ARNOLD ROTH
BATHING
HUMANITY IS DIVIDED INTO TWO CAMPS ~ 1· BATH PEOPLE -
ACHTUNG!
-AND 2· SHOWER PEOPLE!
IT IS A WELL KNOWN FACT THAT THE MAN WHO INVENTED BATHING....
....ALSO INVENTED SHOWERS!
BATHING MAKES A PROFOUND DIFFERENCE:
BEFORE
AFTER
AFTER-AFTER
2-26
©1961, New York Herald Tribune Inc.
Trade Mark Reg. U. S. Pat. Off.
TURKISH STEAM BATHS ENTRANCE
TURKISH STEAM BATHS ENTRANCE
EXIT
ORIGINALLY, PEOPLE BATHED IN RIVERS-
-THEN, POOLS-
-TUBS-
-AND, FINALLY, THE MODERN, GLASS-ENCLOSED SHOWER!
ARNOLD ROTH

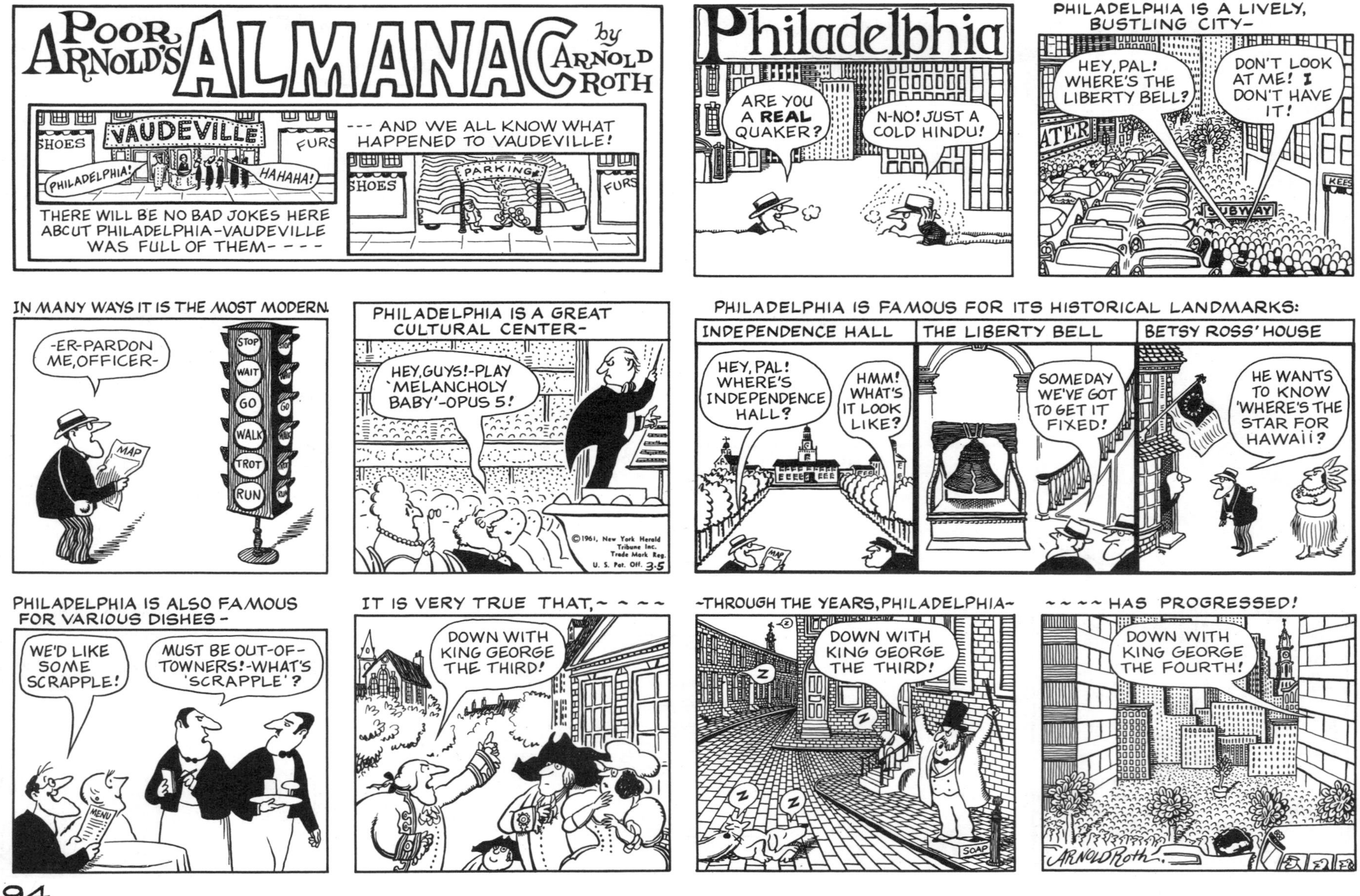
POOR ARNOLD'S ALMANAC by ARNOLD ROTH
VAUDEVILLE
SHOES
FURS
PHILADELPHIA!
HAHAHA!
THERE WILL BE NO BAD JOKES HERE ABOUT PHILADELPHIA-VAUDEVILLE WAS FULL OF THEM- - - -
--- AND WE ALL KNOW WHAT HAPPENED TO VAUDEVILLE!
PARKING
SHOES
FURS
Philadelphia
ARE YOU A **REAL** QUAKER?
N-NO! JUST A COLD HINDU!
PHILADELPHIA IS A LIVELY, BUSTLING CITY-
HEY, PAL! WHERE'S THE LIBERTY BELL?
DON'T LOOK AT ME! I DON'T HAVE IT!
SUBWAY
IN MANY WAYS IT IS THE MOST MODERN.
-ER-PARDON ME, OFFICER-
MAP
STOP
WAIT
GO
WALK
TROT
RUN
PHILADELPHIA IS A GREAT CULTURAL CENTER-
HEY, GUYS!-PLAY `MELANCHOLY BABY'-OPUS 5!
©1961, New York Herald Tribune Inc. Trade Mark Reg. U. S. Pat. Off. 3-5
PHILADELPHIA IS FAMOUS FOR ITS HISTORICAL LANDMARKS:
INDEPENDENCE HALL
HEY, PAL! WHERE'S INDEPENDENCE HALL?
HMM! WHAT'S IT LOOK LIKE?
MAP
THE LIBERTY BELL
SOMEDAY WE'VE GOT TO GET IT FIXED!
BETSY ROSS' HOUSE
HE WANTS TO KNOW 'WHERE'S THE STAR FOR HAWAII?
PHILADELPHIA IS ALSO FAMOUS FOR VARIOUS DISHES-
WE'D LIKE SOME SCRAPPLE!
MUST BE OUT-OF-TOWNERS!-WHAT'S 'SCRAPPLE'?
MENU
IT IS VERY TRUE THAT,~ ~ ~ ~
DOWN WITH KING GEORGE THE THIRD!
-THROUGH THE YEARS, PHILADELPHIA-
DOWN WITH KING GEORGE THE THIRD!
SOAP
~ ~ ~ ~ HAS PROGRESSED!
DOWN WITH KING GEORGE THE FOURTH!
ARNOLD ROTH

POOR ARNOLD'S ALMANAC
by ARNOLD ROTH
Beards
THE FIRST BEARDS BELONGED TO CAVEMEN.
BEATNIK!
CAVE WOMEN CHOSE TO DO WITHOUT THEM.
MOST ANCIENT PEOPLES WORE BEARDS....
BY THE WAY- WHO DOES YOUR BEARD?
...BUT THE ROMANS SHAVED.
NO
BUS STOP
SMOKING
GO
BEATNIK!
HOHO HOHOHO HOHOHO HOHO HO
SINCE THEN, THE WORLD HAS BEEN SPLIT IN TWO:
Beatniks!
Baldniks!
GLUE
DO-IT-YOURSELF DEPT.
"HOW TO GROW YOUR OWN BEARD."
1. THROW AWAY YOUR RAZOR!
WOW! MY LUCKY DAY!
2. BUY A LARGE SCARF TO GET THROUGH 'AWKWARD' STAGE.
Before
After
3. WAIT IT OUT- -COLD TURKEY!
4. HOW TO TELL WHEN IT'S 'DONE'!
YOU LOOK LIKE A BUM!
MEN'S FURS DEPT.
"HOW TO WEAR A BEARD."
ARNOLD ROTH
I. BE NONCHALANT!
II. TAKE KIDDING IN GOOD SPIRITS!
HA-HA-HA-A-AAAGH!
BANG-BANG
III. TAKE CARE OF IT!
YOU'RE MOULTING, AGAIN!
IV. WEAR IT WITH DIGNITY!
BUS

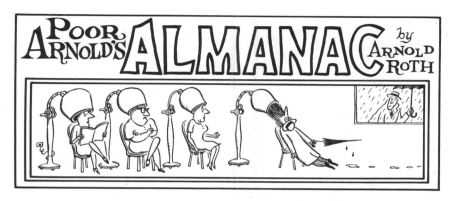

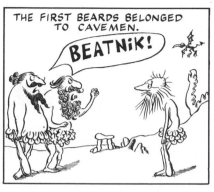

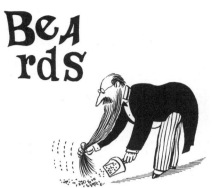

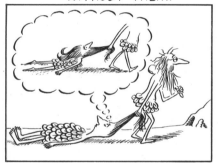

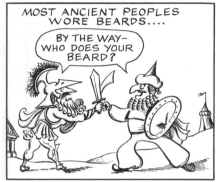

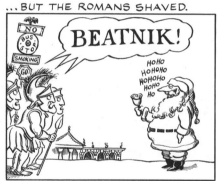

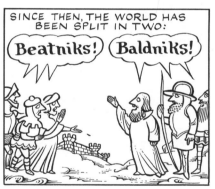

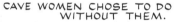

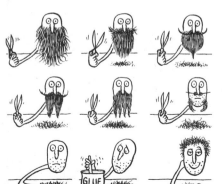

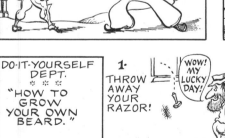

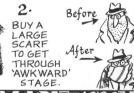

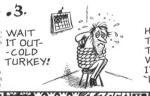

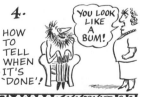

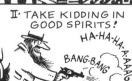

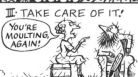

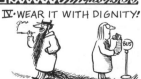

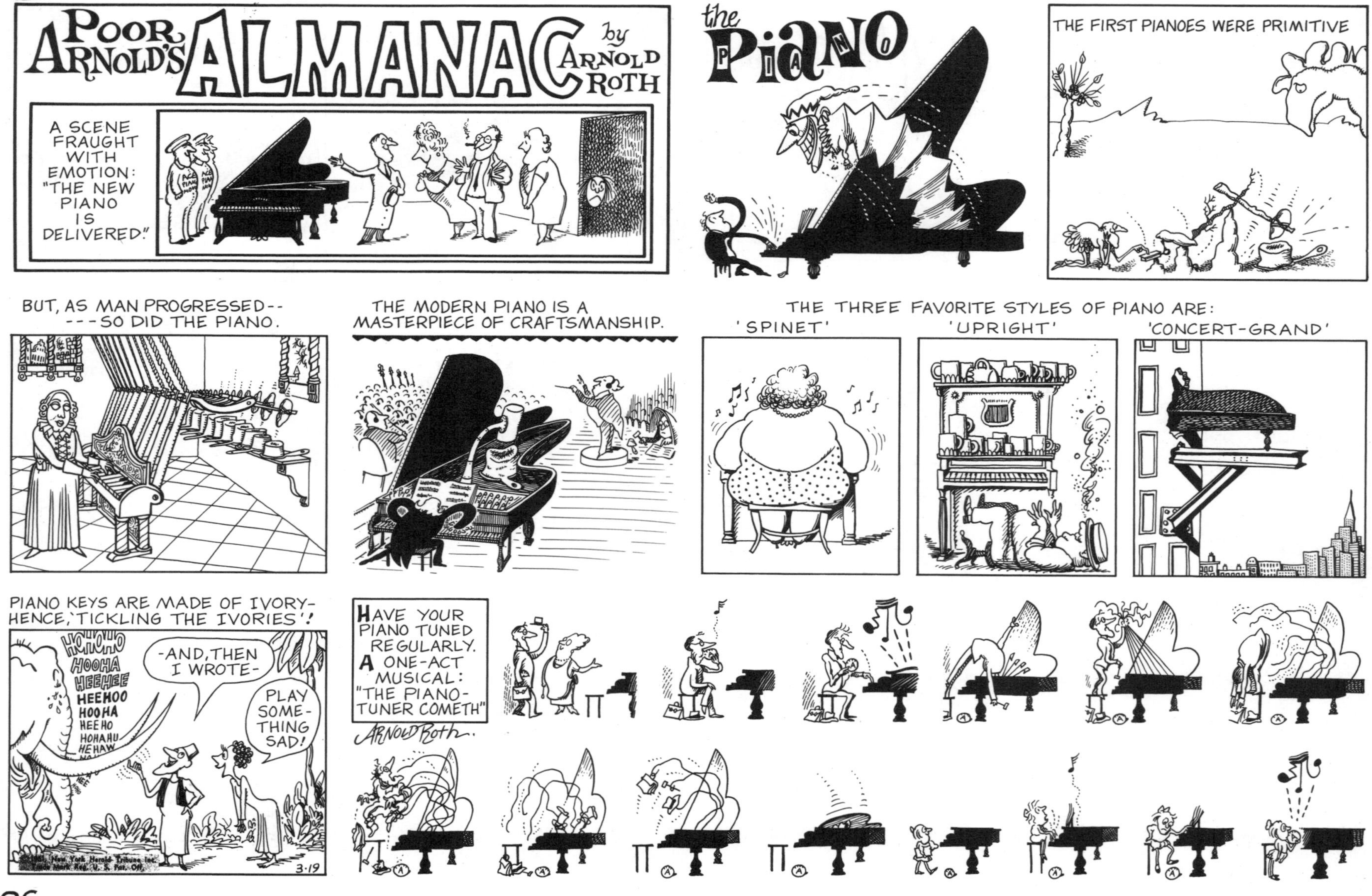

POOR ARNOLD'S ALMANAC by ARNOLD ROTH
A SCENE FRAUGHT WITH EMOTION: "THE NEW PIANO IS DELIVERED."
the PIANO
THE FIRST PIANOES WERE PRIMITIVE
BUT, AS MAN PROGRESSED-- ---SO DID THE PIANO.
THE MODERN PIANO IS A MASTERPIECE OF CRAFTSMANSHIP.
THE THREE FAVORITE STYLES OF PIANO ARE:
'SPINET'
'UPRIGHT'
'CONCERT-GRAND'
PIANO KEYS ARE MADE OF IVORY- HENCE, 'TICKLING THE IVORIES'!
HOHOHO
HOOHA
HEEHEE
HEEHOO
HOOHA
HEEHO
HOHAHU
HEHAW
-AND, THEN I WROTE-
PLAY SOME-THING SAD!
©1961 New York Herald Tribune Inc. Trade Mark Reg. U. S. Pat. Off.
3·19
HAVE YOUR PIANO TUNED REGULARLY.
A ONE-ACT MUSICAL: "THE PIANO-TUNER COMETH"
ARNOLD ROTH

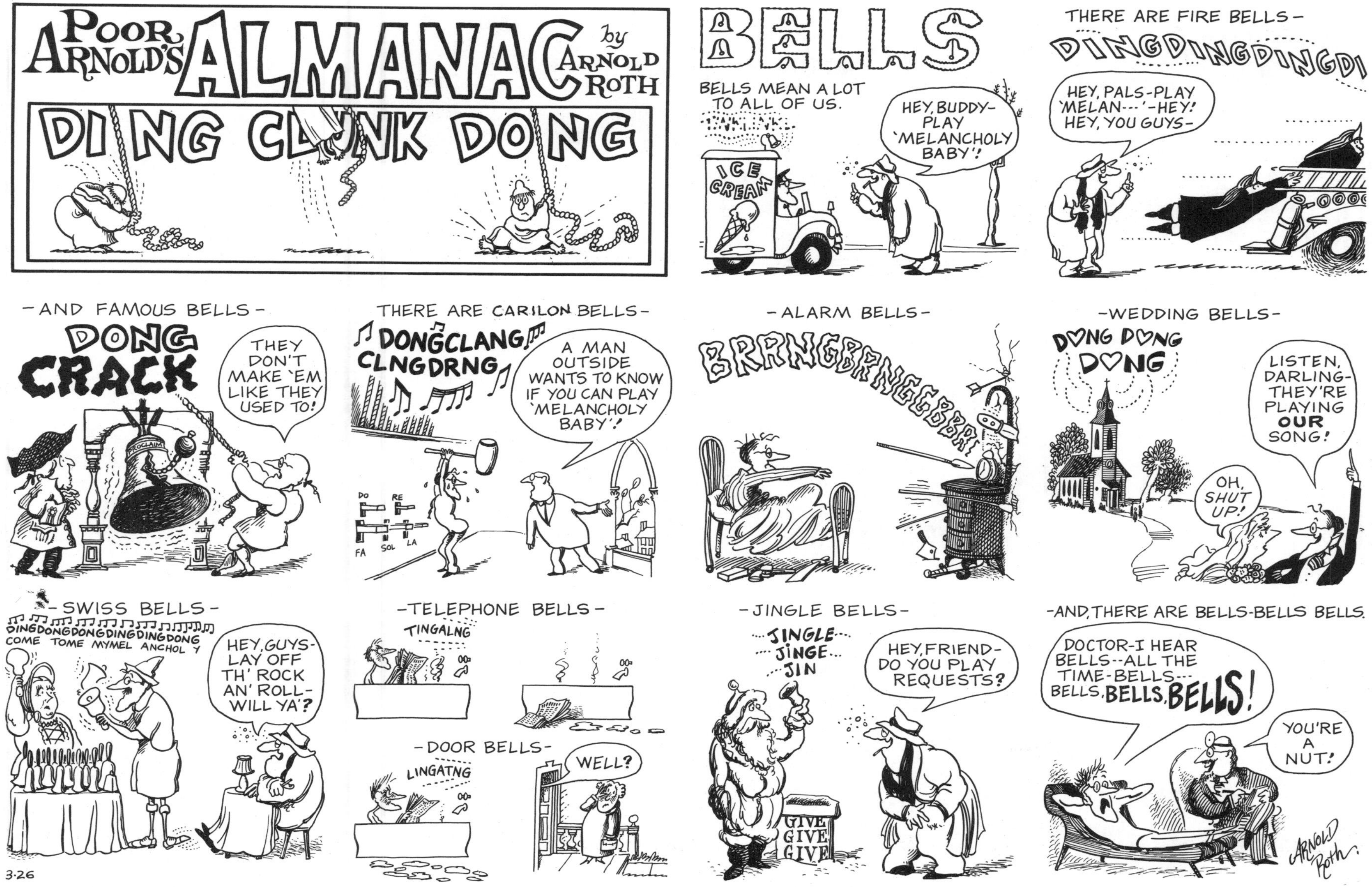
POOR ARNOLD'S ALMANAC by ARNOLD ROTH
DING CLUNK DONG
BELLS
BELLS MEAN A LOT TO ALL OF US.
ICE CREAM
HEY, BUDDY- PLAY 'MELANCHOLY BABY'!
THERE ARE FIRE BELLS-
DINGDINGDINGDINGDI
HEY, PALS-PLAY 'MELAN---'-HEY! HEY, YOU GUYS-
-AND FAMOUS BELLS-
DONG CRACK
PROCLAIM
THEY DON'T MAKE 'EM LIKE THEY USED TO!
THERE ARE CARILON BELLS-
DONGCLANG CLNGDRNG
DO RE FA SOL LA
A MAN OUTSIDE WANTS TO KNOW IF YOU CAN PLAY 'MELANCHOLY BABY'!
-ALARM BELLS-
BRRNGBRNGGBRR
-WEDDING BELLS-
DONG DONG DONG
LISTEN, DARLING- THEY'RE PLAYING **OUR** SONG!
OH, SHUT UP!
-SWISS BELLS-
DINGDONGDONGDINGDINGDONG
COME TOME MYMEL ANCHOL Y
HEY, GUYS- LAY OFF TH' ROCK AN' ROLL- WILL YA'?
-TELEPHONE BELLS-
TINGALNG
-DOOR BELLS-
LINGATNG
WELL?
-JINGLE BELLS-
JINGLE JINGE JIN
HEY, FRIEND- DO YOU PLAY REQUESTS?
GIVE GIVE GIVE
-AND, THERE ARE BELLS-BELLS BELLS.
DOCTOR-I HEAR BELLS--ALL THE TIME-BELLS--- BELLS, BELLS, BELLS!
YOU'RE A NUT!
ARNOLD Roth
3·26

POOR ARNOLD'S ALMANAC

by ARNOLD ROTH

'THE RAINMAKER'

THE SUN DRAWS WATER **UP** FROM THE SEA INTO CLOUDS--

--THE CLOUDS DUMP IT DOWN AGAIN -AND THAT'S HOW WE GET RAIN & STUFF!

IN SOME PARTS OF THE WORLD IT NEVER RAINS....

HELP! HELP! THE SKY IS FALLING DOWN!

..... IN MOST PLACES, IT RAINS OCCASIONALLY...

AT LEAST IT DOES THE FARMERS SOME GOOD!

....WHILE IN OTHERS, IT RAINS ALL THE TIME.

BY JOVE, LORD MOULDY-FIGG, IT'S STOPPED RAINING!

WHAT'D YOU EXPECT? THOSE SCIENCE CHAPS WITH THEIR H-BOMBS WERE BOUND TO **RUIN** OUR WEATHER!

4·2

RAIN IS LIKE BASEBALL--SOME PEOPLE LIKE IT AND SOME PEOPLE DON'T.

INNING	1	2	3	4	5	6	7	8	9	
PILTRIN	12	8	6	29						
FURZE	0	0	0							

98

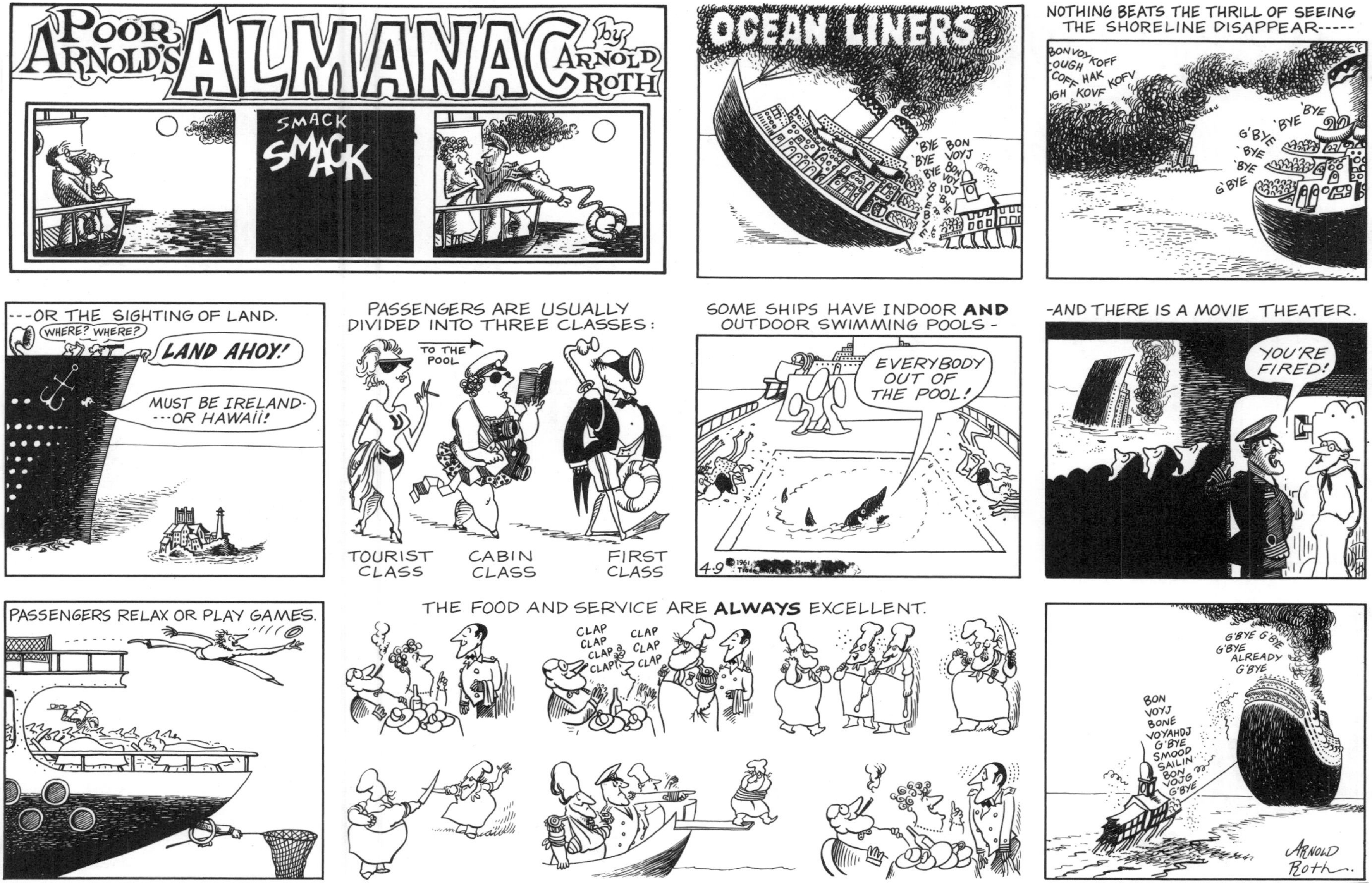
POOR ARNOLD'S ALMANAC by ARNOLD ROTH
SMACK
SMACK
OCEAN LINERS
'BYE BON VOYJ
'BYE BYE BON VOY IDJ
B'YE BYE
NOTHING BEATS THE THRILL OF SEEING THE SHORELINE DISAPPEAR-----
BONVOY KOFF
COUGH HAK
COFF KOVF KOFV
UGH
G'BYE 'BYE 'BYE
'BYE
'BYE
G'BYE
---OR THE SIGHTING OF LAND.
WHERE? WHERE?
LAND AHOY!
MUST BE IRELAND---OR HAWAII!
PASSENGERS ARE USUALLY DIVIDED INTO THREE CLASSES:
TO THE POOL
TOURIST CLASS
CABIN CLASS
FIRST CLASS
SOME SHIPS HAVE INDOOR AND OUTDOOR SWIMMING POOLS -
EVERYBODY OUT OF THE POOL!
4-9 ©1961 [redacted]
-AND THERE IS A MOVIE THEATER.
YOU'RE FIRED!
PASSENGERS RELAX OR PLAY GAMES.
THE FOOD AND SERVICE ARE ALWAYS EXCELLENT.
CLAP CLAP CLAP CLAP
CLAP CLAP CLAP
G'BYE G'BYE
G'BYE ALREADY
G'BYE
BON
VOYJ
BONE
VOYAHDJ
G'BYE
SMOOD
SAILIN
BON
VOJG
G'BYE
ARNOLD Roth

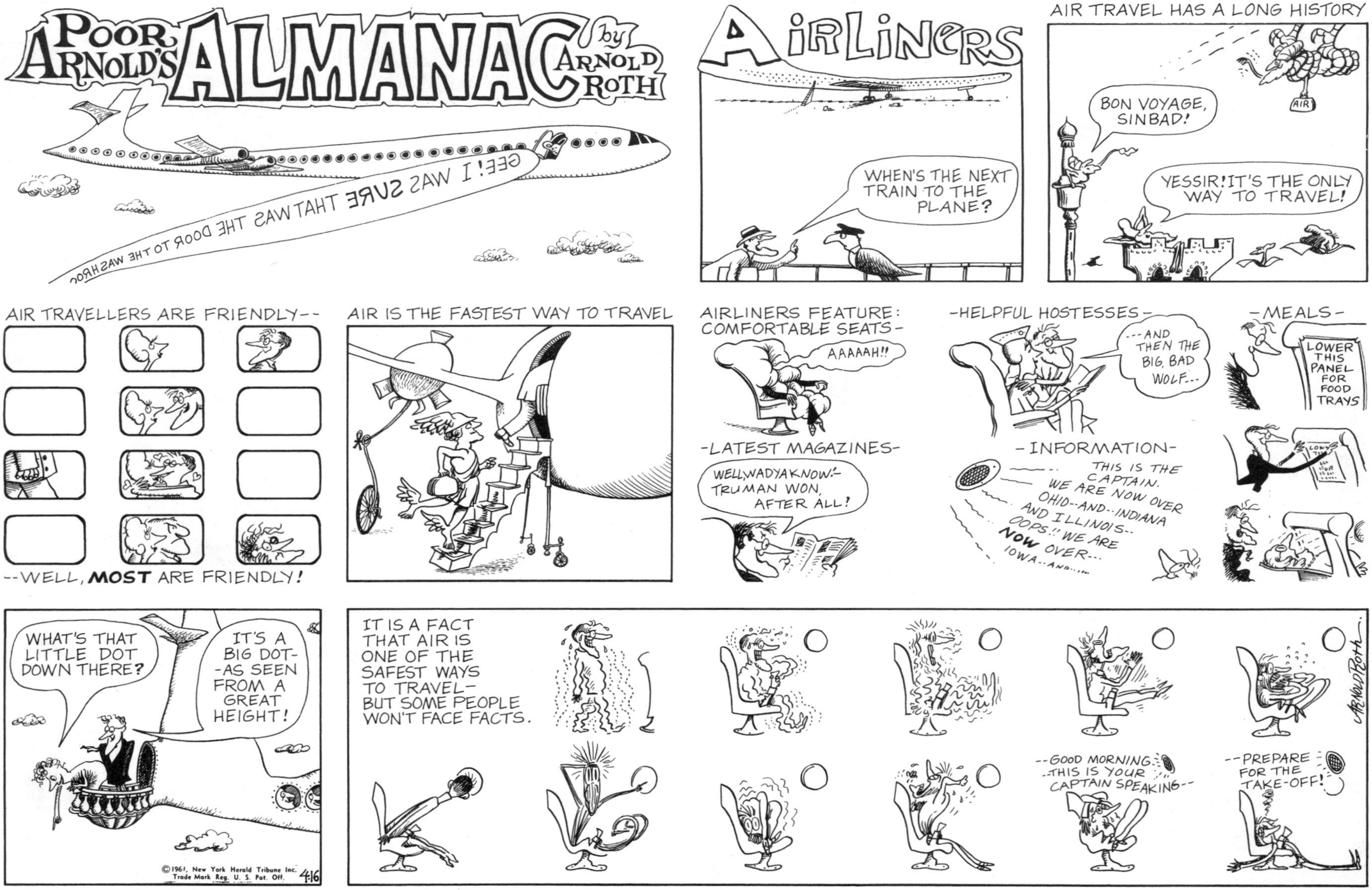
POOR ARNOLD'S ALMANAC by ARNOLD ROTH
GEE! I WAS SURE THAT WAS THE DOOR TO THE WASHROO
AIRLINERS
WHEN'S THE NEXT TRAIN TO THE PLANE?
AIR TRAVEL HAS A LONG HISTORY
BON VOYAGE, SINBAD!
AIR
YESSIR! IT'S THE ONLY WAY TO TRAVEL!
AIR TRAVELLERS ARE FRIENDLY--
--WELL, MOST ARE FRIENDLY!
AIR IS THE FASTEST WAY TO TRAVEL
AIRLINERS FEATURE: COMFORTABLE SEATS-
AAAAAH!!
-LATEST MAGAZINES-
WELL, WADYAKNOW!- TRUMAN WON, AFTER ALL!
-HELPFUL HOSTESSES-
---AND THEN THE BIG, BAD WOLF---
-INFORMATION-
THIS IS THE CAPTAIN. WE ARE NOW OVER OHIO--AND--INDIANA AND ILLINOIS-- OOPS!! WE ARE NOW OVER--- IOWA--AND---
-MEALS-
LOWER THIS PANEL FOR FOOD TRAYS
WHAT'S THAT LITTLE DOT DOWN THERE?
IT'S A BIG DOT- -AS SEEN FROM A GREAT HEIGHT!
©1961, New York Herald Tribune Inc. Trade Mark Reg. U. S. Pat. Off.
4-16
IT IS A FACT THAT AIR IS ONE OF THE SAFEST WAYS TO TRAVEL- BUT SOME PEOPLE WON'T FACE FACTS.
ARNOLD ROTH
--GOOD MORNING- -THIS IS YOUR CAPTAIN SPEAKING--
--PREPARE FOR THE TAKE-OFF!

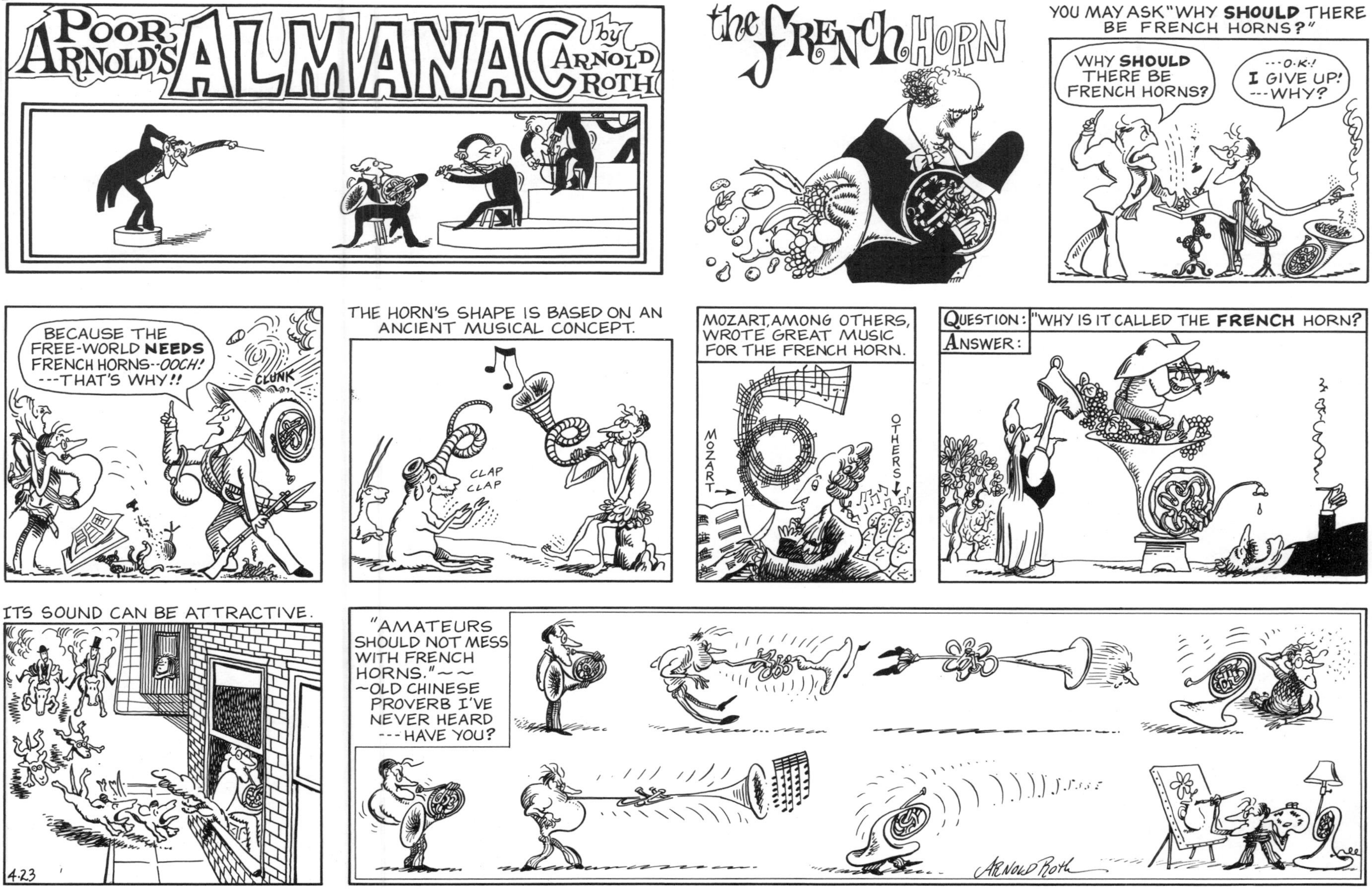
POOR ARNOLD'S ALMANAC by ARNOLD ROTH
the FRENCH HORN
YOU MAY ASK "WHY SHOULD THERE BE FRENCH HORNS?"
WHY SHOULD THERE BE FRENCH HORNS?
---O.K.! I GIVE UP! ---WHY?
BECAUSE THE FREE-WORLD NEEDS FRENCH HORNS--OOCH! ---THAT'S WHY!!
CLUNK
THE HORN'S SHAPE IS BASED ON AN ANCIENT MUSICAL CONCEPT.
CLAP CLAP
MOZART, AMONG OTHERS, WROTE GREAT MUSIC FOR THE FRENCH HORN.
MOZART
OTHERS
QUESTION: "WHY IS IT CALLED THE FRENCH HORN?
ANSWER:
ITS SOUND CAN BE ATTRACTIVE.
"AMATEURS SHOULD NOT MESS WITH FRENCH HORNS."~~ ~OLD CHINESE PROVERB I'VE NEVER HEARD ---HAVE YOU?
4.23
ARNOLD ROTH

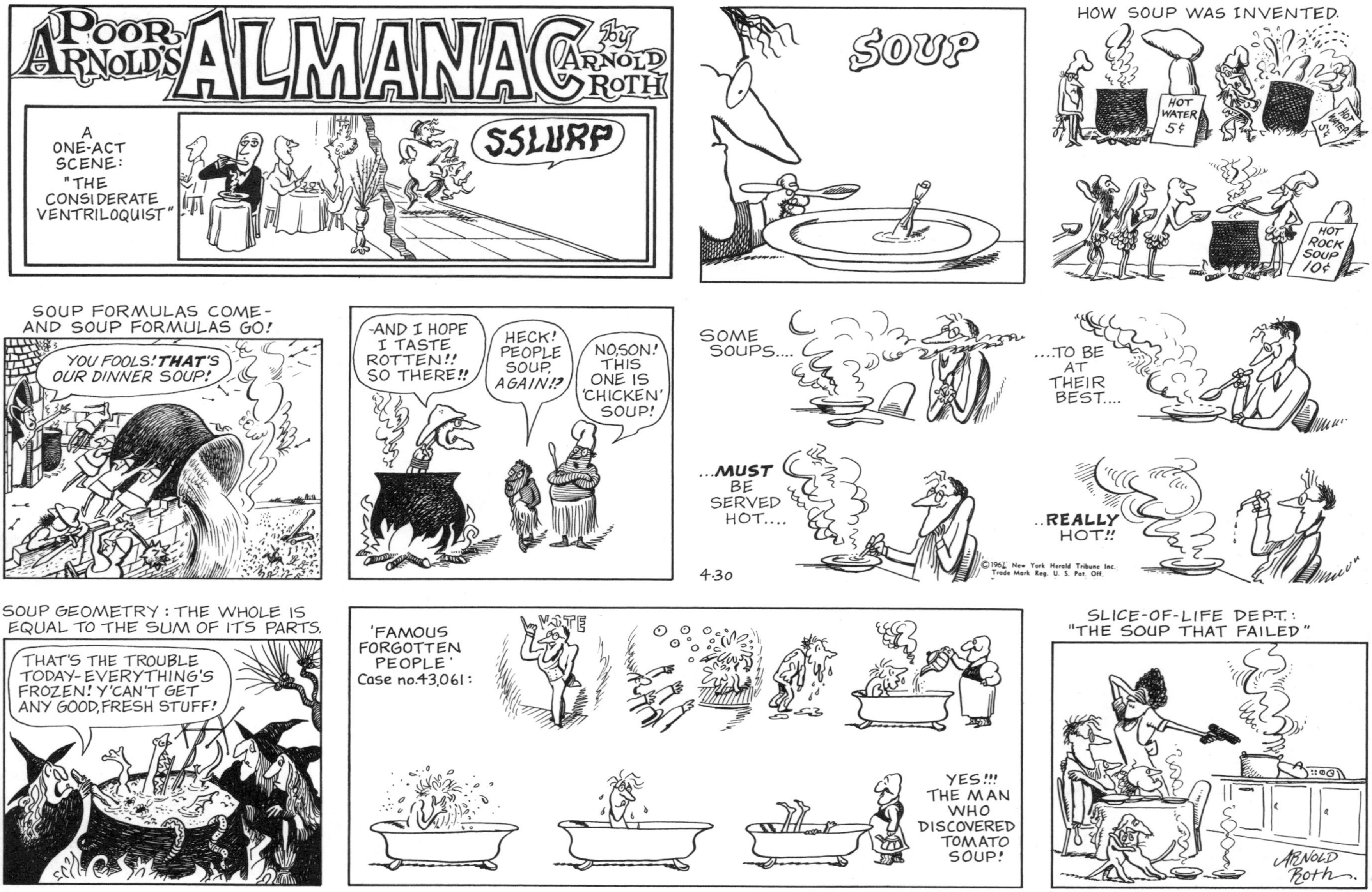

POOR ARNOLD'S ALMANAC
by ARNOLD ROTH
A ONE-ACT SCENE: "THE CONSIDERATE VENTRILOQUIST"
SSLURP
SOUP
HOW SOUP WAS INVENTED.
HOT WATER 5¢
HOT WATER 5¢
HOT ROCK SOUP 10¢
SOUP FORMULAS COME - AND SOUP FORMULAS GO!
YOU FOOLS! THAT'S OUR DINNER SOUP!
-AND I HOPE I TASTE ROTTEN!! SO THERE!!
HECK! PEOPLE SOUP, AGAIN!?
NO, SON! THIS ONE IS 'CHICKEN' SOUP!
SOME SOUPS....
....TO BE AT THEIR BEST....
...MUST BE SERVED HOT....
..REALLY HOT!!
©1962 New York Herald Tribune Inc. Trade Mark Reg. U. S. Pat. Off.
4-30
SOUP GEOMETRY: THE WHOLE IS EQUAL TO THE SUM OF ITS PARTS.
THAT'S THE TROUBLE TODAY- EVERYTHING'S FROZEN! Y'CAN'T GET ANY GOOD, FRESH STUFF!
'FAMOUS FORGOTTEN PEOPLE' Case no. 43,061:
VOTE
YES!!! THE MAN WHO DISCOVERED TOMATO SOUP!
SLICE-OF-LIFE DEPT.: "THE SOUP THAT FAILED"
ARNOLD Roth

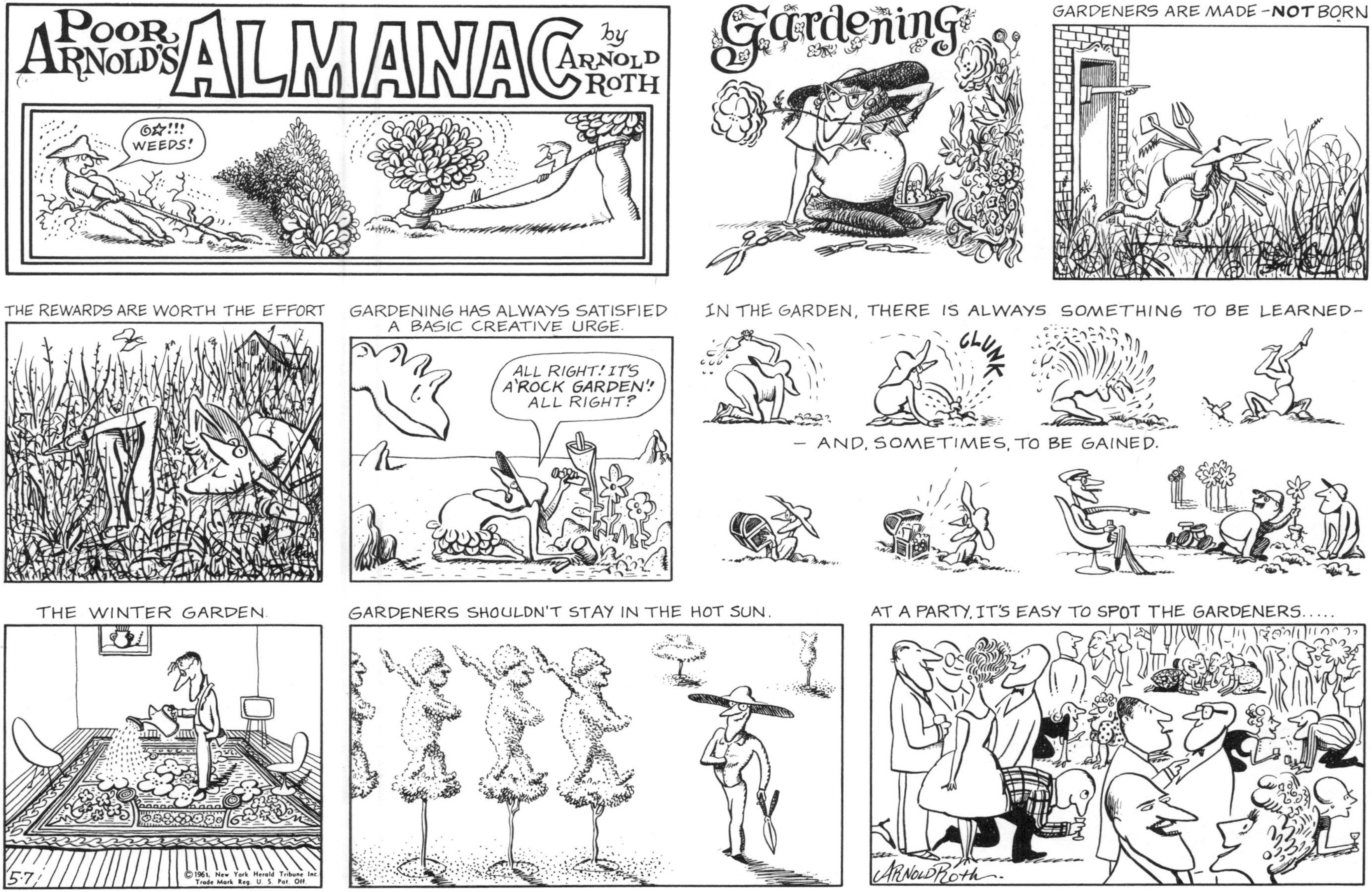
POOR ARNOLD'S ALMANAC
by ARNOLD ROTH
G☆!!! WEEDS!
Gardening
GARDENERS ARE MADE - NOT BORN
THE REWARDS ARE WORTH THE EFFORT
GARDENING HAS ALWAYS SATISFIED A BASIC CREATIVE URGE.
ALL RIGHT! IT'S A 'ROCK GARDEN'! ALL RIGHT?
IN THE GARDEN, THERE IS ALWAYS SOMETHING TO BE LEARNED-
CLUNK
- AND, SOMETIMES, TO BE GAINED.
THE WINTER GARDEN.
5·7
© 1961, New York Herald Tribune Inc.
Trade Mark Reg. U. S. Pat. Off.
GARDENERS SHOULDN'T STAY IN THE HOT SUN.
AT A PARTY, IT'S EASY TO SPOT THE GARDENERS.....
ARNOLD ROTH

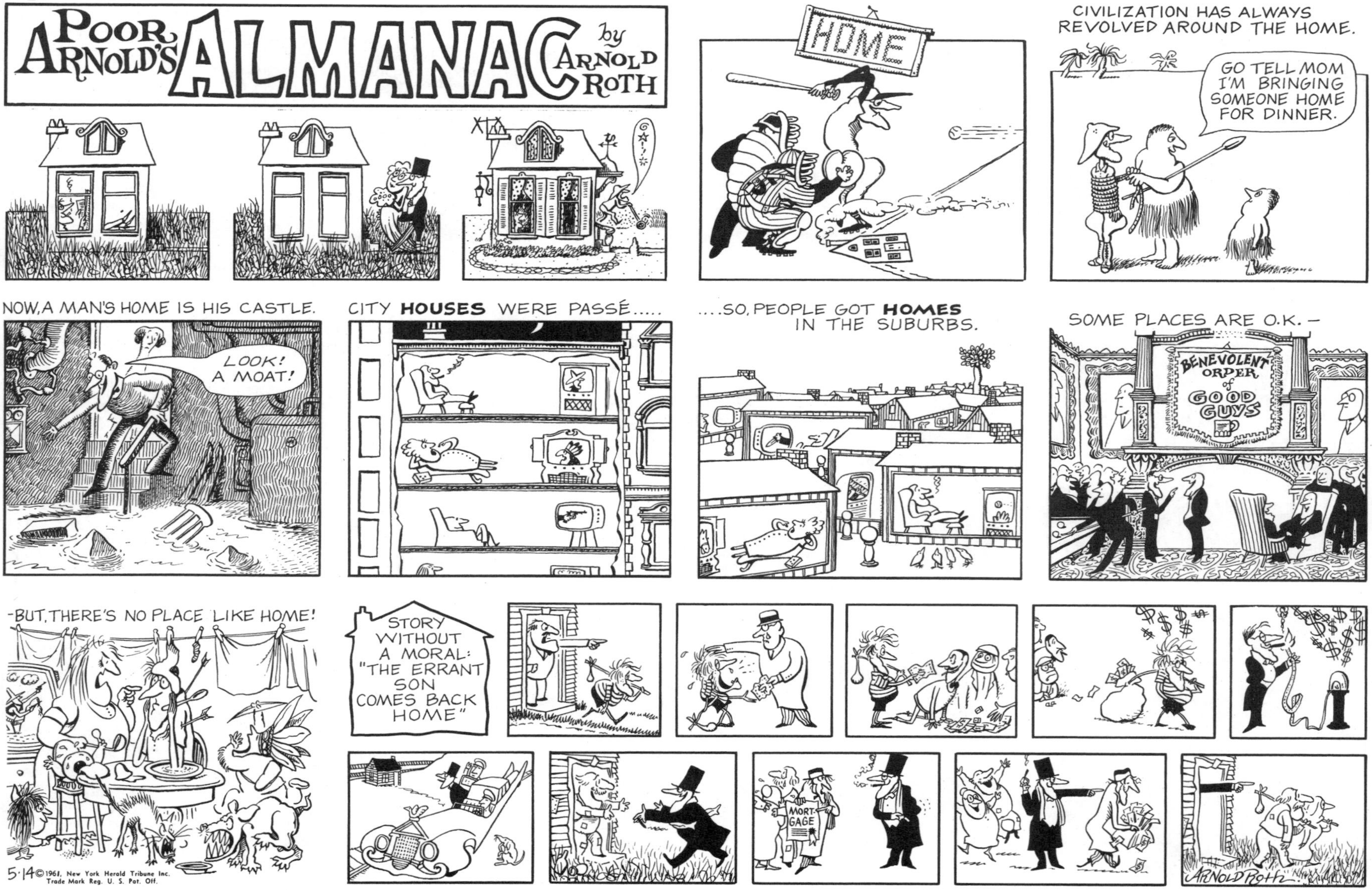

POOR ARNOLD'S ALMANAC by ARNOLD ROTH
HOME
CIVILIZATION HAS ALWAYS REVOLVED AROUND THE HOME.
GO TELL MOM I'M BRINGING SOMEONE HOME FOR DINNER.
NOW, A MAN'S HOME IS HIS CASTLE.
LOOK! A MOAT!
CITY **HOUSES** WERE PASSÉ.....
....SO, PEOPLE GOT **HOMES** IN THE SUBURBS.
SOME PLACES ARE O.K. –
BENEVOLENT ORDER of GOOD GUYS
–BUT, THERE'S NO PLACE LIKE HOME!
STORY WITHOUT A MORAL: "THE ERRANT SON COMES BACK HOME"
MORT-GAGE
ARNOLD ROTH
5·14 ©1961, New York Herald Tribune Inc.
Trade Mark Reg. U. S. Pat. Off.

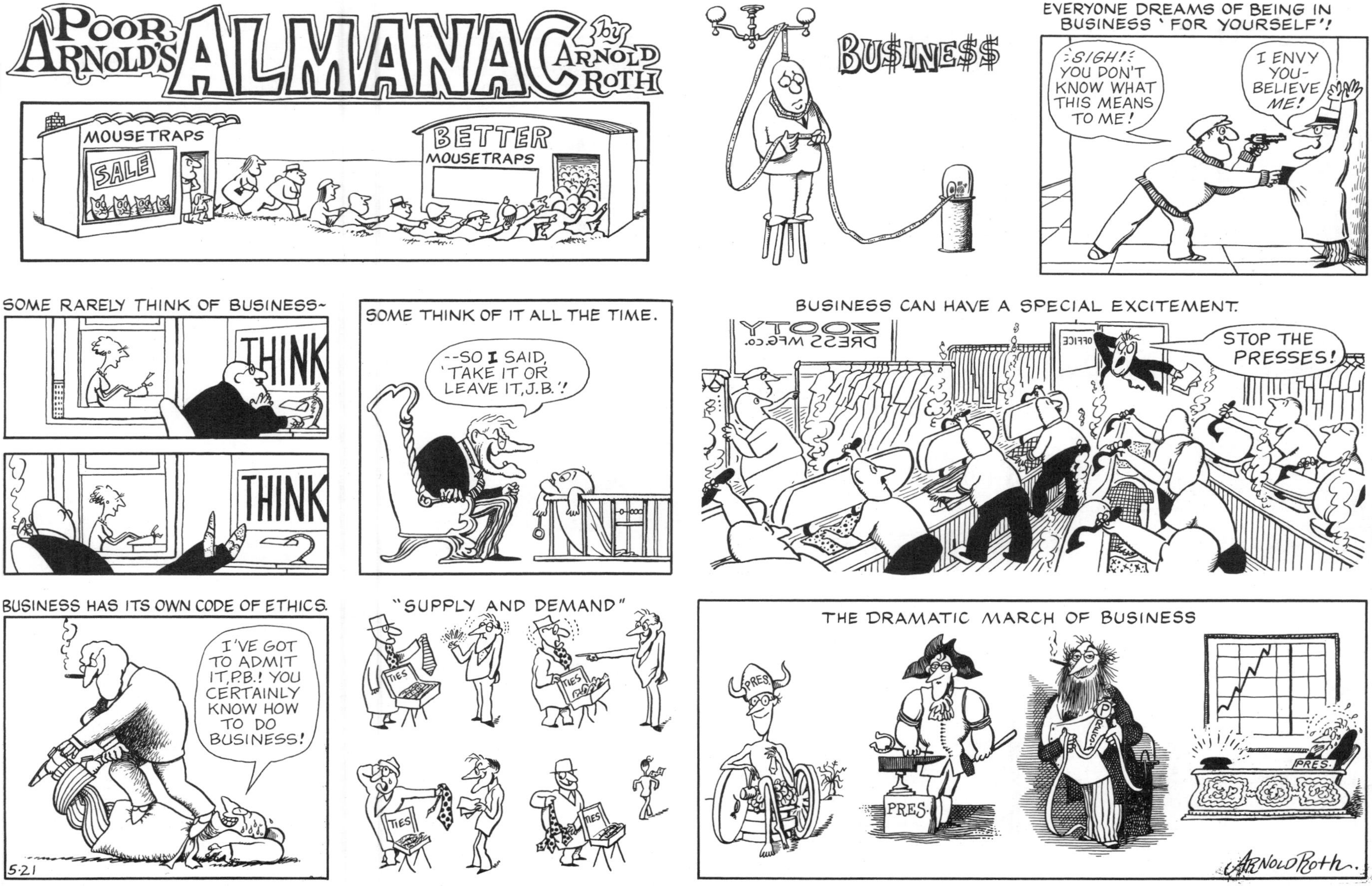

POOR ARNOLD'S ALMANAC by ARNOLD ROTH
MOUSETRAPS
SALE
BETTER MOUSETRAPS
BU$INE$$
EVERYONE DREAMS OF BEING IN BUSINESS 'FOR YOURSELF'!
:SIGH!: YOU DON'T KNOW WHAT THIS MEANS TO ME!
I ENVY YOU- BELIEVE ME!
SOME RARELY THINK OF BUSINESS~
THINK
THINK
SOME THINK OF IT ALL THE TIME.
--SO I SAID, 'TAKE IT OR LEAVE IT, J.B.'!
BUSINESS CAN HAVE A SPECIAL EXCITEMENT.
STOP THE PRESSES!
BUSINESS HAS ITS OWN CODE OF ETHICS.
I'VE GOT TO ADMIT IT, P.B.! YOU CERTAINLY KNOW HOW TO DO BUSINESS!
5·21
"SUPPLY AND DEMAND"
TIES
TIES
TIES
TIES
THE DRAMATIC MARCH OF BUSINESS
PRES.
PRES.
PRES.
PRES.
ARNOLD ROTH

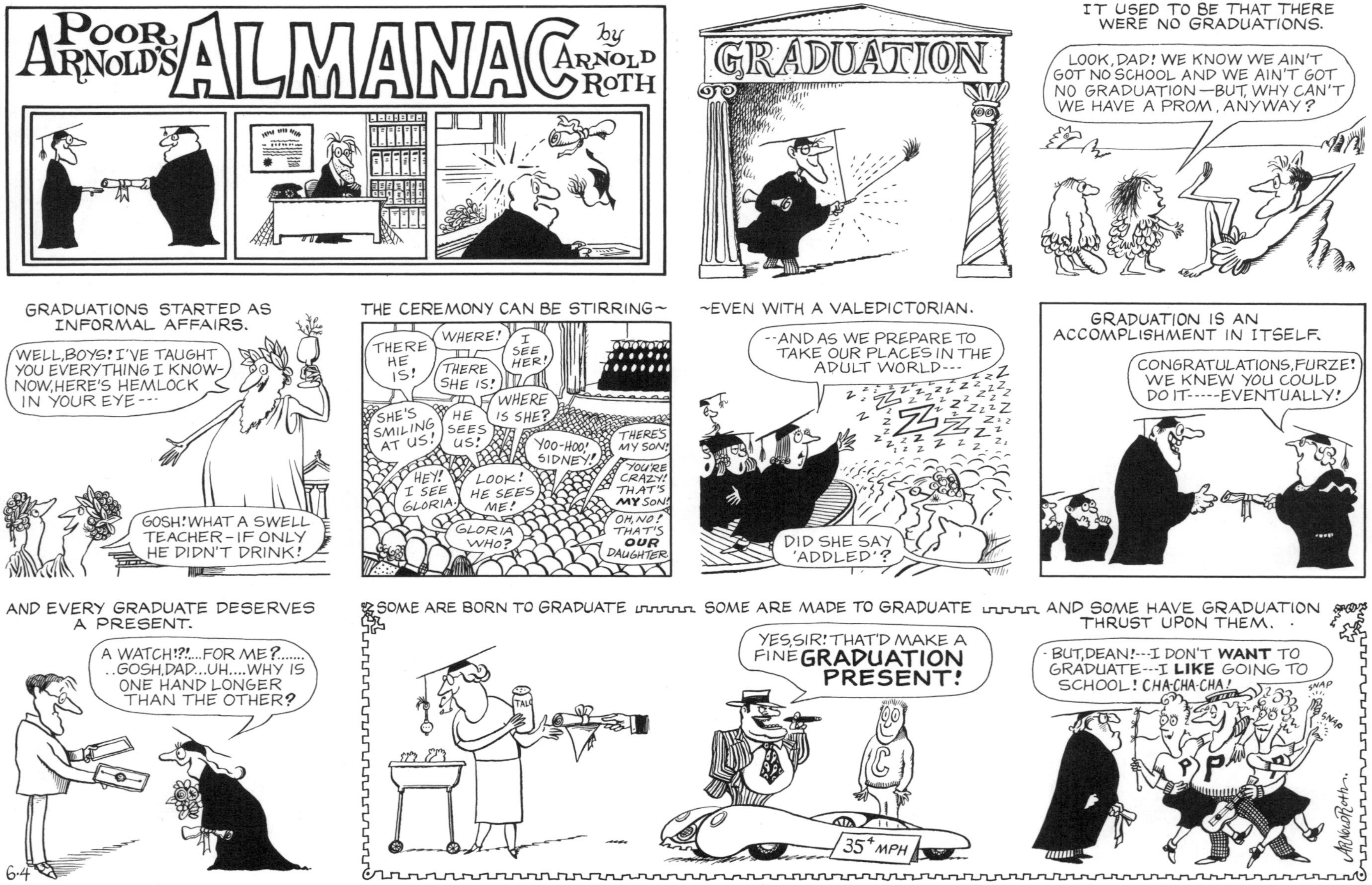
POOR ARNOLD'S ALMANAC
by ARNOLD ROTH
GRADUATION
IT USED TO BE THAT THERE WERE NO GRADUATIONS.
LOOK, DAD! WE KNOW WE AIN'T GOT NO SCHOOL AND WE AIN'T GOT NO GRADUATION—BUT, WHY CAN'T WE HAVE A PROM, ANYWAY?
GRADUATIONS STARTED AS INFORMAL AFFAIRS.
WELL, BOYS! I'VE TAUGHT YOU EVERYTHING I KNOW—NOW, HERE'S HEMLOCK IN YOUR EYE---
GOSH! WHAT A SWELL TEACHER—IF ONLY HE DIDN'T DRINK!
THE CEREMONY CAN BE STIRRING~
THERE HE IS!
WHERE!
I SEE HER!
THERE SHE IS!
WHERE IS SHE?
SHE'S SMILING AT US!
HE SEES US!
YOO-HOO! SIDNEY!
THERE'S MY SON!
YOU'RE CRAZY! THAT'S **MY** SON!
HEY! I SEE GLORIA.
LOOK! HE SEES ME!
GLORIA WHO?
OH, NO! THAT'S **OUR** DAUGHTER
~EVEN WITH A VALEDICTORIAN.
--AND AS WE PREPARE TO TAKE OUR PLACES IN THE ADULT WORLD---
DID SHE SAY 'ADDLED'?
GRADUATION IS AN ACCOMPLISHMENT IN ITSELF.
CONGRATULATIONS, FURZE! WE KNEW YOU COULD DO IT-----EVENTUALLY!
AND EVERY GRADUATE DESERVES A PRESENT.
A WATCH!?!...FOR ME?.......GOSH, DAD...UH....WHY IS ONE HAND LONGER THAN THE OTHER?
6-4
SOME ARE BORN TO GRADUATE
TALC
SOME ARE MADE TO GRADUATE
YES, SIR! THAT'D MAKE A FINE **GRADUATION PRESENT!**
MPH
AND SOME HAVE GRADUATION THRUST UPON THEM.
BUT, DEAN!--I DON'T **WANT** TO GRADUATE---I **LIKE** GOING TO SCHOOL! CHA-CHA-CHA!
SNAP
SNAP
ARNOLD ROTH

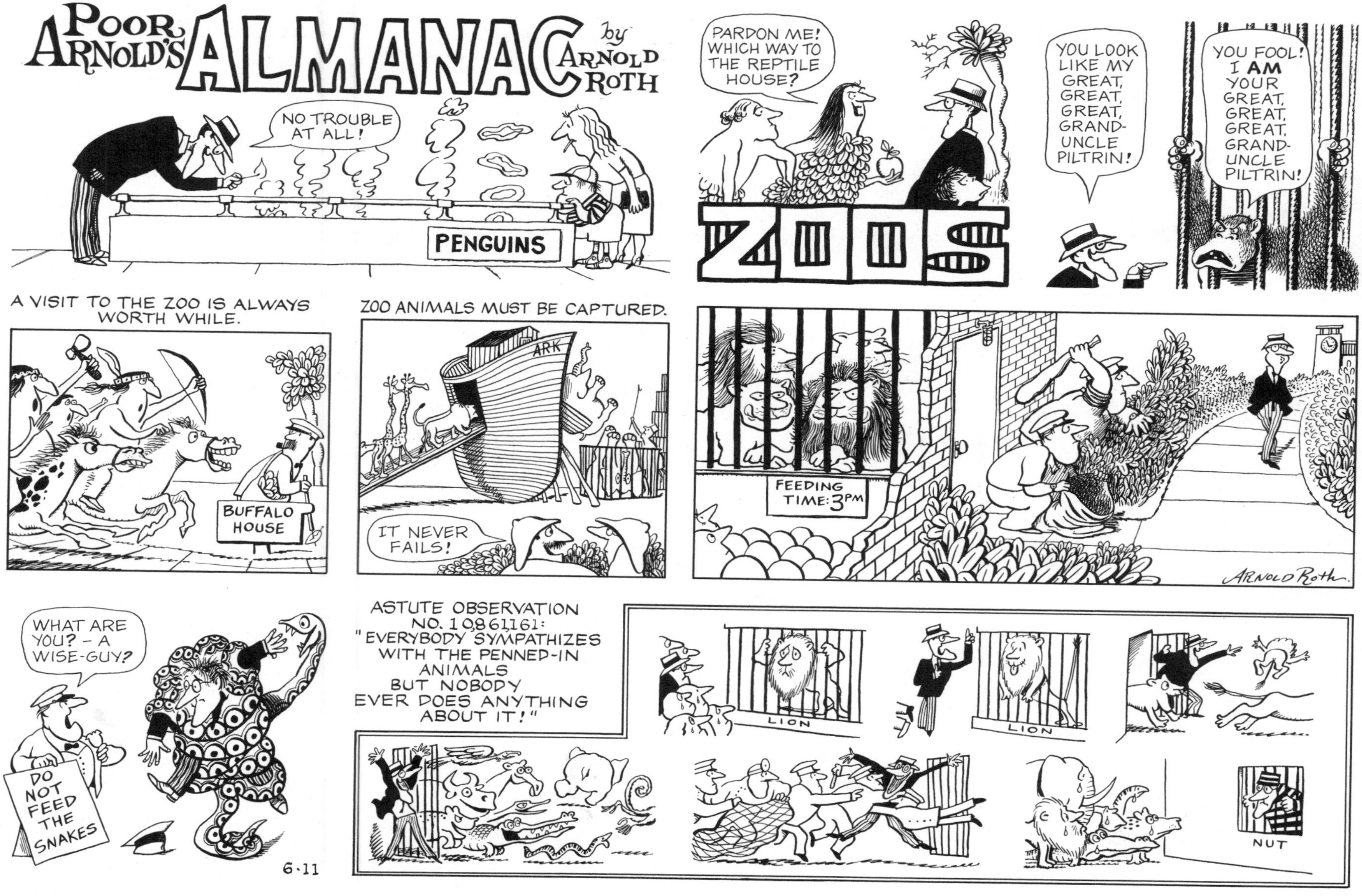

POOR ARNOLD'S ALMANAC by ARNOLD ROTH
NO TROUBLE AT ALL!
PENGUINS
PARDON ME! WHICH WAY TO THE REPTILE HOUSE?
ZOOS
YOU LOOK LIKE MY GREAT, GREAT, GREAT, GRAND-UNCLE PILTRIN!
YOU FOOL! I AM YOUR GREAT, GREAT, GREAT, GRAND-UNCLE PILTRIN!
A VISIT TO THE ZOO IS ALWAYS WORTH WHILE.
BUFFALO HOUSE
ZOO ANIMALS MUST BE CAPTURED.
ARK
IT NEVER FAILS!
FEEDING TIME: 3PM
ARNOLD ROTH
WHAT ARE YOU? – A WISE-GUY?
DO NOT FEED THE SNAKES
6·11
ASTUTE OBSERVATION NO. 10,861,161: "EVERYBODY SYMPATHIZES WITH THE PENNED-IN ANIMALS BUT NOBODY EVER DOES ANYTHING ABOUT IT!"
LION
LION
NUT

When POOR ARNOLD'S ALMANAC was halted, Arnold Roth had two strips written and sketched out but not drawn: they are presented here in their unfinished form.

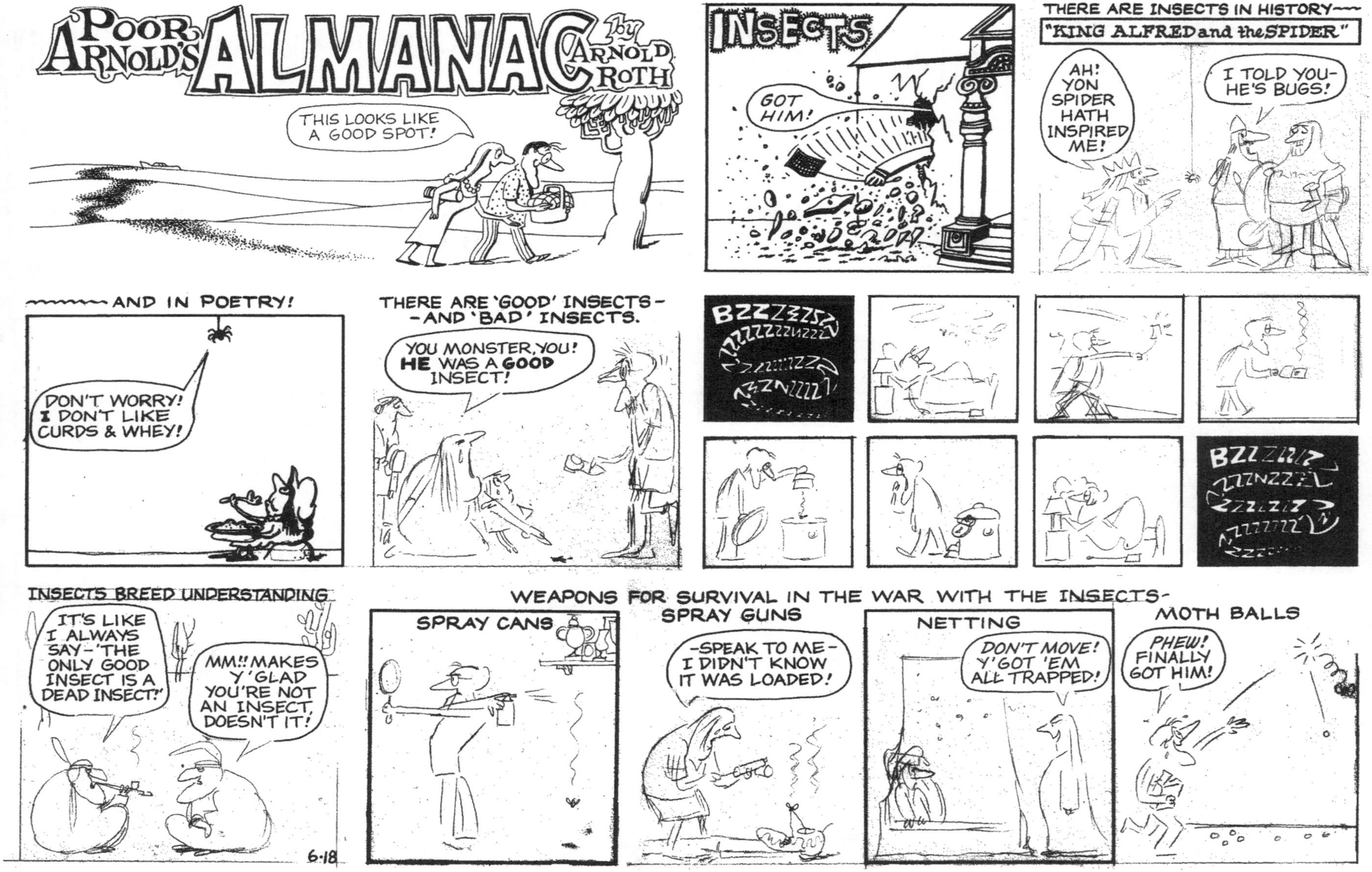
POOR ARNOLD'S ALMANAC by ARNOLD ROTH
THIS LOOKS LIKE A GOOD SPOT!
INSECTS
GOT HIM!
THERE ARE INSECTS IN HISTORY
"KING ALFRED and the SPIDER"
AH! YON SPIDER HATH INSPIRED ME!
I TOLD YOU- HE'S BUGS!
AND IN POETRY!
DON'T WORRY! I DON'T LIKE CURDS & WHEY!
THERE ARE 'GOOD' INSECTS- -AND 'BAD' INSECTS.
YOU MONSTER, YOU! HE WAS A GOOD INSECT!
INSECTS BREED UNDERSTANDING
IT'S LIKE I ALWAYS SAY-'THE ONLY GOOD INSECT IS A DEAD INSECT!'
MM!! MAKES Y'GLAD YOU'RE NOT AN INSECT, DOESN'T IT!
6-18
WEAPONS FOR SURVIVAL IN THE WAR WITH THE INSECTS-
SPRAY CANS
SPRAY GUNS
-SPEAK TO ME- I DIDN'T KNOW IT WAS LOADED!
NETTING
DON'T MOVE! Y'GOT 'EM ALL TRAPPED!
MOTH BALLS
PHEW! FINALLY GOT HIM!

POOR ARNOLD'S ALMANAC

by ARNOLD ROTH

OH! OH! HERE COMES SUMMER, AGAIN!

SUMMER

ALL OF YOU MUST WRITE A COMPOSITION CALLED "WHAT I DID LAST SUMMER"!

NATURE PROVIDES SIGNS THAT SUMMER HAS BEGUN.

IT'S HOT OUTSIDE!

IT'S ONE OF THOSE NEW, LIGHT-WEIGHT, SUMMER SUITS!

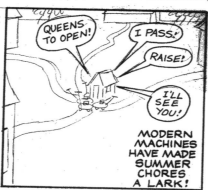

QUEENS TO OPEN!

I PASS!

RAISE!

I'LL SEE YOU!

MODERN MACHINES HAVE MADE SUMMER CHORES A LARK!

A SUMMER DRAMA: "MY SUN, MY SUN"

SUMMER IS EDUCATIONAL.

G☆☽ⅶⱮ☀ ☾☉☆☒ⓒ FLYS!

WOW, POP! **THEY**'RE BETTER'N THE BIRDS AND BEES!

6·25

SUMMER IS THE STRENUOUS, OUTDOOR SEASON.....

...ATHLETICS...

..NATURE STUDY...

...BASEBALL...

...SWIMMING...

...SIGHTSEEING.

You may receive absolutely free of charge our fabulous color catalogue featuring collections of cartooning by such masters as Winsor McCay (Little Nemo), Harold Gray (Little Orphan Annie), Walt Kelly (Pogo), Hal Foster (Prince Valiant), V.T. Hamlin (Alley Oop), Jules Feiffer, R. Crumb, and many, many more by: calling 1-800-657-1100; visiting our web site at www.fantagraphics.com; or writing to us the old fashioned way at 7563 Lake City Way; Seattle, WA 98115.